Christ and Controversy

Christ and Controversy

The Person of Christ in Nonconformist Thought and Ecclesial Experience, 1600–2000

ALAN P. F. SELL

☙PICKWICK *Publications* • Eugene, Oregon

CHRIST AND CONTROVERSY
The Person of Christ in Nonconformist Thought and Ecclesial Experience, 1600–2000

Copyright © 2011 Alan P. F. Sell. All rights reserved. Except for brief quotations in critical publications or reviews, no part of this book may be reproduced in any manner without prior written permission from the publisher. Write: Permissions, Wipf and Stock Publishers, 199 W. 8th Ave., Suite 3, Eugene, OR 97401.

Pickwick Publications
An Imprint of Wipf and Stock Publishers
199 W. 8th Ave., Suite 3
Eugene, OR 97401

www.wipfandstock.com

ISBN 13: 978-1-61097-669-5

Cataloguing-in-Publication data:

Sell, Alan P. F.

Christ and controversy : the person of Christ in nonconformist thought and ecclesial experience, 1600–2000 / Alan P. F. Sell.

xii + 218 pp. ; 23 cm. Includes bibliographical references and indexes.

ISBN 13: 978-1-61097-669-5

1. Jesus Christ—History of doctrines—17th century. 2. Jesus Christ—History of doctrines—18th century 3. Jesus Christ—History of doctrines—19th century. 4. Jesus Christ—History of doctrines—20th century 5. Dissenters—Religious—Great Britain—History—17th century. 6. Dissenters—Religious—Great Britain—History—18th century. 7. Dissenters—Religious—Great Britain—History—19th century. 8. Dissenters—Religious—Great Britain—History—20th century. I. Title.

BT203 S45 2011

Manufactured in the U.S.A.

*Dedicated to Donald K. McKim,
interpreter of the faith par excellence*

Ere the blue heavens were stretched abroad.
    From everlasting was the Word;
With God he was; the Word was God;
    And must divinely be adored
        —Isaac Watts, 1674–1748

Let earth and heaven combine,
    And joyfully agree,
To praise in songs divine
    The incarnate Deity,
Our God, contracted to a span,
    Incomprehensibly made man.
        —Charles Wesley, 1707–88

Heav'n be amazed! see thy Maker
    Thy only Creator, and thy God
Cloath'd in human Flesh, and welt'ring
    (Pierc'd and wounded) in his Blood;
Pity drew him down from Heaven,
    Mercy, Grace, and ardent Love,
    Made him part with all his Glory
In the blissful Realms above.
        —William Williams, 1717–91

High beyond imagination
    Is the love of God to man;
Far too deep for human reason;
    Fathom that it never can;
Love eternal
    Richly dwells in Christ the Lamb.
        —William Gadsby, 1773–1844

My Master was a worker,
    With daily work to do,
And he who would be like Him
    Must be a worker too.
Then welcome honest labour,
    And honest labour's fare.
For where there is a worker,
    The Master's man is there.
        —William George Tarrant, 1853–1928

Contents

Preface • ix
Abbreviations • xi

1 Introduction • 1
2 Classical Affirmations and Alternative Stances in the Seventeenth Century • 7
3 Nonconformist Christology in the Eighteenth Century • 22
4 Representative Ecclesial Repercussions in Eighteenth-Century England • 61
5 Representative Ecclesial Repercussions in Eighteenth-Century Wales • 83
6 Christological Contributions and Ecclesial Developments, 1800–1891 • 89
7 The Proliferation of Nonconformist Christology, 1891–1950 • 121
8 The Decline of Nonconformist Christological Endeavour, 1950–2000 • 173
9 Epilogue • 179

Bibliography • 183
Index of Persons • 199
Index of Places • 207
Index of Academies, Colleges, and Universities • 211
Index of Subjects • 215

Preface

My purpose in writing this book is stated in the Introduction. Here I wish to make four explanatory points, and then to render thanks.

First, readers will swiftly discern that a considerable number of Nonconformist divines appear in this book. It would have made for a very unwieldy volume if the bibliographical and biographical references to every one of them had been exhaustively presented. Accordingly, I have referred in the main to readily available dictionaries, yearbooks, and online resources. These will, in turn, direct those who consult them to further relevant literature.

Secondly, as far as possible (the information is not always known, and some, especially among the earlier Baptists and Methodists, were theological autodidacts) I have indicated where the Nonconformist divines were educated. This is of particular interest in the case of those who attended Dissenting academies, which were of interestingly differing theological complexions. For example, Northampton Academy is best described as "mixed," since students and tutors alike were found on the continuum from more theologically conservative to more theologically liberal; whereas the academy sponsored by the King's Head Society was as avowedly Calvinistic as that at Warrington was avowedly liberal.[1] None of which is to imply that the alumni of these several types necessarily evinced the characteristics desired by their tutors; clearly they did not, and one of the intriguing aspects of this story, as it would be if certain other doctrines were in view, is to observe the changes in doctrinal stance that some ministers underwent as their lives proceeded.

Thirdly, the terms "Congregational" and "Independent" were used interchangeably from about 1640. Except when referring to the names of local churches, or to book titles, I have used "Congregational" on the ground that in Britain and in other parts of the world "Independent" is

---

1 See further, Sell, *Philosophy, Dissent and Nonconformity 1689–1920*, ch. 2.

nowadays used by local churches and denominations whose roots, and in some cases whose polity and doctrines, are distinct from those of classical Congregationalism.

Fourthly, the authors of the epigraphs represent the traditions with which we are concerned: Watts the Congregationalist, Wesley the evangelical Arminian Methodist, Williams the Calvinistic Methodist, Gadsby the Baptist, and Tarrant the Unitarian.

I am grateful for the assistance of Alice Ford-Smith of Dr. Williams's Library, London; John Briggs of the Baptist Historical Society; David Woodruff of the Strict Baptist Historical Society Library, and Robert Pope of the University of Wales Trinity Saint David. The ceaseless encouragement of Karen, my wife, means more to me than I can say.

I thank Dr. K. C. Hanson and Dr. Robin Parry of Wipf and Stock, and their colleagues, for the interest they have shown in my work, and for their care in bringing it to the light of published day.

I dedicate this book to Donald K. McKim, whom I first met in 1984 at Dubuque Theological Seminary, where he was a greatly valued professor. We at once became firm friends, and such we remain. I have followed his subsequent career with great interest, and have benefited greatly from his writings. As an interpreter and propagator of the Christian faith he excels to an unusual degree in the diverse roles of scholar, teacher, preacher and editor.

Alan P. F. Sell
Milton Keynes, UK

Abbreviations

THE NAMES OF EDITORS and publication details will be found in the Bibliography

DECBP	*Dictionary of Eighteenth-Century British Philosophers.* Edited by John W. Yolton, John Valdimir Price, and John Stephens
DEB	*Dictionary of Evangelical Biography.* Edited by Donald M. Lewis
DHT	*The Dictionary of Historical Theology.* Edited by Trevor A. Hart
DMBI	*A Dictionary of Methodism in Britain and Ireland.* Edited by John A. Vickers
DNCBP	*Dictionary of Nineteenth-Century British Philosophers.* Edited by W. J. Mander and Alan P. F. Sell
DSCBP	*Dictionary of Seventeenth-Century British Philosophers.* Edited by Andrew Pyle
DTCBP	*Dictionary of Twentieth-Century British Philosophers.* Edited by Stuart Brown
DWB	*The Dictionary of Welsh Biography.* Edited by John Edward Lloyd and R. T. Jenkins
DWBO	*The Dictionary of Welsh Biography Online.* Edited by Brynley F. Roberts
ODCC	*The Oxford Dictionary of the Christian Church.* 3rd ed. Edited by F. A. Livingstone.
ODNB	*The Oxford Dictionary of National Biography.* Edited by Colin Matthew and Brian Harrison, and online, Lawrence Goldman

SI	The Charles Surman Index of Ministers at Dr. Williams's Library, London, and online
UGAYB	*The Unitarian General Assembly Year Book*
URCYB	*The United Reformed Church Year Book*
WTW	*Who They Were*. Edited by John Taylor and Clyde Binfield

1

Introduction

CONFRONTED BY A VAST territory, in this book I shall understand by "Nonconformist," not the Roman Catholics, but the most long-standing traditions of English and Welsh historic Dissent: the Congregationalists, Baptists, and Presbyterians (some of whom segued into Unitarianism); together with those later arrivals on the Nonconformist scene, the Methodists, both Calvinistic and Arminian, and the orthodox Presbyterians of varying stripes who came together in the Presbyterian Church of England (1876). I shall not refer to those who have come and gone (the Muggletonians and Sandemanians, for example), or to those groups—the Plymouth Brethren and the Pentecostal and Black Churches among them—that have been formed since 1800. My terminus year is 2000.

I begin with a statement of the obvious: there is not a "Nonconformist Christology" that is distinct from all others. What we find is that from the time of the English Reformation onwards Nonconformists have concerned themselves with a miscellany of Christological topics; but that is not all. Christology has been far more than an armchair hobby or the subject of coffee house discussions. It has played a significant role in Nonconformist ecclesial experience. It is not an exaggeration to say that more secessions within Nonconformity have been prompted by, or at least justified by reference to, divergent views of the person of Christ than by any other aspect of Christian doctrine. Certainly the doctrines of creation, the particular theories of the atonement, and party lines regarding the last things have not, in England and Wales, led to as much troubling of the Nonconformist ecclesial waters as have differing views concerning Christ's person.

This study is abstractive in nature. It is possible, no doubt legitimate, and many would say necessary, to construe the whole of Christian doctrine—from creation to eschatology—through a Christological lens, but in this book the focus is strictly upon the person of Christ as such. Thus, for example, the discussion is conducted more or less in isolation from soteriology. I shall not dwell upon the Christological offices of prophet, priest, and king, because they are more readily accommodated under the heading of Christ's work. I do not, of course, think that Christ's person can satisfactorily be dissociated from his work. On the contrary, Christ does what he does because he is who he is; the incarnation precedes the cross, both temporally and logically. It is undeniable that throughout the Christian ages (except when specific doctrinal questions are in view, as here) the question of Christ's person has been raised in consequence of the understanding—indeed, in many cases of the personal appropriation—of his work. Thus the earliest Christians did not occupy themselves by pondering the two nature doctrine of the person of Christ. They had found forgiveness, new life, salvation in Christ crucified and risen, and their question was, "If this is what Jesus has done, who must he be?"[1] This is the question that many Nonconformists (and others) have sought to answer as they have taken the cross as their starting-point for theological reflection. P. T. Forsyth was characteristically to the point: "Our approach to Christology," he declared, "is through the office of Christ as Saviour. We only grasp the real divinity of His person by the value for us of His Cross."[2] Forsyth's student, H. F. Lovell Cocks underscored the point: "What Christ is can only appear in what He has done for us."[3] The same theologian may sum the matter up: "The earliest believers did not first believe in Christ's deity, and then receive the forgiveness of God and the reconciliation through Him. It was the other way about."[4] With this I agree, but Christians have nevertheless interpreted Christ's person in

---

1. I have developed this point more fully in *Aspects of Christian Integrity*, ch. 2; and in *Enlightenment, Ecumenism, Evangel*, ch. 13. In my book, *Christ Our Saviour* I proceed from Christ's work to his person.

2. Forsyth, *The Church and the Sacraments*, 33. For Forsyth (1848–1921), who was educated at Aberdeen University, Göttingen University and New College, London, see DHT, ODCC, ODNB, SI, WTW.

3. Lovell Cocks (1894–1983), untitled paper on Christology in the Lovell Cocks papers at Dr. Williams's Library, London. For this unduly neglected theologian see ODNB, SI, WTW; Sell, *Commemorations*, ch. 13.

4. Lovell Cocks, untitled paper on Christology.

a variety of ways, and it is perfectly proper to present and discuss their findings. As before, I have P. T. Forsyth on my side: "The theology of the incarnation is necessary to explain our Christian experience and not our rational nature, nor our religious psychology."[5]

Again, apart from the question of the relation of the Father to the Son, I shall refer to the doctrine of the Trinity only so far as that is necessary to sketch the Trinitarian context within which discussion of the person of Christ and, indeed, the ecclesial disruptions to which I shall refer, are alike rooted; and I shall not pursue the theme of the believer's union with Christ which is central to the Christian doctrine of humanity. Yet again, the pursuit of apologetic attempts to "prove" the divinity of Christ from his miracles, or the scrutiny of the several quests of the historical Jesus, would take us too far afield. To repeat, the focus here is upon the person of Christ as this has been discussed in, and as it has shaped, the major streams of English and Welsh Nonconformity. We shall find among the running themes from the seventeenth to the end of the nineteenth century that of the eternal generation of the Son; we shall witness the procession of some Nonconformists from either Calvinism or Arminianism (sometimes through Arianism) to Unitarianism—a clamant issue with ecclesial implications in the long eighteenth century and to a lesser extent subsequently; we shall note the way in which, in the wake of modern biblical criticism, and inspired by certain aspects of German theology, some Nonconformists developed kenotic Christologies; we shall consider some modern assessments of the Chalcedonian Formula; and we shall discover that from about 1950 onwards Nonconformist theologians have not produced substantial systematic studies of Christ's person. I emphasize the term "theologians" because I cannot here accommodate biblical scholars; nor can I plough the rich field of Nonconformist hymnody, from which (to step into a hornet's nest) it was, conceivably, once more possible for Nonconformists at large to imbibe more aspects of Christological doctrine than is always possible from some latter day hymnic effusions.[6] Unless the context indicates a wider reference, I shall throughout mean "the doctrine of the person of Christ" when using the term "Christology."

5. Forsyth, *The Person and Place of Jesus Christ*, 9.

6. I hasten to moderate this unsanctified thought by recognizing that the bulk of Charles Wesley's 6,000-plus hymns are no longer sung, and that even Isaac Watts could perpetrate godly doggerel.

Two cautionary words must be uttered before we proceed. First, in treating the subject of Christ's person we cannot avoid the fact that we are thereby confronted by mystery. I do not invoke mystery in order to excuse a refusal to think, still less with a view to sanctifying irrationalism. Two Nonconformists saw point I have in mind: "If by a doctrine of the person of Christ we mean a theory that will explain his person, it is from the nature of the case impossible. The idea of the God-man, however inevitable it may be, is in itself but a symbol; it is not a fully intelligible notion."[7] Furthermore, "We dare not forget that no part of Christian doctrine is more exposed to the menace of mere intellectualism than Christology."[8]

At the same time, faith seeks understanding, and to respond to the intellectualist menace by suppressing our questions and resting upon blind faith would be a sad exchange; it would also betoken a failure to attempt an answer to the question that Jesus posed to his disciples, "Who do you say I am?" (Matt 16:15). The history of the doctrine of the person of Christ is in large part the history of attempts to answer that question. One of the most significant attempts made is that of the theologians who devised the Chalcedonian Formula, to which I referred in passing, which was promulgated in the year 451. I mention it now because it enshrines many of the Christological issues that were still alive when the Nonconformists came upon the scene and, indeed, that remain alive to this day. It reads as follows:

> Following the holy Fathers, we all with one accord teach men to acknowledge one and the same Son, our Lord Jesus Christ, at once complete in Godhead and complete in manhood, truly God and truly man, consisting also of a reasonable soul and body; of one substance [*homoousios*] with the Father as regards his Godhead, and at the same time of one substance with us as regards his manhood; like us in all respects, apart from sin; as regards his Godhead, begotten of the Father before the ages, but yet as regards his manhood begotten, in the last days, for us men and for our salvation, of Mary the Virgin, the God-bearer [*Theotokos*]; one and the same Christ, Son, Lord, Only-begotten, recognized *in two natures without confusion, without change, without division, without separation*; the distinction of natures

---

7. Micklem, *Ultimate Questions*, 98. For Micklem (1888–1976) see ODNB, SI, WTW. He was educated at New and Mansfield Colleges, Oxford, and Marburg University.

8. Whale, *Christian Doctrine*, 106. For Whale (1896–1997), see ODNB, SI, WTW.

being in no way annulled by the union, but rather the characteristics of each nature being preserved and coming together to form one person and subsistence [*hupostasis*], not parted or separated into two persons, but one and the same Son and Only-begotten the Word, Lord Jesus Christ; even as the prophets from earliest times spoke of him, and our Lord Jesus Christ himself taught us, and the creed of the Fathers has handed down to us.[9]

Positively, the major claims are that Jesus Christ is fully human and fully divine; that he has two distinct natures, but is not two distinct persons, but one; and that he was eternally the Son of God—"begotten of the Father before the ages" (eternal generation). Negatively, the view of Arius (d. 336) (opposed by Athanasius {c. 296–373}) that Christ was the Father's pre-eminent creature—a subordinate divinity, and that there was a time when the Son of God was not, is repudiated, for Christ is declared to be eternal and of one substance with the Father. Again, the "four famous adverbs" (italicized above) rule out the views of Eutyches (c.378–454) that Christ's humanity was absorbed into his divinity; of Apollinarius (c. 310–c. 390), who, in teaching that the human soul of Jesus was replaced by the divine Logos, emphasised Christ's divinity at the expense of his humanity; and of Nestorius (post 351—post 451), who was long thought to have maintained that in the incarnate Christ there was both the eternally begotten Son, and the Son born of Mary.[10] Here are themes that shall be resumed as we proceed. We shall see that the Chalcedonian Formula is open to criticism; but my point here is that the Chalcedonian divines cannot be rebuked for, to put it crudely, not elucidating the mechanics of the incarnation. They knew when they were confronted by mystery, and their Formula was a confession, not an hypothesis, still less a full-blown explanation. We may permit the Anglican theologian, John Burnaby, to draw the moral for us: "In principle . . . Chalcedon warns us against *all* theories of Incarnation. For theories must aim at making an idea of an event intelligible; and they can only do that by bringing their subject into line with the rest of our experience. But the event of the Incarnation is strictly unique, and therefore can have no parallel: we can never *understand* how God could become man."[11]

9. Bettenson, ed., *Documents of the Christian Church*, 73.

10. On the basis of fresh evidence, modern scholars have qualified the traditional view of Nestorius' thought, but it would take me too far afield to pursue the point now.

11. Burnaby, *The Belief of Christendom*, 86.

The second cautionary word is this: denominations as we have come to know them—that is, as bodies having central organizational and disciplinary structures (not to mention pension plans)—are creatures of the nineteenth century. In the earlier centuries of Nonconformist life there was considerable fluidity of "tendency," so that a minister might be trained at Bristol Baptist College and subsequently serve Congregational and/or Unitarian churches; while churches themselves might now wear one label, now another. Thus, for example, on the one hand, the church at Carlton, Bedfordshire, began Congregational, and retained its high Calvinism by becoming first Baptist, and then Strict and Particular Baptist. On the other hand, a number of General Baptist and Presbyterian churches had become Unitarian by the end of the eighteenth century. In other words, Carlton retained its doctrinal stance by changing its denominational label, while others changed their denomination because their doctrines changed. Few churches, however, could emulate the fluidity of opinion found at Stainland Congregational church, Halifax, whose minister, the Idle-trained John (?) Hanson answered a query as to his church's denomination thus: "We have Wesleyans, Independents, and Church-people; an Independent parson in the pulpit, a Baxterian clerk, a Roman Catholic organ, and a drunken player, so you may call us what you like."[12]

---

12. Miall, *Congregationalism in Yorkshire*, 367. For Hanson, see SI.

2

Classical Affirmations and Alternative Stances in the Seventeenth Century

SINCE WE SHALL BE entering a doctrinal thicket, we shall do well to take our bearings from the Christological clauses in some of the confessions and declarations of faith drawn up by the several Dissenting traditions, having regard to the fact that such documents were normally intended as records of things commonly believed by the authors and those they represented, and not as statements requiring formal assent— least of all if such assent were construed as a condition of church membership. In the words of the Preface (largely the work of John Owen) to the Congregational *Savoy Declaration of Faith and Order* (1658), "The *Spirit of Christ* is in himself too *free*, great and generous a Spirit, to suffer himself to be used by any humane arm, to whip men into belief; he drives not, but *gently leads into all truth*, and *perswades* men to *dwell in the tents* of *like precious Faith*; which would lose of its preciousness and value, if that sparkle of freeness shone not in it."[1] The general objectives of the authors of *Savoy* and kindred documents were to adhere closely to the Bible on the one hand, and to be open to further guidance of the Holy Spirit on the other.

What, then, of their Christological affirmations? To the Baptists we are indebted for a number of early confessions, and I can refer to a sample only. In 1596 the Separatist-Baptist church, a portion of which was in London while the majority of the members were exiled in Holland, published *A True Confession*. We here learn that

---

1. Matthews, ed., *The Savoy Declaration*, 53. For Owen (1616–83) see DHT, ODCC, ODNB, SI. He was educated at Queen's College, Oxford.

touching his person, the Lord Jesus . . . is the everlasting Son of God, and the engraven form of his Person; co-essential, co-equal, and co-eternal, God with him and with the Holy Ghost, by who he hath made the worlds, by whom he upholdeth and governeth all the works he hath made; who also when the fullness of time was come, was made man of a woman . . . to whit of Mary that blessed Virgin, by the Holy Ghost coming upon her . . . and was also in all things like unto us, sin only excepted.[2]

According to John Smyth's *Short Confession of Faith in XX Articles* (1609) "Jesus Christ is true God and true man, viz. the Son of God taking to himself, in addition, the true and pure nature of a man, out of a true rational soul, and existing in a true human body. . . . Jesus Christ, as pertaining to the flesh, was conceived by the Holy Spirit in the womb of the Virgin Mary . . ."[3] The repetition of 'true' for emphasis is significant, but Smyth (?1570–1612) is not as specific as others as to the eternal generation of the Son or the divinity of Christ. He is, in fact, a General Baptist, who denies original sin, repudiates the Calvinist doctrine of election, and affirms that human beings have the ability to repent and believe. There is a marked contrast between his confession and *A True Confession*.

Lumpkin notes that "The seven Particular Baptist Churches of London used [*A True Confession*] as a model when they drew up their earliest confession, the *London Confession* in 1644."[4] They declare that God is a Spirit, and further explain that "In this Godhead there is the Father, the Son, and the Spirit; being every one of them one and the same God; and therefore not divided, but distinguished from one another by their several properties . . ."[5] Seven clauses later we come to an affirmation concerning Jesus's birth of the Virgin Mary in the words of *A True Confession*.

Because it was largely followed by both the *Savoy Declaration* and the Particular Baptists' *Second London Confession* (1677) we may take the *Westminster Confession* of 1647 as representing the doctrinal position of the bulk of seventeenth-century Dissent. Drafted largely by

---

2. Lumpkin, *Baptist Confessions of Faith*, 84. Spelling modernized throughout.

3. Ibid., 100. For Smyth (1570?–1612), see ODCC, ODNB. He was educated at Christ's College, Cambridge.

4. Ibid., 81.

5. Ibid., 156.

Presbyterians, the Congregationalists Thomas Goodwin (1600–1680), Philip Nye (1596?–1672), William Bridge (1600?–1670), Sidrach Simpson (1600?–1655) and Jeremiah Burroughes (1599–1646) were prominent members of the Westminster Assembly, and the first three were among those who later drafted the *Savoy Declaration*.[6] The teaching of *Westminster* on the person of Christ is divided between the section on the Trinity and that on Christ the mediator, thus:

> In the unity of the Godhead there be three Persons, of one substance, power, and eternity; God the Father, God the Son, and God the Holy Ghost. [*The Second London Confession* elaborates, "each having the whole Divine Essence, yet the essence undivided"]. The Father is of none, neither begotten nor proceeding, the Son is eternally begotten of the Father; the Holy Ghost eternally proceeding from the Father and the Son. [*The Second London Confession* inserts: "all infinite, without beginning, therefore but one God, who is not to be divided in nature and Being; but distinguished by several peculiar, relative properties, and personal relations; which Doctrine of the Trinity is the foundation of all our Communion with God, and comfortable Dependence upon him {the last two clauses taken from *Savoy*}]. . . . The Son of God, the second person in the Trinity, being very and eternal God, of one substance, and equal with the Father, [*The Second London Confession* adds, 'who made the World, who upholdeth and governeth all things he hath made] did, when the fullness of time was come, take upon him man's nature, with all the essential properties and common infirmities thereof, yet without sin: being conceived by the power of the Holy Ghost in the womb of the Virgin Mary, of her substance. [*The Second London Confession* elaborates here]. So that two whole, perfect, and distinct natures, the Godhead and the manhood, were inseparably joined together in one person, without conversion, composition, or confusion. Which person is very God and very man, yet one Christ, the only Mediator between God and man.'"[7]

In the *Westminster-Savoy-Second London* line of confessions we find the bones of the Christologies of such voluminous theologians as John Owen, and of such catechetical writers as Thomas Watson

---

6. For all five, see ODNB, SI. Goodwin was educated at Queens' College, Cambridge; Nye at Brasenose College and Magdalen Hall, Oxford; Bridge and Burroughes at Emmanuel College; and Simpson at Emmanuel and Queens' Colleges, Cambridge.

7. *The Westminster Confession*, II, VIII.

(d. 1686).[8] Thus Owen declares that Christ "was truly, really, completely a divine person from eternity, which is included in the notion of his being the Son, and so distinct from the Father. . . . His being so was not a voluntary contrivance or effect of divine wisdom and goodness, his eternal generation being a necessary internal act of the divine nature in the person of the Father."[9] He adds that at the incarnation the perfect Son of God, who could never become what he was not, assumed the "substantial adjunct" of human nature[10] which, in his case, was full of grace and free from sin.[11] For his part, the Presbyterian Thomas Watson, convinced that "As feathers will be blown every way, so will feathery Christians"[12] set about expounding the Westminster Assembly's *Shorter Catechism*. His popular objective notwithstanding, he cannot avoid technical language altogether. Thus of Christ he writes that "He is co-essential with God the Father. The Godhead subsists in Christ."[13] As if to compensate, he also has recourse to homely similitudes, thus: "In the body of the sun, there are the substance of the sun, the beams, and the heat; the beams are begotten of the sun, the heat proceeds both from the sum and the beams; but these three, though different, are not divided; they all three make but one sun: so is the blessed Trinity . . ."[14] Hence, "While Christ was on the earth by his bodily presence, he was at the same time in the bosom of the Father by his divine presence. (John 3:13)."[15]

Enough has been said to justify the assertion that up to the end of the seventeenth century the main lines of Dissenting Christology, as expounded in their major formal declarations of faith and propounded by some of their major theologians, were consistent with classical orthodox thought on the person of Christ, albeit that thought was now processed by Puritan minds. Alternative views were already being canvassed, however, and to these we must now turn.

---

8. For Watson, see ODNB; SI. He was educated at Emmanuel College, Cambridge.
9. J. Owen, *Works*, I, 13.
10. Ibid., 15. For a fuller exposition of the hypostatical union, see ibid., 223–35.
11. Ibid., II, 63–66.
12. Watson, *A Body of Divinity*, 1.
13. Ibid., 110.
14. Ibid., 109.
15. Ibid., 111.

I

Our particular concern is with "Socinianism" and "Arianism." The Christology of Fausto Paolo Sozzini (1539–1604), known as Socinus, was publicized in the *Racovian Catechism* of 1605. Here appeal is made to the sufficiency of Scripture, and there is no requirement that assent be given to the doctrinal assertions made. Jesus Christ was a real man who did not exist prior to his miraculous conception (*contra* the eternal generation of the Son); who was filled with God's spirit (not construed as the third person of the Trinity); and whose teaching was authenticated by the miracles he performed. Arianism takes its name from the heresiarch, Arius (d. 336). Arian Christology focuses upon the relations between the Father and the Son. Jesus Christ was not Son of God from eternity, for that which is generated requires a prior generator. Although an original creation of God, Jesus was a creature only. We thus see that both Socinianism and Arianism proclaim different varieties of Christological subordinationism. We shall see that while Arians were to be found throughout the eighteenth century—Micaijah Towgood[16] among them—some of that persuasion found Arianism an unstable position and embraced first Socinianism and then the humanitarianism of Unitarianism; others arrived at the latter destination without passing through an Arian phase.[17] To offer a broad generalization (always a questionable thing to do where the eighteenth century is concerned): in the first half of the century the weight of concern on the part of divines was upon the Father-Son relationship, while in the second half of the century attention was increasingly directed towards the (human) nature of the Son as such. All of which had ecclesial implications. We can at once detect the difference between Arian and Socinian Christology and that of the formal Nonconformist confessions from which we set out. By the same token we can predict the terms of the broadsides that the orthodox were to launch against those deemed heterodox. What R. W.

---

16. For Towgood (1700–1792), see SI; Sell, *Dissenting Thought*, ch. 7. He was educated at Taunton Academy under Henry Grove.

17. For a broad review of Arianism, see Wiles, *Archetypal Heresy*. For Arianism in England see Colligan, *The Arian Movement*. Jeremy Goring questions Colligan's reference to an Arian *movement* in England, and suggests that if there was one, it was confined to the Church of England. See his "Introduction" to Bolam, *et al*, *The English Presbyterians*, 22. In my view there was no movement in the sense of an organised party in either Nonconformity or the Church of England; we are concerned with individually espoused doctrinal tendencies of varying temperature, emphasis and clarity.

Dale wrote of the Arianism that was denounced by the Council of Nicea (325) applies *a fortiori* to Socinianism, and it will serve as a summary statement of the protest:

> It was of the very substance of the Christian Gospel that, in Christ, heaven and earth, God and Man, had been brought together; and if Christ was only a creature, no matter how glorious, God was still at a distance from our race. It was the fundamental assumption of Arianism that the Infinite and Eternal God *could* not come near to men; but the Church knew, for itself, that He had come near; it has seen in Christ the glory of God, and had found God in Him.[18]

But this is to anticipate. We must return to the seventeenth century when, in 1609, the *Racovian Catechism* first reached England. From this we learn that "by nature [Jesus] was truly a man; a mortal man while he lived on earth, but now immortal."[19] He was not, however, "a mere or common man," but was "the only begotten Son of God . . . conceived by the Holy Spirit, and born of a virgin . . ."[20] We are further advised that Christ is not divine in the sense of being "of the very essence of God," though if "divine" refers to the Holy Spirit, "united by an indissoluble bond to [Christ's] human nature . . . I certainly do so far acknowledge such a nature in Christ as to believe that next after God it belonged to no one in a higher degree."[21]

Here was a degree Christology expressed in terms at some remove from full-blooded trinitarianism. The denial of the Trinity being illegal, a number of copies of the *Catechism* were burnt in 1614. A few, however, survived, and further underground Socinian literature was circulated, with the result that gradually heterodox ideas began to take root in the minds of some Dissenters and Church of England people alike. This in turn stimulated the "doctrine police" who were only too keen to expose those deemed heretical. Supreme in this regard was Thomas "*Gangraena*" Edwards (1599–1647) who, for example, ferreted out the young preacher, Thomas Webb, who itinerated in London, Essex and Suffolk. Among his catalogue of errors was that of asserting equality with

---

18. Dale, *Christian Doctrine*, (1894), 92.
19. Rees, *The Racovian Catechism*, 51.
20. Ibid., 52–53.
21. Ibid., 55–56.

Christ.²² The Arminian Congregationalist John Goodwin (1594–1665) was rebuked, as were the Congregationalists John Fry and William Erbury (1604–1654), the Baptist Paul Hobson (d. 1666) and other Baptists in Bath and Bristol, who held that Jesus's human nature was, like that of all human beings, defiled by original sin.²³ The Presbyterian Ralph Josselin (1617–1683) was also favourably disposed to the general thrust of Socinian biblicism and rationality.²⁴

In 1652 John Biddle (1616–62),²⁵ who had taught at Oxford and was now a schoolmaster in Gloucester, published an English version of the *Racovian Catechism* in Holland, and his own study of the Bible persuaded him that Jesus was not co-equal with God. He further believed that the Holy Spirit was independent of God and Jesus—an argument he advanced in his *XII Arguments Drawn Out of the Scripture: Wherein the Commonly-Received Opinion Touching the Deity of the Holy Spirit is Clearly and Fully Refuted* (1647). In the following year he published *A Confession of Faith, Touching the Holy Trinity, according to Scripture*. He here confesses belief in the "one most high God . . . the Father of our Lord Jesus Christ, the first Person of the holy Trinity."²⁶ Jesus is Lord of the Church, the second cause of our salvation and "consequently, the immediate object of our Faith and Worship."²⁷ He is the second Person of the Trinity, who is our Brother and helper, having "no other than a humane nature, and therefore in this very nature, is not onely a Person . . . but also our Lord, yea our God."²⁸ The impression thus far is of a tension between language and concepts, and this is strengthened when Biddle's next article reminds us that although worship is due to Christ in view of his sovereignty over us, "yet he is not the most high God, the same with the Father, but subordinate to Him."²⁹ This subordination notwithstanding, we must not infer "that by this account there will be another God, or

---

22. Edwards, *Gangraena*, 1646, I.ii.21–22. For Edwards, a Church of England clergyman, see ODNB.

23. Ibid., I.ii.1. For Webb (birth and death dates unknown), see SI. For Goodwin and Erbury, both of whom were of Queens' College, Cambridge, the latter thereafter Brasenone College, Oxford, see ODNB, SI. For Hobson, see ODNB.

24. See H. John McLachlan, *Socinianism*, 120. For Josselin, see ODNB, SI.

25. For whom, see ODCC, ODNB.

26. Biddle, *A Confession of Faith*, 1.

27. Ibid., 9.

28. Ibid., 19.

29. Ibid., 29.

two gods."[30] Biddle's efforts were rewarded with a term in prison, where he remained until freed under Oliver Cromwell's "Act of Oblivion" in 1652. On his release Biddle translated and published more Socinian tracts, and in 1654 there appeared *A Twofold Catechism: The One Simply Called A Scripture Catechism; The Other, A Brief Scripture Catechism for Children.* In the former he adduces scriptural verses from which we are expected to infer that Jesus the Son of God, conceived by the Holy Spirit and born of Mary, was not eternally generate.[31] Again Biddle was sent to gaol, where he died a martyr's death. It remains to add that Biddle's writings are replete with quotations from the Bible, as befits one who stoutly maintained the sufficiency of Scripture and believed that the arguments of his orthodox opponents could be refuted therefrom. The latter, persuaded to the contrary, took up their pens and attended self-fortifying meetings, such as the nine gatherings of the Wirksworth Presbyterian Classis held between June 1655 and July 1657, where anti-Socinian apologetic weaponry was honed.[32] No less orthodox was the Presbyterian, Philip Henry (1631–1696), who summed up his view thus: "though Jesus Christ was truly man, yet he was not a *mere* man, but God-man.... Christ our Redeemer, is God. This is the main doctrine of the gospel. If this fail, all fails."[33]

The biggest gun to sound against Biddle was that of John Owen, and with this we are reminded that our concern is not with armchair theological musings; many felt that heterodoxy threatened the stability of the nation. Accordingly, in 1654 Owen was commanded by the Council of State to write a refutation of Socinianism. The result was his *Vindiciae Evangelicae; or, The Mystery of the Gospel Vindicated and Socinianism Examined* (1655). Criticisms of some of Richard Baxter's animadversions upon the death of Christ,[34] and of the "perverse" expositions of Grotius on the deity of Christ, are to be found in Owen's work, the (vast) bulk of which concerns Biddle's *Catechism* and the *Racovian Catechism.* He counters Biddle's rejection of the view that God subsists in three persons. He refers to Cerinthus, Paul of Samosata, Arius and others, declaring that "God made their memory to rot, and their names

---

30. Ibid., 42.

31. Biddle, *A Twofold Catechism,* 29–30.

32. See H. J. McLachlan, *Socinianism,* 206.

33. Henry, *The Life of the Rev. Philip Henry,* 345. For Philip Henry, see also ODNB, SI. He was educated at Christ Church College, Oxford.

34. For Baxter (1615–91), the moderate episcopalian, see DHT, ODCC, ODNB.

to be an abomination to all generations."³⁵ In less *ad hominem* fashion, albeit with somewhat tortuous logic, he proceeds to argue as follows:

> By the subsisting of God in any person, no more is intended than that person's being God. If that person be God, God subsists in that person. If you grant the Father to be a person (as the Holy Spirit expressly affirms him to be, Heb. 1:3) and to be God, you grant God to subsist in that person. . . . The Son is God, or is not. To say he is not God, is to beg that which cannot be proved. If he be God, he is the Father, or he is another person. If he be the Father, he is not the Son. That he is the Son and not the Son is sufficiently contradictory. If he be not the Father, as was said, and yet be God, he may have the same nature and substance with the Father (for of our God there is but one essence, nature. or being), and yet be distinct from him. That distinction from him is his personality,—that property whereby and from whence he is the Son.³⁶

Owen concedes that in respect of the divine circumincession—a "barbarous term"—the schoolmen were unduly "curious in their inquiries" and "bold in their expressions," and thinks that the term can be lost without any prejudice to the doctrine of the Trinity.³⁷ He does, however, stand by the doctrine of the eternal generation of the Son, which Biddle rejects. He contends that since Christ is the Son by whom all the worlds were made (Heb 1:2), he had his sonship before his incarnation, and "when he had his sonship he had his generation."³⁸ Owen's *Vindiciae Evangelicae* includes more that seventy pages in which he defends the deity of Christ against the *Racovian Catechism*. Happily, in his later work, *A Brief Declaration and Vindication of the Doctrine of the Trinity* (1669), he is more concise in stating the nub of his case. He notes that according to the *Racovian Catechism* Christ is "by no means" a mere man; yet in answer to their next question, "hath he a divine nature also?" the Socinians reply, "By no means; for this is contrary to right reason." If asked how this assertion is to be reconciled with the claim that Christ is more than a mere man, they reply, "because he was born of a virgin"—the very claim that "Scripture, and all men of right wits, grant to

---

35. J. Owen, *Works*, XII, 72.
36. Ibid., 72–73.
37. Ibid., 73.
38. Ibid., 74.

be an invincible reason to prove him to be a man, and, as he was born of her, no more."[39] When the *Catechism* protests that Jesus was endowed with the Spirit, wrought miracles, was raised from the dead, and had all power given to him, and thus "by these degrees he came to be God," Owen retorts that "all men see that the inquiry is about the nature of Christ, and this answer is about his state and condition."[40]

Of the early Baptist confessions of faith it is the *Standard Confession* (1660) of the General Baptists that most clearly manifests what might be termed a tincture of Christological ambivalence. Thus the first paragraph refers to God the Father, but not to the other persons of the Trinity, while the third unequivocally describes the "one Lord Jesus Christ" as "the only begotten Son of God, born of the Virgin Mary . . ." Paragraph eleven offers an alternative to those who repent and profess faith in Christ: they may be baptized either "in the name of the Father, Son and holy Spirit, or in the name of the Lord Jesus." Paragraph twenty-seven asserts the duty of "the true Church of Christ" to "reject all Hereticks."[41] The abiding impression is that there was less than unanimity among the General Baptists of the time concerning the perimeter of acceptable doctrine. For this reason the General Baptist, Matthew Caffyn (bapt. 1628–1714)[42]—the "Battle Axe of Sussex," who had been imprisoned five times prior to the Toleration Act of 1689—was able to steer close to the heterodox wind; and for the same reason his more orthodox peers found it difficult to make their charges stick against him. There was even a geographical distinction between the generally more latitudinarian General Baptists of Kent and Sussex and those of Buckinghamshire, whose Christian inheritance included Lollardy. The latter charged Caffyn with blasphemy at Aylesbury in 1672, and he was perceived as prevaricating in his replies. He did, indeed, express his puzzlement concerning the person of Christ, and he in turn has puzzled subsequent historians as to his Christological views. Some regard him as having been influenced by the German Anabaptist Melchior Hoffman (c. 1500–c. 1543), who taught that since humanity as a whole is under the curse of sin and death, Jesus could not be our redeemer if his flesh were Mary's flesh and blood; and this would mean that redemption had not yet occurred. Positively,

---

39. Ibid., II, 413–14.
40. Ibid., 414.
41. Lumpkin, *Baptist Confessions*, 225, 228, 230.
42. For whom, see ODNB.

Hoffman declared that the eternal Word became incarnate. This is clearly a variety of docetism, and it does not seem that Caffyn embraced it: indeed he published denunciations of the doctrine, not least as it was espoused by some Quakers. It seems more likely that Caffyn tended in the direction of Caspar Schwenckfeld's view that Christ's truly human flesh was given to him by the Father, and that Mary was the vehicle for his birth on earth.[43] However this may be, immediately following the Aylesbury meeting Thomas Monk rushed into print with *A Cure for the Cankering Error of the New Eutycians: Who (Concerning the Truth) Have Erred; Saying That Our Blessed Mediator Did Not Take His Flesh of the Virgin Mary*. In 1679 Monk joined with fifty-four General Baptists from Buckinghamshire, Hertfordshire, Bedfordshire, and Oxford in publishing an *Orthodox Creed*. Their Christological section is a medley of positive affirmations regarding the co-equality of the persons of the Trinity and the eternal generation of the Son, and negative ones designed to rule out adoptionism, Arianism, Socinianism, and Melchiorism:

> We confess and believe, that the Son of God, or the eternal word, is very and true God, having his personal subsistence of the father alone, and yet for ever of himself as God; and of the father as the son, the eternal son of an eternal father; not later in the beginning. There never was any time when he was not, not other in substance . . . not metaphorical, or subordinate God; not a God by office, but a God by nature, coequal, coessential, and coeternal with the father and the holy ghost. . . . [T]he second person in the sacred Trinity, took to himself a true, real, and fleshly body, and reasonable soul, being conceived in the fullness of time by the holy ghost, and born of the virgin Mary, and became very and true man.[44]

For good measure they appended in full the Apostles, Nicene, and Athanasian Creeds, and urged their catechetical use among young and old alike.

Caffyn was again challenged at the General Baptist Assemblies of 1691 and 1693. On the latter occasion the question was put,

> whether Christ as he was the Word of God John 1:1, Albeit that he was God yet he is not of the Uncreated Substance of his fa-

---

43. Having already written this, I am pleased to find myself in agreement with Stephen R. Holmes. See Cross and Wood, eds, *Exploring Baptist Origins*, 129.

44. Lumpkin, *Baptist Confessions*, 299–300.

> ther But God made him a creature only And secondly that this Creature was made flesh & Blood & Bones in the Virgins Womb Not by takeing flesh of the Virgin Mary But ye Matter (viz) the Word was turned into flesh in the Virgins Wombe being
>
> Audibly read was universally owned to be an error in the Terms aforesaid. Bror Smart charging Bror Caffin with owneing the last aforementioned Ques. Bror Caffin was acquitted by far the greater part of the Assembly.[45]

With this the Assembly firmly set its face against Melchiorism, and failed to convict Caffyn of it.

Yet again, at the Assembly of 1700, the messengers from Buckinghamshire and Northamptonshire brought a further charge against Caffyn. It was "Agreed that the Defence Bror Mathew Caffin made in the Assembly and his Acknowledgement was in the satisfaccon of the Assembly." Thus, as on previous occasions, Caffyn escaped church discipline. Meanwhile in 1696 a more orthodox General Association was constituted over against the General Assembly. The breach was temporarily healed in 1704, when, on the basis of a document written at the behest of the Assembly entitled, "The Unity of the Churches," six articles were agreed as being the basis of union. The critical Christological clause reads as follows: "We do believe, that there is but one Lord Jesus Christ, the second Person in the Trinity, and the only begotten Son of God; and that he did, in the fullness of time, take to himself our nature, in the womb of the blessed Virgin Mary, of whom, *in respect of the flesh*, he was made; and so is true God, and true Man, our Immanuel."[46] The words I have italicized indicate that, however the opinions of Caffyn were to be understood, the drafters thought it necessary to rule out any suggestion of Melchiorism. However, when at the Assembly of 1705 formal assent to the articles was required as a condition of membership of the Assembly, a further breach ensued and another Assembly was constituted, largely comprising representatives from Kent, Sussex, East Anglia and the West.[47]

---

45. Whitley, ed., *Minutes*, 41.
46. Lumpkin, *Baptist Confessions*, 340.
47. See Whitley, ed., *Minutes*, xx–xxiii. For my fuller account of the Caffyn affair see Sell, *Testimony and Tradition*, 52–56.

Classical Affirmations and Alternative Stances

It was only to be expected that the views heard by messengers at the various assemblies would influence church life on the ground.[48] The General Baptist ministers, Richard Allen, Benjamin Keach (1640–1704), Mark Key and Shad Thames joined the Particular Baptists between 1679 and 1689.[49] The Particular Baptists of Smarden, Kent, expelled the General Baptists in 1706,[50] while by 1716 there were three varieties of Baptist causes at Cranbrook, Kent.[51]

Lest it be thought that Christological issues disturbed the General Baptists of the south-east only, mention may be made of the situation in Shrewsbury, where the church members were disturbed by the views of Richard Newton, a glover, who had been prosecuted on at least twenty-four occasions for not attending the Parish Church, and whose son, Habakkuk followed suit. In 1692 the church members, led by Brother Brown, addressed their concern to the General Baptist Assembly, and received the following advice in reply: "Whereas we, are Informed that you are troubled wth. Severall persons who teach & maintain Socinianisme or Doctrines contrary to the Articles of our faith Our Advice unto you is That you call in the assistance of the Sister Churches in your parts & take such method to reclaim them as shall be judged most Necessary & so wee bid you heartily farewell."[52] At the same time the Association wrote "To our Beloved Bror Richd. Newton," urging him to "forbear & Desist troubling of the peace and welfare of our Brethren But if you should persist in these errors which we pray that you might not we have sent Advice to our Brethren what to do in that Case."[53]

During last two decades of the seventeenth century the orthodox Dissenters kept their flags flying in a variety of ways. In 1697, for example, Pastor Thomas Badland and forty-one church members of "A Particular Church of Christ in Worcester," signed their local covenant, which in the wake of recent persecutions in Worcester, is staunchly Trinitarian. It opens with the assertion that "there is one only God, the Father," it

---

48. I draw the following examples from Sell, *Testimony and Tradition*, 56.

49. Torbet, *A History of the Baptists*, 64. For Keach (1640–1704), see ODNB.

50. See Packer, *The Unitarian Heritage in Kent*, 10; Anon., "Baptist Churches in the Weald," 374.

51. For the local influence of Caffyn, see Kensett, *History of the Free Christian Church in Horsham*.

52. Collis, *Shropshire*, 94.

53. Ibid.

affirms that the Son is "God, and one with the Father [who] did take to him our nature, and became man, being conceived of the Holy Ghost in the Virgin Mary, and born of her, and named Jesus Christ." The concluding paragraph begins, "We do take this one God for our only God, and our chief good, and this Jesus Christ for our only Lord, Redeemer, and Saviour, and this Holy Ghost for our Sanctifier..."[54] Again, in his exposition of the *Westminster Shorter Catechism,* Thomas Watson denounces "the execrable opinion of the Socinians, who deny the Divinity of the Lord Jesus, and make him to be a creature only, but of a higher rank."[55] He grants that "The Trinity is purely an object of faith; the plumbline of reason is too short to fathom this mystery; but where reason cannot wade, there faith may swim."[56]

The 1690s saw a spate of publishing on all sides of the Christological question, and from all quarters. The Church of England businessman, Thomas Firmin (1632–1697),[57] sponsored a series of *Unitarian Tracts* (from 1694), among the anonymous contributors to which was the clergyman Stephen Nye (1647/8–1719),[58] whose father, John (bapt. 1620, d. 1686?),[59] had written an anti-Socinian tract, and whose great uncle was Philip Nye of the Westminster Assembly and *Savoy Declaration*. Nye's objective was to combat tritheism, to which charge William Sherlock had laid himself open in his *Vindication of the Doctrine of the Trinity* (1691), and this he did in a manner reminiscent of Sabellianism. Nye is remembered as the first to use the term "Unitarian" on the title page of a book published in England.[60] Meanwhile the Presbyterians and the Congregationalists had cemented a "Happy Union" in 1690. This was a union of ministers, not of churches, and one of the fruits was the establishment of a common Fund for the support of the Dissenting interest. However, the Union failed in 1693, when the Congregationalists—above all Isaac Chauncy (1632–1712)—accused the Presbyterians—especially Daniel Williams (1643?–1715)—of Socinianism; to which charge the

---

54. Anon., *A Fac-Simile Copy of the Original* Covenant, 39–40. For Badland (1634–98), see SI.

55. Watson, *A Body of Divinity*, 110.

56. Ibid., 112.

57. For whom, see ODNB.

58. For whom, see ODNB.

59. For whom, see ODNB.

60. The book is, *A Brief History of the Unitarians, called also Socinians*, London, 1687.

Presbyterians responded by inviting the Congregationalists to disavow antinomianism, which they refused to do.[61] The Congregationalists withdrew from the Fund, created their own, and henceforward sought to support more orthodox Dissenters. In the following year, in his Pinner's Hall Lecture, the Congregationalist, Nathaniel Mather (1630–97), branded Williams a semi-Socinian, in consequence of which the Presbyterians established their own Salters' Hall Lecture. The Congregationalists kept up their anti-Socinian pressure—in 1695 Williams was again accused of Socinianism, this time by Stephen Lobb (1647?–1699).[62] Among other Presbyterians who, like Watson, were not inclined to heterodoxy were Richard Frankland (1630–1698), the tutor whose northern academy, owing to prevailing adverse legislation, was unavoidably peripatetic,[63] and Oliver Heywood (1629–1702).[64] In 1697 Frankland published his orthodox *Reflections on a Letter Writ by a Nameless Author . . . and on His Bold Reflections on the Trinity*, and his friend, Heywood, contributed a Preface. Heywood expresses entire sympathy with Frankland's views and, with reference to Socinianism and Arianism he laments, "Surely, 'tis a thousand Pities that in England, a Goshen, a Land of Light, where the Gospel-Sun hath shined in its Meridian Splendor, such black Fogs should rise out of the bottomless Pit as to darken our Horizon."[65] Yet another Presbyterian William Bates (1625–1699),[66] led an appeal to the King against Socinianism—one of the stimuli to the Blasphemy Act of 1698. This Act, the objective of which was "the more effectual suppressing of blasphemy and profaneness," was directed against those who, having been educated in, or having made profession of, the Christian religion, now denied any of the persons of the Trinity to be God. First offenders were excluded from civil office—a disability removed if they recanted within four months of their conviction; additional civil disabilities and three years' imprisonment followed a second offence.[67]

61. For Chauncey, educated at Harvard University, and Williams, see ODNB, SI.

62. For whom, see SI.

63. See Sell, *Church Planting*, 26–28; Sell, *Philosophy, Dissent and Nonconformity*, 10, 24–25. The academy relocated on five occasions between 1683 and 1689. For Frankland, who was educated at Christ's College, Cambridge, see ODNB, SI.

64. For whom, see ODNB. He was educated at Trinity College, Cambridge.

65. Quoted by Nicholson and Axon, *The Older Nonconformity in Kendal*, 185.

66. For whom, see ODNB, SI. He was educated at Cambridge and Oxford Universities.

67. See Bennett, *Laws Against Nonconformity*, 188–89.

3

Nonconformist Christology in the Eighteenth Century

It is manifestly the case that throughout the long eighteenth century (and, indeed, down to the present day), there were Nonconformists who upheld the classical doctrines regarding Christ's eternal generation and divine-human nature. Prominent in this regard were the high Calvinist[1] Baptist John Gill (1697–1771), and the evangelical Calvinist Baptist, Andrew Fuller (1754–1815).[2] Gill affirms that "Christ the Son of God . . . in the fullness of time was made of a woman, or became incarnate."[3] He is especially concerned to defend the doctrine of the eternal generation of the Son; indeed after his *Declaration of Faith and Practice* was entered in the Church Book at Southwark, where he was minister, he added a further clause to underline the doctrine and to exclude the pre-existarian notion that the human soul of Jesus existed eternally. He was convinced that if eternal generation were denied the distinction between the persons of the Trinity, and the relation between the first and second persons, would be lost. Fuller similarly excludes both pre-existarianism and adoptionism when he writes that "Christ is

---

1. By an hyper-Calvinist I mean one who will not freely offer the gospel, and who denies that all persons have a duty to repent and believe in Jesus Christ. The proximate influence here is that of Joseph Hussey (1659–1726), the Presbyterian turned Congregationalist, among whose Cambridge church members was John Skepp (1675–1721), who in turn influenced John Brine (1703–1765), his successor at Currier's Hall, and John Gill, in whose ordination service in 1720 he took part. See further, Sell, *The Great Debate*, 52–54, 78. By a "high Calvinist" I mean one who does not hold the "hyper" position, but who is a double predestinarian. By a "moderate Calvinist" I mean one who, frequently under evangelical influence and/or because of the repudiation on moral grounds of deterministic understandings of predestination, questions some aspects of Calvinistic scholasticism.

2. For Gill, see DEB, ODNB; for Fuller, see DEB, ODCC, ODNB.

3. Gill, *A Complete Body of Doctrinal and Practical Divinity*, I, 198.

called the Son of God antecedently to his miraculous conception, and consequently he did not become such by it.... [I]n the order of nature the Father must have existed before the Son; but, in that of duration, he never existed without the Son. The Father and the Son, therefore, are properly eternal."[4]

But (and this is what makes the long eighteenth century the doctrinal minefield that it is) some authors were influenced by heterodox opinions that were in the intellectual air of the time. Indeed, when writing the words I have just quoted, Gill had the Arians and Socinians in his sights, while Fuller was in pursuit of Joseph Priestley and the Socinians/Unitarians, as we shall see.

As we brace ourselves to dip a toe into the turbulent doctrinal waters of the period we must bear a number of factors in mind. First, and most easily overlooked amidst the proliferation of polemical pamphlets and books, is the simple fact that a sizeable number of divines evinced little or no interest in doctrinal squabbling, and some had little interest in doctrine at all. Thus, we learn that John Reynall (1736-1800),[5] who studied under Caleb Ashworth (d. 1775)[6] at Daventry Academy, "was unfriendly to controversy, and seldom dwelt on speculative points of theology.... He was fond of rural pursuits and recreations, as well as of his books."[7] From the same Academy came Henry Procter (1733-1808), who "had some knowledge, and a great deal of anecdote, and he had a considerable library of useful books." He presided over the decline of the united Presbyterian charges of Stafford and Stone, where he served from 1789 until his death in 1808, by which time had outlived his faculties and was "only the ruins of a man."[8] Such men were not the stuff of which doctrinal gladiators are made.

4. Andrew Gunton Fuller, ed., *The Works of Andrew Fuller*, 944.

5. For whom, see SI.

6. For Ashworth, see ODNB, SI; Sell, "Caleb Ashworth of Daventry: his academy, church and students," forthcoming. He was educated under Doddridge at Northampton Academy.

7. Murch, *West of England*, 516, 517. We should note the important distinction to be drawn between the early academies in which a broad general education was given to men not all of whom were destined for the ministry, and later Nonconformist theological colleges the principal objective of which was the supply of adequately trained ministers. Of the latter, the Countess of Huntingdon's college at Trefeca was a pioneer. See further, Sell, *Philosophy, Dissent and Nonconformity*, 27–54.

8. G. E. Evans, *Midland Churches*, 126. Matthews, *Staffordshire*, wrongly names him William on p. 111, but corrects the error on p. 260. For Procter, see SI.

Again, others thought it unbecoming and a poor witness to Christ that ministers should be at loggerheads over doctrinal points. On 6 July 1753 Peter Baron (d. 1759?) addressed a letter to Henry Walrond, minister at Barnstaple. Baron, co-pastor first with John Enty (d. 1743) and then with John Moore (d. 1760) at Batter Street, Plymouth, was ordained on July 19, 1704. He retained vivid and distressing memories of the doctrinal discord preceding and following the Salters' Hall conference of 1719 (of which more shortly). His letter to a younger colleague trained at Tiverton under John Moore (d. 1730), comes as from one "overtaken with age, and bowed down with infirmities." He pleads for preservation of "the honour of God, of Christ, and the Holy Sprit," and laments that "The bad lives of some, and the fierce contentions of other professing christians [sic] will, I fear, make me go sorrowing to the grave."[9] With regard to the key issue of Trinitarian subscription, he recalls that:

> The silence of some, and the declarations of others, in terms that were not liked, brought on such animosities, distractions, and divisions, between Ministers and people, as I hoped never to see or hear more. Many learned and good men, who I doubt not, are now in heaven, and others going thither, fell under great hardships and sufferings that I did not then foresee, whom I heartily pitied, helping some of them, according to my narrow abilities, in their distress. Observing these sad and rueful effects, I long since determined never to say or do what might bear hard upon my brethren, who are accomplished with learning, do lead good lives, do believe in the divine authority of the sacred scriptures, and particularly all that therein is expressly said of God the Father, of God the Son and of God the Holy Ghost.

Then with reference to recent deliberations of the Assembly of the Protestant Dissenting Ministers of Devon and Cornwall, he declares that:

> People should not entertain groundless jealousies, or throw out uncharitable surmises concerning worthy Ministers, who live well, and preach well; and so render their labours useless, and their lives grievous, to the great discouragement of others to prepare for and enter on the Ministry, to the dissolving our general Assembly, to the shutting up the doors of many churches, and to

---

9. For Baron, Walrond (educated at Tiverton Academy), Enty (educated at Taunton Academy), Moore and Moore, see SI.

the destroying, in this part of the world, Nonconformity, which I am fully persuaded is the cause of Christ.[10]

It was the easiest thing in the eighteenth-century world for a person of such a charitable and peaceable disposition to find himself labelled by the orthodox as at least a fellow-traveller with the heterodox. This may have been the fate of the Presbyterian Thomas Whitaker (d. 1778), who ministered at Call Lane, Leeds from 1727 to 1776. Of this "plain, serious, practical preacher" it is written that "as he sedulously avoided all points of controversy at a time when some of the most essential doctrines of the Gospel were denied, his love for those doctrines may be regarded as questionable. A considerable number of his hearers were at least suspicious on the subject, and left him to attend the preaching of Mr. Edwards."[11] Whitaker had succeeded his father, also Thomas, in the pastorate at Call Lane, and his son William, educated under Caleb Ashworth at Daventry, served as his assistant. With the passage of time the chapel came to be used by General Baptists, and there is a suggestion that Whitaker himself may have moved in that direction.

In the two following chapters I shall record a number of instances of secession; but secession was not the only option when church members disagreed with the doctrinal position of their ministers: opponents could, for example, remain *in situ* and cause a fuss. Thus, in 1753 James Ritchie (1698–1763), an MD of Glasgow University, removed from Alston, Cumberland, to Mixenden, Yorkshire, on receiving the call of the Presbyterians there. He had begun his ministry at Ravenstonedale in 1733 (in which connection we shall meet him again), and he was an Arian. This greatly displeased Benjamin Patchett, one of his elders, who published, *A Short Inquiry into the Proper Qualification of Gospel Ministers: With Some Directions How We, Who Are Hearers, May Know Whether the Doctrines our Ministers Deliver from the Pulpit are According to God's Mind and Will, or Not* (1759). Patchett "was in the habit of calling out to the minister in the pulpit when anything displeased him. He was much respected and feared."[12] Such provocations notwithstanding, Ritchie remained in post until his death in October 1763. Yet another

10. Manning, *A Sketch*, 55, 56–57, 58. Manning (1781–1856) was educated at Towgood's Exeter Academy.

11. Miall, *Congregationalism in Yorkshire*, 304. For the Whitaker ministers, see SI.

12. Ibid., 318, though note that Ritchie came to Mixenden from Alston, not Alton as stated by Miall.

option open to the non-seceding disgruntled was taken by the saints at Mixenden. Ritchie was succeeded there by the heterodox Thomas Evans (d. 1779) and David Gronow (d. 1796), both trained at Carmarthen Academy, the former an Arian, the latter a Unitarian who "seems, from his entries in the church registers, to have only imperfectly understood and written the English language."[13] They were followed by Daniel Jones, of whose origins and opinions little is known, and then came a great doctrinal contrast. In 1791 James Rattray (1748–1806), an alumnus of Glasgow University, accepted the call to the pastorate. "He," we learn, "was a zealous Calvinist, little to the satisfaction of his hearers." He is said to have been "starved out."[14]

Next, we need to be alive to the fact that some possessed of sensitive doctrinal antennae were not immune to the temptation to indulge in the tactics we nowadays associate with the tabloid press. In fact some appear to have yielded to the temptation to scurrility and defamation with zeal and glee. Nicknaming was rife, and although such former nicknames as "Quaker" and "Methodist" have acquired respectability, those who first coined them were motivated by disapproval. We might also note that those thus labelled could "give as good as they got," as when John Wesley, deeming the high Calvinist Toplady "too dirty a writer for me to meddle with,"[15] left him to Sellon the baker-preacher, who lambasted Toplady with fourteen epithets, some of which, as Toplady wryly noted—Papist, Socinian, Mahometan, Atheist—were mutually exclusive.[16] For his part, the high Calvinist Presbyterian Thomas Edwards had earlier inveighed against the (unusually) Arminian Congregationalist, John Goodwin, describing him as "a monstrous sectary, a compound of Socinianism, Arminianism, Libertinism, Antinomianism, Independency, Popery, yea and of Scepticism . . ."[17] Needless to say, such invective failed to convert

13. Ibid., 319.

14. Ibid., though note that Miall names him James. Ritchie, Evans, Gronow, Jones, and Rattray are in SI.

15. Quoted by Tyerman, *The Life and Times of the Rev. John Wesley*, III, 83. The bibliography on Wesley (1703–91) is vast, but a beginning can be made with DEB, DHT, DMBI, ODCC, ODNB. He was educated at Christ Church, Oxford.

16. Toplady, *Complete Works*, 50. See further, Sell, *Enlightenment, Ecumenism, Evangel*, ch. 12.

17. T. Edwards, *Gangraena*, III, 114. More than a century on, Toplady hounded Goodwin in the Introduction to his vast tome, *Historic Proof of the Doctrinal Calvinism of the Church of England*, 1774. Of Goodwin it was said that "he was a man by himself; was against every man, and had every man almost against him." See Granger, *A Biographical History*, III, 42.

the accused, some of whom were more than adept at turning the tables on their accusers—among them the Presbyterian Arian, Samuel Bourn the Younger (1689–1754):

> Calling a Man *Arian* or *Arminian* has sometimes produced the same Effects among the Dissenters, as calling him *Presbyterian* has amongst our Church Bigots; or as calling him *Heretick* has done amongst the Papists. He becomes the Object of vulgar Hatred, and every Zealot has a Stone to throw at him, as if he was a *mad Dog*.
>
> But a little Reflection will inable you to see, that as in the Mouth of a Papist, *Heretick* is usually the Mark or Denomination of an upright, conscientious Christian; and as in the Mouth of a Church Bigot, *Presbyterian* means a honest Protestant; so in the Mouth of a Dissenting Zealot, *Arian* and *Arminian* are almost certain Marks of a sincere, inquisitive, learned Man.[18]

In a letter to Samuel Palmer of 27 March 1777, Job Orton remarked on the use of doctrinal terms as weapons by members of the Old Meeting, Kidderminster, where Benjamin Fawcett was minister: "You have probably seen Mr. *Fawcett's* 'Candid Reflections upon the Trinity.' I think it will for ever ruin his reputation among the warm zealous people, who are very stiff and bigoted, and call every minister an *Arian* who does not use their favourite phrases and doxologies, though they know nothing of the matter."[19]

It must be conceded that some hostile writers may have thought that one out of a catch-all range of epithets, however mutually contradictory, might hit the target, for some divines were less than forthright in the matter of self-labelling, and this for a variety of reasons. "Why," asked the Arian Presbyterian, James Peirce (1674–1726), "should we I pray, be denominated from Arius? Did we ever propose any particular veneration for him? Do we pretend, nay, do we not most positively deny, that we have received our opinions from him?"[20] Peirce, like many

---

18. [S. Bourn], *An Address to Protestant* Dissenters, 17. For Bourn, see ODNB, SI; Sell, *Dissenting Thought*, ch. 7. He was educated at Manchester Academy.

19. Orton, *Letters to Dissenting Ministers*, II, 182–83. For Orton (1717–83) and Fawcett (1715–80) see ODNB, SI. Orton and Fawcett were educated under Philip Doddridge at Northampton Academy, Palmer under Caleb Ashworth at the continuation academy at Daventry.

20. Peirce, *The Evil and Cure of Divisions*, 25. This was a sermon preached on March 15, 1719, on the occasion of the opening of a new meeting house in Exeter following Peirce's ejection from his former charge in the city. For Peirce, see ODNB, SI. He was educated at the universities of Utrecht and Leiden.

others appealed to the principle of the sufficiency of Scripture—a point to which I shall return. Almost twenty years later Samuel Bourn felt it appropriate to repeat the point: "Are Men, who profess to have *no other* Master of their Faith but *Jesus* Christ, and to derive all their Notions about revealed Religion from the New Testament, Arians? Can any conscientious Men call them so, while they profess not to have received one Notion from him, to have no acquaintance with him, and to have seen none of his Writings, and while they disclaim such as are reported to be his peculiar tenets?"[21] In an earlier generation John Knowles (1600?–1685) had declared that he had never met anyone known to be a Socinian; that he had heard of Socinus, but that "I have never read over one Book of his; all his works I never saw as yet."[22] This would appear to be the ambiguity of one who was anxious not to invite punishment under the law for the open profession of anti-Trinitarian views. Knowles says that he had never "read over one Socinian book"—presumably from cover to cover; and that he had not seen all his works. He did, however, have two significant treatises by Socinus in his library.[23]

With reference to the eighteenth century, Robert Halley observed with hindsight that many ministers "said little about controverted doctrines," and that Arianism "was a comfortable resting-place for some of the Presbyterian ministers so long as they could contrive to say nothing about it."[24] There is a suggestion of implied duplicity in this judgment and, indeed, when Daniel Phillips (1716–1800), who ministered at Sowerby from 1753 to 1783 told a ministerial colleague that "there was not a person in his congregation who knew his real sentiments on religious subjects [which were heterodox]," Job Wilson, then aged seven, overheard this conversation and was shocked by what he took to be his minister's dishonesty.[25] No doubt some ministers were hypocritical; pos-

---

21. S. Bourn, *An Address to Protestant Dissenters*, 51.

22. Knowles, *An Answer to Mr. Ferguson's Book*, 4. For Knowles, see ODNB, SI.

23. See H. John McLachlan, Socinianism, 280.

24. Halley, *Lancashire*, II, 382. For Halley (1796–1876), see DEB, ODNB, SI. He was educated at Homerton College.

25. See Powicke, *A History of the Cheshire County* Union, 17. But Powicke states that Wilson was born at "Sowerby, near Halifax," where the unnamed minister served. He was in fact born at Sowerby, North Yorkshire, and then the minister I have named, and his dates at Sowerby, 1753–87, fit the anecdote; as does the fact that Phillips was educated at Carmarthen and at Findern under Ebenezer Latham (1688–1754)—two academies with a "liberal" reputation at the time. For Phillips, see SI. Job Wilson (1765–1838),

sibly some were discreet in order to hold their flocks together and secure their stipends, but the discretion of others was definitely in the interests of a catholicity rooted in the fundamentals of the faith and a non-sectarian attitude towards what they regarded as secondary doctrinal refinements. Thus, of John Jennings (1687/8–1723), his tutor at Kibworth Academy, Philip Doddridge (1702–1751) wrote, "He furnishes us with all kinds of authors upon every subject, without advising us to skip over the heretical passages for fear of infection. It is evidently his main care to inspire us with sentiments of Catholicism."[26] This educational approach was viewed askance by those who thought that it made for doctrinal confusion and undermined orthodoxy. We should remember, however, that the vocation of the Dissenting academy tutors was to provide a higher education to those who were otherwise excluded from it, and that while many of their students were ordinands, others were not, and the academies were not ministerial training seminaries.

Some of those deemed heterodox simply believed, as the Presbyterian Samuel Chandler (1693–1766) did—in reply to the Congregationalist Calvinist John Guyse (1680–1761),[27] that there was no place for "the bringing of party differences into our pulpits." Such behaviour, he thought, was a probable cause of "the cold, low, and withering state of religion."[28] The Arian Micaijah Towgood was similarly minded, and for this he was praised by his memoirist: "Would to God, that all ministers of religion, like this amiable preacher, could be induced to drop

---

for whom, see SI, later trained for the ministry at Northowram Academy. Following a year of itinerant ministry in Cheshire he served at Northwich and Middlewich in the same county. For Latham, see ODNB, SI. He was educated at Shrewsbury Academy and Glasgow University.

26. Letter of Doddridge to Samuel Clark of St. Albans, [22] September 1722. See Nuttall, *Calendar*, no. 35. See further, Sell, *Philosophy, Dissent and Nonconformity*, 49–50, 218. In this book mention is made of all of the Dissenting academies and Nonconformist theological colleges to be referred to subsequently in this paper, with special reference to the place of philosophy in the curriculum, and to the contributions to that discipline made by their tutors, professors and alumni. For Jennings, who was educated at Attercliffe Academy under Timothy Jollie, see SI; for Doddridge, see DEB, ODCC, ODNB, SI.

27. For whom, see ODNB, SI. He was educated at Saffron Walden Academy under William Payne (d. 1726), for whom, see SI.

28. Chandler, *A Letter to the Rev. Mr. John Guyse*, 88. For Chandler and Guyse, see ODNB, SI. For Chandler, see also Sell, *Hinterland Theology*, ch. 4 and *passim*. He was educated at Leiden University and at the academies at Bridgewater and Gloucester/Tewkesbury.

their disputes at the shrine of piety . . ."[29] The reference to Towgood cautions us that not all those deemed Arian we likeminded in all respects; for whereas Towgood may be called a "high Arian" because he did not forbid the worship of Christ at the Lord's Supper, his younger contemporary, the Arian Richard Price (1723–1791),[30] did not think that Christ was a proper object of worship. We might also note that what one person perceived as virtues might, by another, be suspected as revelatory of doctrinal slipperiness. Thus, for example, in his funeral sermon on the death of Henry Grove (1683–1738), the Presbyterian academy tutor at Taunton, James Strong (1686?–1738) remarked, "He was very charitable in his sentiments of those that were of different opinions from himself . . . I never knew him earnest and zealous for, or against, any particular principles"[31]—claims that the ultra-orthodox would have regarded as damning indeed.

Mixed motives—or, at least, a variety of motives—those deemed heterodox may have had,[32] but what united them—whether they were Socinians or Arians—was their appeal to the sufficiency of Scripture and their perceived obligation to bring reason to bear upon their belief systems. When we recall that earlier ones among them had lived through the turmoil of Civil War and had been appalled at the activities of some of the Commonwealth sectaries; and that memories of this period lingered strongly in the minds of those of their eighteenth-century successors who encountered an evangelical "enthusiasm" that seemed to them to border on the irrational if not the fantastic, their general stance is by no means to be condemned out of hand. They were determined to go no farther than the Bible would take them, and to eschew

29. Manning, "A sketch," 426.

30. For whom, see DECBP, DWB, ODCC, ODNB, SI. He was educated at Llwynllwyd and Hoxton academies.

31. Strong, *The Suddenness of Christ's coming*, 26. For Grove (1684–1738), see DECBP, ODNB, SI; Sell, *Dissenting Thought*, ch. 6; Sell, *Testimony and Tradition*, ch. 5. For Strong, see ODNB, SI. He was educated at Taunton Academy.

32. Certainly the judgment of A. G. Matthews requires qualification: "In intellectual ability and in the moral earnestness which refused to use orthodox formulae because they were orthodox, and also in their zeal for a practical as well as merely doctrinal profession of Christianity, the Arians were ahead of their opponents." See *Staffordshire*, 109. This is the verdict of a Congregationalist of who, like some others of his denomination and generation, was relieved to have seen the back of scholastic Calvinism. The fact is that there was intellectual ability, moral earnestness—and there were moral lapses—on both sides of the doctrinal fence.

the opinions of men on the ground that "When Men set up their own fallible Interpretations for Standards of Faith . . . they visibly detract from the Authority and Sufficiency of the Holy Scriptures, and lay unjust Restraints upon our Consciences."[33] We might almost say that they became proto-fundamentalists—liberal ones, no doubt, but nevertheless mirror images of later conservative fundamentalists; for both parties thought that they were reading truth straight off the text; and in the case of the liberals, if they could *not* find terms in the biblical text they saw no obligation to adopt or endorse them. Thus with reference to the traditional Trinitarian-*cum*-Christological lexicon John Taylor of Norwich (1694–1761) thundered against:

> high swelling Words of Vanity; such as *Entity, Tri-Unity, Quoddity, Quiddity, Formalities, Essentialities, Primalities, Consubstantiality, necessary Emanation, hypostatical Union, mutual Circumplexion, a Trinity of Modes, Communication of Properties, Oeconomical, Co-essential, Co-equal, Co-eternal.* These, Christians, are barbarous Sounds, unknown to the pure and divine Mouth of thy Saviour, and the inspired Voice of his Apostles, whereby the Principles of Religion . . . have been worked into pompous Nonsense and profound Darkness.[34]

A roll-call of some of Taylor's publications emphasises his commitment to Scripture: *The Scripture Doctrine of Original* Sin, 1740; The *Lord's Supper Explained upon Scripture Principles*, 1756; *The Scripture Account of Prayer*, 1761; and *A Scheme of Scripture Divinity*, 1762. The problem is that the orthodox could and did write under analogous titles, and could express identical motives. Thus, for example, "I must not pin my faith upon the sleeve of any person or persons on earth, though never so holy or learned, as not knowing whither they may carry it; the best of men are but men at best: both God and man will expect from me, that I be able to render a Scripturall Reason of my faith and conscience."[35] Those are the quoted words of the Calvinist Congregationalist, Thomas Goodwin, than whom few were more orthodox. The moral is that all who came

---

33. Dodson, *Moderation and* Charity, 13. For Dodson, see SI. He entered the ministry in 1708, was at Penruddock from 1712 to 1721, and then removed first to Faringdon and thence to Marlborough.

34. J. Taylor, *A Narrative*, 13. For Taylor, see ODNB, SI; Sell, *Dissenting Thought*, ch. 7. He was educated at Findern and Whitehaven academies.

35. Anon, *Independency accused*, 1.

to the Scriptures in the seventeenth and eighteenth centuries, like all who have come to them in any century, have come with their presuppositions, and have engaged in acts of interpretation. Samuel Chandler made no bones about it: "My orthodoxy consists in believing as well as I can, from the best knowledge I can gather from Scripture; and I think that every honest man will form his principles according to the best of his understanding, and according to what he apprehends to be the mind of God in Christ."[36] There is, however, a difference of tone in the appeal to Scripture sufficiency as between the orthodox and the heterodox. The latter were much more likely to emphasise the right of private judgment, and to exalt the place of reason. The thought of Locke was in the air they breathed, and he had written,

> When [God] illuminates the Mind with supernatural Light, he does not extinguish that which is natural. If he would have us assent to the Truth of any Proposition, he either evidences that Truth by the usual Methods of Natural Reason, or else makes it known to be a Truth, which he would have us assent to, by his Authority, and convinces us that it is from him, by some Marks which *Reason* cannot be mistaken in. *Reason* must be our last judge and Guide in every Thing.[37]

The Presbyterian Arian divine, George Benson (1699–1762), educated at Whitehaven Academy under Thomas Dixon (1680–1729) and at Glasgow University, was one of many who took the point. He argued that "By our *reason*, we are to make trial of what is offered to us, as a *revelation* from God. Otherwise; how could we distinguish between the *Koran of Mahomet*, and the *Bible*?"[38]

With hindsight, and with reference to his own kind James Martineau (1805–1900)[39] declared that "The earlier Unitarians, notwithstanding their repute of rationalism, drew their doctrine out of the Scriptures, much to their own surprise, and did not import it into them."[40] It remains only to add that the heirs of those who embraced

---

36. Chandler, *A Second Letter*, 97.

37. Locke, *An Essay concerning Human Understanding*, IV.xix.14. On this and related matters, see Sell, *John Locke*, ch. 3.

38. Benson, *The Reasonableness of the Christian* Religion, I, 158. For Benson and Dixon, see ODNB, SI.

39. For whom, see DNCBP, ODNB.

40. Quoted by H. McLachlan, *The Unitarian* Movement, 13. For Martineau, see ODCC, ODNB.

Arianism, Socinianism or Unitarianism, or who adopted two or three of them in sequence, maintained the doctrine of Scripture sufficiency until the middle of the nineteenth century; by which time, under the influence of modern biblical criticism with its critique of the evidential value of miracles, the doctrine waned in Unitarian circles.[41]

I

As we delve more deeply into eighteenth century Christology we shall find that as the century proceeds a bolder Unitarianism begins to replace the somewhat milder Socinianism and the inherently unstable Arianism of earlier decades. We are not here speaking of solid schools, parties or movements, but rather of overlapping tendencies, which tendencies varied in strength, and were more or less articulate as between one individual and another. The advent of Methodism, whether Calvinistic or Arminian, will not be found to add new dimensions to the discussion of such oft-reiterated themes as the relation of the Son to the Father, the eternal generation of the Son, and the two natures of Christ. We should also be aware that although by now the so-called Toleration Act of 1689 was on the statute book, there were still many ways in which those who regretted its passing and who wished to turn the clock back—and such people may be found throughout the eighteenth century—could cause difficulties for the Dissenters who, although now granted freedom to worship, were subject to second-class citizenship in respect of educational, professional and civic opportunities. Of particular relevance to Christology is the fact that penalties for denying the Trinity could legally be imposed upon those pronounced guilty.

Thus, for example, the Presbyterian minister, Thomas Emlyn of Dublin (1663–1741), who had become a semi-Arian through reading William Sherlock's defence of the Trinity, was, in 1703, sentenced to more than two years' imprisonment upon the urging of a Baptist, Caleb Thomas. Emlyn's offence was to have published *An Humble Enquiry into the Scripture Account of Jesus Christ: or a Short Argument concerning His Deity and Glory, according to the Gospel* in the previous year. This tract appears in *A Collection of Tracts on the Deity of Christ*, on the title page of which Emlyn describes himself as "a Sufferer in this Cause." One can readily imagine the curdling of orthodox blood when, on the very

---

41. See Ruston, "English Approaches to Socinianism," 430–31.

first page he declares that "Jesus Christ is the chief of all subordinate powers."[42] He proceeds to argue that Christ "is indeed the *Lord of Lords*, but that Notes an Inferior Character, compared with that of *God of Gods* [1 Cor 8:5] . . . if he have a God above him, then he is not the Absolutely Supream God, tho' in relation to Created Beings, he may be a God (or Ruler) over all."[43] Emlyn's reading of the Bible persuades him that "the Man Christ is sufficient, by help from God, to manage his Universal Spiritual Kingdom" and accordingly, "I see no reason there will be to oppose those *Unitarians* who think him to be a sufficient Saviour and Prince, tho' he be not the only Supream God."[44] God, he says, expects Jesus to deliver his kingdom up to him, and this indicates the subordination of the Son to the Father.

That Emlyn had previously distressed the orthodox is clear from his tract, *A True Narrative of the Proceedings of the Dissenting Ministers of Dublin against Mr. Thomas Emlyn*, (1691). This is revealing both of his Christological puzzlement, his determination to settle his mind, and his reliance upon the sufficiency of Scripture:

> I own I had been settled in my notions from the time I read Dr. *Sherlock's* book of the Trinity, which sufficiently discovered how far many were gone backward toward polytheism; I long tried what I could do with some *Sabellian* turns, making out a Trinity of somewhats in one single mind. I found that by the tritheistical scheme of Dr. *Sherlock* and Mr. *Howe*, I best preserved a Trinity, but I lost the Unity: by the *Sabellian* scheme of modes and subsistences, and properties, &c. I best kept up the divine Unity; but then I had lost a Trinity, such as the Scripture discovers, so that I could never keep both in view at once. But after much serious thought, and study of the holy Scriptures, with many concerned addresses to the Father of lights, I found great reason, first to doubt, and after by degrees, to alter my judgment, in relation to formerly received opinions of the Trinity, and the *supreme Deity* of our Lord Jesus Christ. . . . I did not make reason the rule of my faith, but employed it to judge what was the meaning of that written rule or word of God; and thus was led to form notions

---

42. Emlyn, *An Humble Enquiry*, 1. For Emlyn, see ODNB, SI. He was educated at Cambridge University and Sulby Academy, Northamptonshire.

43. Ibid., 2.

44. Ibid., 4.

different from what others had taught me, without regard either to *Arius* or *Socinus*, not agreeing wholly with either.[45]

By none of this was the Presbyterian Matthew Henry (1662–1714) impressed. He records a visit from Emlyn, newly released from gaol, thus: "He was with me to-day, Sept. 1, 1705, and adheres to the Arian heresy. I had a deal of talk with him, endeavoured to shew him that even his own principles are nearer to the orthodox than the Socinian, which yet he was inclined to speak favourably of."[46] Henry summed up his own attitude thus: "It was a pleasure to Socinus, that arch-heretick, that he had no master: we wish it had been his fate to have had no scholars."[47]

That others were, like Henry, eager to maintain Calvinistic orthodoxy is exemplified by the fact that when in 1711 Bernard Foskett (1685–1758) went to Henley-in-Arden to join John Beddome (1697–1724) in ministering to a widely-scattered Baptist constituency that included the church at Alcester,[48] that church drew up *A Short and Compendius Confession of Faith Held by the Church of Christ Meeting at Aulcester in the County of Warwick Who are Baptized by Immersion upon a Personal Profession of Faith*. The second and third clauses of their Confession are as follows:

> We believe that this [one] God subsists in three distinct personalities and yet these three are one undivided essence . . .
>
> We believe that the Father is God, the Son of God, and the Holy Spirit is God; all equal in power, authority and glory & we believe this God is the only object of Divine worship and Adoration.[49]

In the following clause the Alcester Baptists affirm their commitment to the sufficiency of Scripture (as did their heterodox peers). But even as they were doing this the Baptist John Gale (1680–1721),[50] who was connected with the significant Paul's Alley (Particular Baptist)

---

45. Emlyn, *Works*, I, 15–16.

46. J. B. Williams, ed., *Memoir of . . . Matthew Henry* (1828), 180. For Henry, see also ODCC, ODNB, SI.

47. Ibid., 181.

48. See Hayden, *Continuity and Change*, 64–65. For Foskett, see DEB, ODNB; Sell, *Philosophy, Dissent and Nonconformity*, 42–43 and *passim*. He studied medicine in London prior to entering the ministry.

49. Hayden, *Continuity and Change*, 212.

50. For whom, see ODNB.

Church in London, began to influence members in a semi-Arian direction. Gale had graduated PhD at Leiden University at the age of nineteen, and when he was later offered the Leiden DD if he assented to the high Calvinistic articles of the Synod of Dort, he declined. Whereas Gale was able to maintain good relations in his Baptist circle, Martin Tomkins (d. 1755),[51] the minister of Stoke Newington Presbyterian Church, was not so fortunate. On July 13, 1718, he delivered a sermon in which he advanced six reasons for denying that "the Doctrine of the Trinity, or of the Deity of Christ, according to what is generally reckon'd to be the Orthodox Notion—is a *Fundamental Doctrine of Christianity.*"[52] He was dismissed from his charge, and twenty years on no other Presbyterian church had called him.

In 1719 the growing agitation over the Trinity in the West Country became a storm that broke over the head of James Peirce of Exeter. This phase of the Trinitarian discussion had been notably stimulated by the Anglican, Samuel Clarke, Rector of St. James', Piccadilly, who had published *The Scripture Doctrine of the Trinity* in 1712. Clarke thus fuelled a debate that had begun when Arthur Bury (1624–1713), describing himself as "a true son of the Church of England," published his anti-Trinitarian tract, *The Naked Gospel* in 1690, the year after he had been expelled from the Rectorship of Exeter College, Oxford. Clarke held that while there were three divine persons, "The Father (or first Person) Alone is Self-existent, Underived, Unoriginated, Independent; made of None, begotten of None, Proceeding from None."[53]

As we saw, Peirce had studied in the Netherlands. He was as staunch a Calvinist when he returned home as he had been when he left. Indeed, in 1708 he deplored the heterodoxy of his friend William Whiston. He never accepted the label "Arian," but came to believe "that there is but one God the Father, because the Scriptures are express in saying so, but we cannot be so certain that he Father, Son, and Holy Ghost are one God, because the Scripture never so much as once says so."[54] He thus denied that the three persons together constituted the one God. The dissemination of such ideas led to the calling of the Salters' Hall conference of 1719. The subject of discussion was the Trinity but,

---

51. For whom, see ODNB.
52. Tomkins, *The Case of Mr. Martin Tomkins*, 23.
53. S. Clarke, *The Scripture Doctrine of the Trinity*, 243.
54. Peirce, *Plain Christianity Defended*, Pt. I, 29.

as Edmund Calamy (1671–1732) observed, that doctrine was "not the point in question."[55] The participants in fact divided over whether or not formal subscription to the doctrine of the Trinity were appropriate. Fifty-three of those who voted favoured subscription, while fifty-seven did not. "The Bible carried it by four," was the judgment of Joseph Jekyl, Master of the Rolls, on the victory of the non-subscribers.[56] It would seem that the Presbyterian Benjamin Avery (d. 1764)[57] and the Congregationalist Nathaniel Lardner (1684–1768)[58] were the only two avowed Arians among the non-subscribers, while Luke Langdon and Martin Tomkins were tending in an Arian direction. These did not join other non-subscribers who, standing on the principle of the sufficiency of Scripture affirmed the Trinity and utterly disowned Arianism.[59] We should not overlook the fact that a number of prominent ministers—the Presbyterian Edmund Calamy and the amiable and non-confrontational Presbyterian Henry Grove among them, took no part in the conference. I have elsewhere noted that the index to the *Works* of Grove that were published in his lifetime contains no specific reference to the Trinity, and while under "Christ" we find entries concerning his death, resurrection, kingly power and second coming, there is no mention of the two-nature doctrine or of the Son's pre-existence.[60] Such silences made Grove suspect in some quarters, and subjected him to the wrath of the high Calvinist John Ball (1655?–1745),[61] Presbyterian minister at Honiton, among whose achievements was that of eliciting a published reply from the naturally peaceable Grove.[62]

The increasingly heterodox tendencies detectable in Dissent in the wake of Salters' Hall would appear to justify the observation of some

---

55. Calamy, *An Historical Account*, II, 414. For Calamy, see ODCC, ODNB, SI.

56. See Whiston, *Memoirs*, I, 220.

57. For whom, see ODNB, SI.

58. For whom, see ODNB, SI. He turned Presbyterian in 1730.

59. See Anon., *An Authentick Account*, 15–16, 25–29. The terms "subscriber" and "non-subscriber" came to be used at the Synod of Ulster in 1721, when members were invited to signify in writing their assent to the *Westminster Confession of Faith*.

60. See Sell, *Testimony and Tradition*, 102.

61. For whom, see ODNB, SI. He was educated at academies near Stourbridge and at Lyme, Dorset, and at Utrecht University.

62. See Ball, *Some Remarks on a new way of Preaching*; H. Grove, *A Letter to the Rev. Mr. John Ball, of Honiton*, in Grove's *Works*, IV, 253–300; Sell, *Dissenting Thought*, 169–76; Sell, *Testimony and Tradition*, 105–6.

scholars that the preponderance of subscribers was over the age of forty, while that of non-subscribers was under forty. It is undeniably the case that some ministers were incited to delve into doctrine more deeply than hitherto as a consequence of the debates surrounding Salters' Hall. Thus, for example, in his funeral oration for the Presbyterian minister Samuel Bourn (1689–1754) Samuel Blyth (1718–1796) recalled that:

> About the time that I am speaking of, the Trinitarian Controversy was carried on with much unjustifiable Heat in the *West of England*, which put our deceased Friend upon thoroughly studying the Points in Debate. With that View he carefully read Dr. *Clark* [sic] on one Hand; and on the other, he read Dr. *Waterland*, with the rest of the *Athanasian* Writers of most Repute at that Day; but, above all, he carefully read his Bible, upon the Points in Question: And such was the Honesty, and the Openness of his Mind, to receive and embrace Truth, wherever he thought he had found it, that, tho' before this impartial Enquiry, he was a professed *Athanasian*, yet after it he altered his Sentiments, and never saw Reason to retract the Change he had made . . . I have heard him declare, that "Next to his Bible, nothing did more towards fixing him in Dr. *Clark's* Scheme than the replies to it. . . . They did more than even what the Doctor had said to support it."[63]

Again, a number of Baptists began to draw firmer doctrinal lines in the wake of Salters' Hall. From 1714 onwards both Particular and General Baptist ministers had met for conversation at the Hanover Coffee House, Finch Lane, London. But the Particulars withdrew on doctrinal grounds in January 1723/4, formed their own fraternal with commitment to Calvinism as the condition of membership. This was the beginning of the influential Baptist Board.[64]

I earlier quoted Joseph Dodson of Penruddock as one committed to the sufficiency of Scripture. What he discerned therein was not, however, to the liking of James Atkinson, of Stainton who, in 1722, published a reply to Dodson entitled, *Jesus Christ the Son, Essentially the Same with God the Father*. We have no difficulty in inferring from this title that Atkinson harboured serious doubts as to the soundness of Dodson's Christology, and a reading of his text confirms the point. Thus, for example, in response to Dodson's claim that "according to the

---

63. Blyth, *The Good Soldier of Jesus Christ*, 12–13. For Blyth see SI.
64. See Raymond Brown, *The English Baptists of the Eighteenth Century*, 41.

Scriptures . . . Christ made the World; and . . . he who made the World is Eternal God," Atkinson declares: "This is a very uncertain Description of the Divinity of Christ, and is no more than what the rankest Arian in the World may say, upon their base and absurd Principles. . . . For who knows in what Sense he takes those Scriptures to say Christ made the World? Whether in the Orthodox or Arian sense? Whether Christ made the World as an Instrument only in the Hand of God; or as He who is the one only Creator of Heaven and Earth?"[65]

We may justifiably infer that Atkinson later reaffirmed his points from the self-explanatory title of two sermons he published in 1726: *The Father, the Word (or Son), and the Holy Ghost, the One True God; Together with the Necessity of Believing it. Prov'd and Apply'd in Two Sermons, on I John v. 7, with a Dedication Plainly Showing the Unreasonableness, Impiety, and Dreadful Effects of Denying Christ to be the Most High God.*[66]

From the late 1720s to the 1740s a good deal of ink was spilled over the somewhat narrower question of the eternal generation of the Son. In 1726 the doughty high Calvinistic Congregationalist, Abraham Taylor (fl. 1721–1740),[67] deeply disturbed by what he perceived as doctrinal declension, tackled a Dissenting giant, and fellow Congregationalist, in his first published work: *The Scripture Doctrine of the Trinity Vindicated in Opposition to Mr. Watts's Scheme of One Divine Person and Two Divine Powers.* This was in reply to Isaac Watts's book, *The Christian Doctrine of the Trinity* (1722).[68] Watts's intention in writing was to assist in reconciling opposing parties in the wake of the Salters' Hall conference. Taylor, however, demanded that Watts seek pardon for having produced a work "full of thick darkness," for "obtruding upon us the Socinian scheme, in a new dress, yet not knowing he does so"; and in particular "for representing the doctrine of the eternal generation of the Son, and the procession of the Spirit, to be a popish and scholastic hypothesis."[69] The following year, Taylor published a two-volume treatise entitled, *The Scripture-Doctrine of the Holy and Ever-Blessed Trinity, Stated and Defended, in Opposition to the Arian Scheme.* In swashbuckling style he welcomes

65. I draw these quotations from Nicholson and Axon, *The Older Nonconformity of Kendal*, 284–85.
66. See Nightingale, *Lancashire Nonconformity*, I (i), 293–94.
67. For whom, see ODNB, SI; Sell, *Hinterland Theology*, ch. 3.
68. For Watts (1674–1748), see DSCBP, ODCC, ODNB, SI.
69. A. Taylor, *The Scripture Doctrine of the Trinity Vindicated*, 115.

Bishop George Bull's critique of Arianism, thinks that Daniel Whitby's reply to it is "more the effect of dotage than anything else,"[70] and maintains against Samuel Clarke that the three persons of the Trinity are one in nature and substance. Christ, he argues is divine because he is consubstantial with the Father, and Christ is eternally generate. He "proves" Christ's divinity from his equality with the Father (a huge begging of the question), from the names ascribed to him, from his attributes, from his accomplishing the work of redemption, and from his being Lord and judge of all. It would seem that Taylor's doctrine was perpetuated at Deptford, for in January 1746–1747, during the ministry of Jenkin Lewis, the church approved and subscribed to a statement of faith, the Christological portions of which are as follows:

1. That there is One God, of infinite, absolute, and incomprehensible perfections.
2. That in this One God there are Three Persons, Father, Son, and Holy Ghost, the same in substance, equal in power and glory.
3. That the Second Person assumed human nature and is true God and real man in one person.[71]

In 1729 the staunchly Calvinistic Congregationalist, John Guyse, preached two sermons on *Christ the Son of God the great Subject of a Gospel Ministry*, to which the Presbyterian, Samuel Chandler (1693–1766) replied. Liable to tease, and almost certainly realising that this was fighting talk, Chandler declared that the precise distinctions between the persons of the Trinity are "of very little importance for us to know" because they are beyond our comprehension.[72] Chandler insists that he is not arguing against "the proper Deity of our Lord Jesus Christ,"[73] but he cannot see that the Bible sanctions the doctrine of eternal generation, and he challenges Guyse to adduce biblical evidence for it. In a prompt reply, Guyse side-steps the question. Chandler came forth with a *Second Letter* in 1730, repeating many of his points and assuring Guyse that "my

---

70. Ibid., xxi.

71. Timpson, *Church History of Kent*, 348–49.

72. Chandler, *A Letter to the Reverend Mr. John Guyse*, 28. For Chandler *versus* Guyse, see Sell, *Hinterland Theology*, 110–13.

73. Chandler, *A Letter*, 33.

temper is naturally cheerful, and all your solemnity hath not spoiled it",[74] but Guyse was not to be drawn further into debate.

The orthodox Congregationalist Thomas Ridgley (1667–1734)—a Salters' Hall subscriber—more eirenic than Abraham Taylor, less reticent/elusive/teasing than Samuel Chandler, nevertheless managed to fire up the redoubtable Baptist John Gill thirty years after his death. The issue was eternal generation. Ridgley thought it unwise on the part of the orthodox to speak of the Father's communicating his essence or personality to the Son; in other words, he would not assent to the doctrine of eternal generation. His motive, however, was orthodox. He wished to hold, against the Arians, that there never was a time when the Son of God was not, but felt that the language of communication could be twisted by Socinians and Arians in a subordinationist direction, and that to speak of eternal generation merely stimulated the heterodox logic that to speak of a generated person is to presuppose a prior generator, to whom the generated is subordinate. Positively, Ridgley asserted "that the divine essence is not communicated by the Father to the Son and Holy Ghost, as imparting or conveying it to them. I take the word 'communicate' in another sense, and say that all the perfections of the divine nature are communicated, that is, equally distributed to, or predicated of, the Father, Son, and Spirit. . . . I cannot but conclude that the divine personality, not only of the Father, but of the Son and Spirit, is as much independent and underived as the divine essence."[75]

Possibly in anticipation of adverse criticism, Ridgley explained his objectives in his Preface.[76] Gill paid scant heed to Ridgley's motives, and took particular exception to the view that "When we read of the Son of God as dependent on the Father, inferior and obedient to him, and yet as being equal with him, and having the same divine nature, we cannot conceive of any character which answers to all these ideas of sonship, except that of Mediator."[77] To Gill this smacked of the Socinian doctrine of

---

74. Chandler, *A Second Letter to the Reverend Mr. John Guyse*, 97.

75. Ridgley, *A Body of Divinity*, (1731), I, 158, 159. For Ridgley, see ODNB, SI; Sell, *Hinterland Theology*, ch. 2.

76. Ridgley, *A Body of Divinity*, I, viii. In the immediate wake of the Salters' Hall conference Ridgley had defended the subscribers' position in a pamphlet entitled, *The Unreasonableness of the Charge of Imposition exhibited against several Dissenting Ministers in and about London*, London, 1719. See Sell, *Hinterland Theology*, 22–23.

77. Ibid., I, 162.

Christ's Sonship by office;[78] he took no account whatsoever of Ridgley's explanation that his reference to the mediatorial office "does not take away any argument by which we prove his deity. When we consider Him as mediator, or speak of the person of Christ as such, we always suppose him to be both God and man";[79] and he completely overlooked Ridgley's stout rebuttal of the Socinian position on this very point: "the Socinians suppose that [Christ's] being called the Son of God, refers only to some dignities conferred upon one whom they suppose to be no more than a man.... Their idea of him, as the Son of God, however extraordinary soever his conception was, argues him to be no more than a creature; but ours ... proves him to be a divine Person, since we never speak of him as Mediator, without including both natures."[80]

As I have elsewhere concluded, "It would seem that Ridgley's 'sin' was to leave himself open to misunderstanding by those who were intent upon misunderstanding him."[81] May it not also be the case that for all his bluster, Gill felt insecure on certain doctrinal points? In the opinion of Roger Hayden, "Gill, unfortunately, often found it easier to assert his negative views rather than to make a clear positive statement about Christian doctrine. He never quite succeeded ... in explaining the eternal sonship of Christ to his own satisfaction, but he was impatient with any who denied the doctrine."[82]

John Gill was no less distressed by the writings of Samuel Bourn, by now a professed Arian, who qualified his professed Trinitarianism as follows:

> If by the doctrine of the *Trinity* you mean the Doctrine of *Father, Son,* and *Holy Spirit*; they [namely, the Baptist preachers within his sights] might have stay'd at home; in regard, as far as I know the Town [Birmingham], this Doctrine is firmly believ'd by every Preacher in the Town, and by all their Hearers.... For my Part, I hold Jesus Christ to be God, or a God ... But I can't bring myself to believe in his *Supreme Deity*, because I believe in the same supreme Deity of God the Father; and it appears to me a plain contradiction to say that there are two Persons or Beings who are

---

78. See Gill, *A Body of Divinity*, 206–7.
79. Ridgley, *A Body of Divinity*, I, 162–63.
80. Ibid., I, 63.
81. Sell, *Hinterland Theology*, 26.
82. Hayden, *Continuity and Change*, 191–92.

both of 'em *Supreme* or *most High God*; and I never yet had Faith eno' to believe two contradictory Propositions.[83]

Gill sallied forth, pulling no punches: "I take him to be a *Heathen*, and not a *Christian*, much less a consistent one, since he gives strong indication of his belief of a supreme and subordinate Deity, a superior God and an inferior one, and both as the objects of religious worship."[84]

Meanwhile James Foster (1697–1753),[85] a General Baptist whose theology took a Socinian turn, became minister at Paul's Alley, Barbican, in succession to John Gale. There he remained until 1744, when he accepted the call to the Congregational church meeting at Pinners' Hall, in succession to Jeremiah Hunt (1768–44).[86] We learn that Foster's disposition was benevolent, but that he "exalted reason to the supreme rank," and was "far gone in the Socinian scheme." Because he "laid but little stress upon the peculiar doctrines of revelation, he was charged by some persons with deism and infidelity. . . . [I]t is no injury to him to observe, that the grand doctrines of human redemption, and divine influence, formed no part of his creed."[87] As his assistant and successor, Caleb Fleming (1698–1779), put it, "he was convinced, the great design of Christ's ministrations was *moral*, viz. to promote virtue, and advance the interests of morality in the world."[88] Foster's Socinianism was chal-

---

83. Bourn, *A Dialogue between a Baptist and a Churchman*, 48. In 1736 Bourn had already published, *An Address to Protestant Dissenters: or an Inquiry into the Ground of their attachment to the Assemblies Catechism*. This drew a reply from the Congregational minister, James Sloss, of Castle Gate Church, Nottingham, entitled, *A Vindication of the Answer to the Sixth Question in the Assembly's Shorter Catechism*, 1738 (not 1728, as printed). For this debate see Sell, *Dissenting Thought*, 236–41. Bourn refused to assent to the *Westminster Confession* at his ordination—a stance which prompted some local minister to boycott the occasion; and later he published catechisms that "improved upon" those of Westminster.

84. Gill, *An Answer to the Birmingham Dialogue-Writer*, 6.

85. For whom, see ODNB, SI. He was educated at the first Exeter Academy.

86. For whom, see ODNB, SI. He was educated at Saffron Walden Academy and the universities of Edinburgh and Leiden.

87. Wilson, *The History and Antiquities of Dissenting Churches*, II, 279–80.

88. Ibid., 280. For Fleming, see ODNB, SI. Of him it is written that he had "the distinction of having destroyed two congregations, one Presbyterian the other Independent [Bartholomew Close and Pinners' Hall], as he had no successor in either." James, *The History of the Litigation and Legislation*, 723. We should not conclude that he achieved this distinction solely by virtue of his Socinianism, for some took exception to his political radicalism, and some of his public utterances suggest that he harboured anti-monarch sentiments. Fleming succeeded Foster at Pinners' Hall in 1758, and remained there until 1778.

lenged in 1746 by Gill's friend, the high Calvinist, John Brine (1703–1765) in a substantial tome, *A Vindication of Some Truths of Natural and Revealed Religion: In Answer to the False Reasoning of Mr. James Foster*. Brine reviews Foster's position on twelve topics, including regeneration, justification and the mediation of Christ, and then appends a lengthy *Dialogue between a Calvinist, a Socinian, and Arminian, a Baxterian, and a Deist*, all of whom he scuppers to his own satisfaction. Foster, however, declined to reply.[89]

Any impression that high Calvinist Baptists alone were concerned about perceived Arianism and Socinianism, and that all was lost for orthodoxy in the West Country will be dispelled by a consideration of the deliberations of the Western Baptist Association between 1733 and 1744. In the wake of the Salters' Hall debate the Association, which hitherto had been open to Baptists of all stripes, now, under the urging of the evangelical Calvinists[90] Bernard Foskett and Hugh Evans (1712–1781) of Broadmead Church, Bristol, and after reflections extending over some years, began to consider requiring assent to the Particular Baptist *Confession* 1689 as a condition of membership.[91] Among other prominent evangelical Calvinist advocates of the *Confession* was Joseph Stennett (1692–1758) who, in an Association sermon at Exeter in 1733 lamented that "The most grievous wounds the Gospel has received, have been in the house of its pretended friends."[92] By 1735, as the discussion proceeded, some were invoking the catholic spirit as a justification of more open membership. In the following year, therefore, Stennett wrote a letter to the churches in which he invited them to "consider the flood of Arian, Socinian, Pelagian and Arminian corruptions, that has overspread the land and broke in upon our churches: and then say whether the revival of these public declarations for the sacred truths of the even-blessed gospel be not seasonable."[93] The eventual upshot was the exclu-

---

89. For other doctrinal skirmishes of Gill and Brine, see Sell, *The Great Debate*, ch. 3.

90. I use the term "evangelical Calvinist" to distinguish Foskett, Evans, and Stennett from Gill and Brine, who, in the wake of Joseph Hussey and John Skepp, declined the free offer of the gospel.

91. For Evans, see DEB, DWB.

92. Stennett, *The Christian Strife for the Faith of the Gospel*, 78. For Stennett, see DEB, ODNB.

93. Quoted from the *Records of the Western Baptist Association, 1733–1744* at the Angus Library, Regent's Park College, Oxford, by Hayden, *Continuity and Change*, 35. Dr. Hayden provides a full account of the discussions, ibid., 30–36.

sion of General Baptists from the Association. Baptists in other parts of England and Wales took similar stock of their doctrinal situation.

Needless to say, the doctrinal qualms of the orthodox did not arrest the flow of heterodox endeavour. Thus in the middle years of the century we find the third Samuel Bourn (1714–1796) publishing two volumes of his *Discourses* (1760), in the second of which he expounds the office and dignity of Christ. Since Bourn's work is regarded by some as marking the high point of Arian teaching in the eighteenth-century, we shall do well to set down the heart of his case.[94]

Bourn's text is Acts 5:31, "Him hath God exalted to be a Prince and a Saviour." He opens with an expression of regret that "Men have rather studied to divide and multiply the characters ascribed to our Saviour in the New Testament, and consequently to perplex our minds in conceiving of them; than to reduce them to one intelligible meaning: and particularly, have applied those titles to the person of our Lord in a *metaphysical* sense, which are given to him in Scripture solely on account of his *office* and *dominion*."[95] Thus, Jesus is indeed "sometimes . . . stiled *a God*: not on account of his metaphysical nature or essence (which Scripture saith not a word of) but on account of the dominion or government, which God hath committed to him for the eternal salvation of men."[96] Moreover, "To this dominion or empire our Saviour rose by his virtue, or his most perfect and exemplary obedience to the divine will."[97] "[*T*]*o us* Christians," he continues, "*there is but one God the Father and one Lord Jesus Chrst*: and . . . when *we confess him to be Lord, it is* to the glory of God, who constituted him Lord . . . Our Lord himself ascribes his own dignity and dominion, and his life also, to the free gift of God."[98] This is the doctrine clearly revealed in the Bible, and it is "sufficient to the faith and practice, comfort and hope of every Christian."[99] Those who live soberly, righteously and piously by this faith "are beyond all doubt the true *disciples of Christ*; and will be acknowledge by him as such."[100]

---

94. For Bourn, educated at Glasgow University, see ODNB, SI.
95. Bourn, *Discourses on Various* Subjects, II, 140.
96. Ibid., 142.
97. Ibid., 145.
98. Ibid., 152.
99. Ibid., 156.
100. Ibid., 157.

With Bourn's work we reach something of a watershed in eighteenth-century Christological discussion. While ideas cannot be turned off like a tap, and while Arians are to be found to the end of the century and beyond, the centre of debate moves from the question of the Son's relation with the Father, to the nature of the Son as such. In other words, the humanity of Christ is increasingly emphasised—by Giles Firmin (d. 1697), Nathaniel Lardner, Paul Cardale (1705–1775), Joseph Priestley (1733–1804) and Theophilus Lindsey (1723–1808), as well as by lesser-known ministers such as Matthew Anstis (1740–1823) of Colyton, Devonshire, of whom it is said that "In rather early life, Mr. Anstis adopted the Unitarian system, and was an avowed believer in "One God and one Mediator between God and men, the *man* Christ Jesus," at a time when the great majority of Unitarians in the West of England, still held Arian opinions concerning the person of Christ."[101] Thus the bridge was erected from Socinianism to a more decided Unitarianism.[102] Among other things, this prompted thirty-one orthodox Dissenters in Kendal to appeal to the Associate (Antiburgher) Presbytery in Edinburgh in April 1763, "praying that ministers might be sent from Scotland to preach the Gospel in Kendal."[103] However, lest we are tempted to lump all of the heterodox together, we should recall that Arianism persisted over against Unitarianism, and was exemplified to the end of the century by Micaijah Towgood (1700–1792), who made his position quite clear:

> His religious opinions were as opposite to those of Dr. Priestley, as to those of Mr. Whitefield and Mr. Wesley; but this did not prevent his entertaining a very high opinion of his abilities and integrity, as will appear from the following letter, written about the year 1779.

---

101. W.B.G., *The Monthly* Repository, XVIII, December 1823, 731. The quotation is mangled by Murch, *West of England*, 339. Anstis's pastorates were brief, and for most of his career he was a schoolmaster. He was educated at Carmarthen Academy, see SI. For Firmin, see ODNB, SI; for Lardner, educated at Hoxton Academy and the universities of Utrecht and Leiden, see ODCC, ODNB, SI; For Cardale, educated at Findern Academy, see ODNB, SI; For Priestley, educated at Daventry Academy under Caleb Ashworth, see DECBP, ODCC, ODNB, SI; for Lindsey, educated at St. John's College, Cambridge, see ODCC, ODNB.

102. Cf. Toulmin, *Memoirs of the Rev.S. Bourn*, Birmingham, 18–19.

103. Sell, *Church Planting. Westmorland Nonconformity*, 42; Nicholson and Axon, *The Older Nonconformity in Kendal*, 343–44. For orthodox Presbyterianism in Kendal see Inglis, *Reminiscences*; Gray, *Presbyterianism in Kendal*, 1908.

> I had never before the pleasure of seeing Dr. Priestley, and I am glad to see a head filled with so much knowledge, connected with a heart adorned with such apparent modesty and benevolence. As to . . . the pre-existence of the Logos . . . I totally disagree with him. He is rather too bold a partisan in the republic of literature.[104]

Towgood also took exception to Priestley neccessarianism, as did Priestley's friend Richard Price[105] who, as I said earlier, remained an Arian but, unlike Towgood, did not favour the worship of Christ. From the other side, and further along the Unitarian road, William Turner (1761–1859) looked back upon John Taylor of Norwich's book, *The Scripture-Doctrine of the Atonement* (1751) with something approaching disdain. It is, he wrote, "an ingenious attempt to construct a scheme which shall be consistent with the moral perfections of the Father of Mercies, and at the same time, enable a man to use the language of reputed orthodoxy. Like all such half measures, however, it is generally allowed to have failed in its object."[106] By 1869 Robert Halley felt able to report that "The decline of Arianism has been so decided that I know not an Arian minister preaching in Lancashire, or indeed in any part of England."[107]

Theophilus Lindsey, left the Church of England in 1773 for Unitarianism without passing through Arianism, and made a significant contribution to the dissemination of Unitarian ideas through the services he conducted at Essex Street, London, from 1774 onwards.[108] He emphasised the Divine Unity, accused Trinitarians of disowning it, denied the name "Unitarian" to those Arians who continued to offer worship to Christ, and regarded Christ's chief function as being that of a moral example. Among Lindsey's critics was the Baptist Robert Robinson (1735–1790) of Cambridge. In 1776 Robinson published, *A Plea for the Divinity of our Lord Jesus Christ*. He here declares, "At pres-

---

104. Manning, *A Sketch of the Life and Writings of the Rev. Micaijah Towgood*, 128–29. The anonymous author of *Observations on the Rev. James Manning's Sketch* took the opportunity of dissenting from a number of Towgood's views, notably the latter's willingness to allow the worship of Christ. See 35 ff.

105. For Price, see D. O. Thomas's exemplary work, *The Honest Mind*.

106. W. Turner, *The Warrington Academy*, 5.

107. Halley, *Lancashire*, II, 417. Arianism lingered longer in Ireland.

108. See further, Ditchfield, "Anti-trinitarianism and toleration in late eighteenth-century British politcs," 39–67.

ent I affirm, because I believe, that Jesus Christ is truly and properly God."[109] (Some of his critics quickly fastened upon the words "at present," and construed them to imply a certain indecisiveness, or openness to a change of opinion, or both). He proceeds to dismiss the Athanasian creed, declaring that Athanasius "was, we think, no saint; but an enormous sinner";[110] and he finds prayer addressed to the several persons of the Trinity unacceptable: the one God is to be worshipped through Jesus Christ the mediator. To those who call themselves Unitarians, Robinson replies, "So are we," immediately adding the clarificatory point, "Our dispute is not, Whether there be one God, or three Gods: but whether the divinity of Jesus Christ be incompatible with the unity of God, which unity both sides believe."[111] Towards the end of his tract Robinson quotes Lindsey and replies to him, thus:

> The reverend Mr. Lindsey says, "That the Lord Jesus is intrusted with a mighty executive power and dominion for the good of his church and people, is plainly revealed to us, Matt. xxviii.18.20. John xiv. &c. How and in what manner he exerciseth this power is wholly unrevealed," . . .
>
> So then! This scheme does not answer its end; like ours it proposes some articles to the belief of its professors, which it does not condescend to explain. I give, however, the preference to the old system of Christ's divinity, because, while it requires me to believe the *mighty dominion* of Jesus, it *reveals* his Godhead, and so accounts for the exercise of it: whereas the new scheme of his mere humanity gives him a dominion in all worlds, while it confines his person and presence, and consequently his influence, to one place, and so leaves his government, not only unsearchable and unrevealed, but absolutely impossible.[112]

Robinson sent a copy of his *Plea* to Lindsey, with whom he had had no previous contact, and the latter replied in *An Examination of Mr. Robinson of Cambridge's Pleas for the Divinity of Christ* (1785), in which he likened Robinson's position to Sabellianism. In Priestley's opinion, "before he died [Robinson] was one of the most zealous *Unitarians*."[113]

---

109. Robinson, *A Plea for the Divinity of our Lord Jesus* Christ, 5. For Robinson, see DEB, ODNB.

110. Ibid.

111. Ibid., 7.

112. Ibid., 100–101.

113. Priestley, *Reflections on Death: A Sermon on occasion of the Death of the Rev.*

In support of this conclusion Priestley feels able to quote from a letter of 7 May 1788 by Robinson to Mr. Marsom: "As to personality in God, a Trinity of persons, I think it the most absurd of all absurdities."[114] This could, of course, be taken as an objection to tritheism. Be that as it may, against the 1788 letter we should set another, written by Robinson to S. Lucas on 16 September 1789: "Believe me, I am neither a Socinian, nor an Arian: . . . I think Jesus a man in whom the fulness of the Godhead dwells. . . . Disputants here want me to take a side; and because I refuse to do so, they represent me as a man void of all principle."[115] As I weigh the matter, I do not think that it may properly be affirmed that Robinson was a Unitarian (though I can understand why some of that ilk may have thought him a good "catch"—they thought the same about Isaac Watts). He upheld the unity of God, he opposed tritheism, he was conscious of mystery and, like Watts at the last, it does not appear that he had resolved the matter of the verbal formulation of the doctrine to his own satisfaction. Indeed, we have it from his own pen that formerly he, like Samuel Clarke, would have agreed that the Trinity was biblically based, and that he "would say so still if I could tell what I meant; but as I cannot I cast that phrase to the bats and the moles"[116]—a sentiment which elicited no compliments from the orthodox. Such Baptist luminaries as Samuel Stennett (1728-1795) and Abraham Booth (1734-1806) "preached against Robinson from their pulpits, and . . . were in return lampooned and be-sermonized by him."[117]

Like Lindsey, Thomas Belsham (1750-1829),[118] a doughty proponent of Unitarian distinctives, thought that Arians like Price were inconsistent in not worshipping Christ, and that the term "Unitarian" should be exclusively used by humanitarians—a desideratum that eluded him. This was the burden of his *Letters upon Arianism, and Other Topics in Metaphysics and Theology, in Reply to the Lectures of the Rev. Benjamin Carpenter* (1808). Carpenter (1752-1816), who entered Caleb

---

Robert Robinson of Cambridge, Delivered at the New Meeting in Birmingham, June 13, 1790, in Rutt, ed., *The Theological and Miscellaneous* Works, XV, 417. Cf. ibid., VII, 26 n.

114. Ibid., n.

115. Robinson, *Miscellaneous Works*, IV, 289-90.

116. Ibid.

117. Dyer, *Memoirs of . . . Robinson*, 295. For Stennett and Booth, see DEB, ODNB. The former was educated at Mile End Academy, London.

118. For whom, see ODNB, SI.

Ashworth's Daventry Academy two years after Belsham, was the Arian Presbyterian minister at Bromsgrove. That Belsham's ambition that "Unitarian" be used exclusively of humanitarians was not realized is evidenced by the fact that without renouncing his Arianism, Price joined the Unitarian Society in 1791, the year of his death, and he was not alone in so doing. I shall return to Belsham shortly, but first it is necessary to summarize Priestley's Christology and then to note some critics of it.

Priestley helpfully provides us with an account of his intellectual development. He was raised among strict Calvinists who wished to send him to John Conder's academy at Mile End, London.[119] "But," writes Priestley, "being at that time an Arminian, I resolutely opposed it, especially upon finding that if I went thither, besides giving an *experience*, I must subscribe to ten printed articles of the strictest Calvinistic faith, and repeat it every six months."[120] In the event Priestley became the first new student enrolled at Daventry Academy, the continuation of Doddridge's Northampton Academy under the charge of Caleb Ashworth.[121] The Daventry students breathed a tolerant air: "Our tutors were of different opinions; Dr. Ashworth taking the orthodox side of every question, and Mr. [Samuel] Clark, the sub-tutor, that of heresy, though always with the greatest modesty."[122]

Priestley left the Academy an Arian, and thus he remained for some years, until, soon after removing to Leeds in 1767, "By reading with care Dr. Lardner's Letter on the Logos, I became what is called a Socinian."[123] The phrase "what is called" is telling; the negative, and accurate, implication is that Priestley had not been reading Socinus himself, for he would not have approved of the latter's toleration of worship addressed to the subordinate Christ. It should be added that Priestley had also been

---

119. For Conder (1714–81), who was educated at Clerkenwell and King's Head academies, see DEB, ODNB, SI.

120. Priestley, *Memoirs*, in *Works*, I pt. 1, 21. For a useful account by David L. Wykes of Priestley's career as minister and teacher see Rivers and Wykes, eds., *Joseph Priestley*, ch. 1.

121. For Caleb Ashworth (d. 1775) see Sell, "Caleb Ashworth: His Academy, Church and Students," forthcoming.

122. Priestley, *Memoirs*, 23. For Clark (1727–69), who was educated under Doddridge at Northampton Academy and, following Doddridge's death, moved to the successor academy at Daventry under Ashworth, see SI, and the paper in the foregoing note.

123. Ibid., 69. Lardner's *Letter*, written in 1735, was not published until 1756.

studying the Bible, and that he was firmly committed to the principle of the sufficiency of Scripture, as the following quotation makes clear: "There is no subject on which the Scriptures are so clear and emphatical as they are on this. The worship of one God, and that one God the maker of all things. . . . [W]hile the *Father*, the *Son* and the *Holy Spirit*, separately considered, are each of them maintained to be true and very God, without the least deficiency of any one attribute of divinity, they cannot, in common sense or common arithmetic, make less than three gods."[124]

As he elsewhere explains, it was "the *Athanasian* doctrine of the Trinity" that gave "men more objects of divine homage than one." By contrast, Peter understood Jesus to be "*a man approved of God*"; Paul insisted that "There is one God, and one mediator between God and man, the man Jesus Christ"—not "the *God*, the *God-man*, or the *super-angelic being*, but simply the *man* Jesus Christ."[125] Here we have the humanitarian Jesus, not the Athanasian Son of God, nor the Socinian subordinate Christ, nor the Arian pre-existent Word. Priestley, like Lindsey and Belsham, protests when Athanasians claim to be Unitarian because they believe in one God; on the contrary, they violate divine unity. As for the Arians, they have no greater title to the name Unitarian, for they ascribe creation to Christ.[126] Consistently with his humanitarianism, Priestley finds the doctrine of the pre-existence of Christ as untenable as that of his divinity.[127] He reiterated his points in tracts and letters on numerous occasions,[128] and did not hesitate to set the Swedenborgians straight on the person of Christ.[129] More generally, he was a tireless apologist for Unitarianism.[130]

Priestley's friend, Price, continued faithful to the Arian position, much to the distress of his uncle, the high Calvinist Samuel Price (d. 1756 aged eighty), co-pastor with, and successor to, Isaac Watts at St. Mary Axe, Bury Street, London, who declared that "he had rather see [his nephew] transformed into a pig, than that he should have been

---

124. Ibid., XVI, 479–80.
125. Ibid., V, 14. Cf. ibid., XVIII, 443.
126. Ibid., VI, 45–49.
127. Ibid., 13–23.
128. See, for example, *Works*, II, 391–97, 449–72; III, 140–41; XXI, 207–14, 229–41.
129. *Works*, XXI, 58–66.
130. See especially *Works* XVIII, 315–572; XIX, 1–110, 245–58.

brought up to be a dissenting minister without believing in the Trinity."[131] Price, however, persisted in believing that while Christ was to be honoured, he was subordinate to the Father, to whom alone worship should be offered. That Price expected opposition to his views is clear from a letter he wrote to William Adams on December 10, 1786. He refers to his forthcoming *Sermons on the Christian Doctrine as received by the different Denominations* (1787), and muses, "Dr. Priestley, Mr. Lindsey, and some others of my *Socinian* friends are full of zeal, and it is probable they will be writing against me; but nothing shall draw me into a controversy."[132] Sure enough, on receiving a copy of the book as a gift from Price, Priestley wrote on January 7, 1787, "we Socinians cannot but think ourselves called upon to make some reply; and tho' *you* may not chuse to enter into the controversy, others may be induced to take it up."[133] Price and Priestley continued to agree to differ, and continued as good friends. Price consistently held to the pre-existence of Christ, as Priestley did not, and regarded Priestley's humanitarian Christology as mistaken and reductionist. Priestley acknowledged this in his funeral oration for Price: "Though, among other things, he differed from me with respect to *the person of* Christ, no man laid more stress than he did on his being a creature of God, equally with ourselves, and no more an *object of* worship than any other creature whatsoever."[134]

Like Priestley, Thomas Belsham had studied under Caleb Ashworth at Daventry Academy. On completing his course he became the junior tutor (1771–1778), and then minister at Angel Street Church, Worcester (1778–1781). In the latter year he returned to Daventry as divinity tutor and pastor but, on having embraced Unitarian views, he resigned in 1789 and removed to the liberal Hackney Academy, where he remained until 1796. He served as pastor at Gravel Pit Meeting, Hackney, from 1794 to 1805. In 1811 he published *A Calm Enquiry into the Scripture Doctrine concerning the Person of Christ*, in which he declared that "Jesus of Nazareth was a man constituted in all respects like other men, subject

---

131. William Morgan, *Memoirs of... Price*, 13. For Samuel Price, who was educated at Attercliffe Academy, see SI.

132. Peach, ed., *The Correspondence of Richard Price*, III, 99.

133. Ibid., 108. In 1788 there was an exchange of letters between Lindsey and Price. Price thought that Lindsey had misrepresented his Arianism. See ibid., 174–75, 177.

134. Priestley, *A Discourse on the Occasion of the Death of Dr. Price*, 25.

to the same infirmities, the same ignorance, prejudice and frailties."[135] As to whether Jesus was sinless: this, to Belsham, was "a question of no great intrinsic moment," and one "concerning which we have no sufficient data to lead to a satisfactory conclusion."[136] Another prominent pioneer of Unitarian Christology was Timothy Kenrick (1759–1804).[137] He studied at Daventry under Ashworth and his successor, Thomas Robins (1732–1810),[138] when Belsham was the junior tutor. Before his course was completed he was appointed junior tutor, and in that capacity he served alongside Belsham on the latter's return from Worcester to Daventry. In 1784 he succeeded Towgood at George's Meeting, Exeter. It appears that at the time of his ordination there his Christology was Arian, but his continuing studies led him to the view that the two important truths to be emphasised were those concerning the unity of God and the full humanity of Christ.[139] In 1799 he made his home the venue of the third Exeter Academy.

G. M. Ditchfield quotes the definition of "Unitarianism" given in the *Monthly Review* (1792). The word applies to those who agree in "denying the Trinity, the pre-existence and atonement of Christ, and the existence of a spiritual principle in man distinct from the body; and maintaining the absolute unity of God, the proper humanity of Christ, the ncecessity and efficacy of good works, and the sufficiency of repentance without a vicarious sacrifice, to obtain pardon from a placable Deity."[140] Professor Ditchfield observes that this was a step too far even for some rational Dissenters, and this was indeed the case; what also strikes me is the way in which the denials precede the affirmations—a not uncommon characteristic of "fighting talk."

It should not be supposed that advancing Unitarianism had the field to itself. By now the Methodists, both Calvinistic and Arminian

---

135. Belsham, *A Calm Enquiry into the Scripture Doctrine concerning the Person of Christ*, 447.

136. Ibid., 450.

137. For whom, see ODNB, SI. On the completion of his studies he served was tutor at Daventry until he removed to Exeter.

138. For Robins, see SI. He was educated at Kibworth, Northampton under Doddridge, and Daventry under Ashworth, whom he succeeded in 1775. In 1781 vocal problems prompted his resignation, and he became a chemist and bookseller in Daventry.

139. See Murch, *West of England*, 441.

140. Ditchfield, "Anti-Trinitarianism and Toleration," 48.

were growing in numbers, and some of their leaders were keen to distance themselves from heterodox Christology.[141] I offer three examples. John Wesley's father, Samuel, was a firm opponent of Socinianism, while his wife, Susanna, thanked God that she had married an orthodox man who had saved her from that very heresy. Their son was no less concerned to rebut the Socinian and Arian errors. In 1742 he published *The Character of a Methodist*, in which he explained with reference to the Bible, in words to which any Socinian and Arian could have assented, that "We believe this written Word of God to be the *necessary and sufficient* Rule"; and then almost immediately he demonstrated that he interpreted the written Word very differently from the heterodox: "We believe Christ to be the eternal supreme God; and herein we are distinguished from the Socinians and Arians."[142] His opposition to Socinianism took a more personal turn when, in a letter of 1785 Wesley urged John William Fletcher (1729–1785) to reply to Priestley's *The History of the Corruptions of Christianity* (1782), because Priestley "is certainly one of the most dangerous enemies of Christianity that is now in the world. And I verily think *you* are the man whom God has prepared to abate his confidence."[143] Fletcher began the task, but died before it was completed. It therefore fell to Joseph Benson (1748–1821) to assemble and expand the work, which appeared in two parts under a self-explanatory title: *A Rational Vindication of the Catholic Faith: Being the First Part of a Vindication of Christ's Divinity; Inscribed to the Rev. Dr. Priestley*, and *Socinianism Unscriptural: or the Prophets and Apostles Vindicated from the Charge of Holding the Doctrine of Christ's Mere Humanity: Being the Second Part of a Vindication of His Divinity; Inscribed to the Rev. Dr. Priestley*. In his portions of the work Benson upheld the doctrine of the divinity of Christ with special reference to the prologue to John's Gospel where Jesus, the Word of God is united with God and hence partakes

---

141. And not only from that. For example, John Wesley took John Taylor of Norwich to task over the latter's book, *The Scripture-Doctrine of Original Sin*. In his reply, *The Doctrine of Original Sin*, Bristol, 1757, Wesley drew upon Isaac Watts's book, *The Ruin and Recovery of Mankind* (1740), to which Taylor had replied in a supplement to the second edition of his *Original Sin*, 1741.

142. J. Wesley, *The Character of a Methodist*, 3.

143. J. Wesley, *The Letters of the Rev. John Wesley*, VII, 265. For Fletcher, see DEB, DMBI, ODCC, ODNB

of his divine nature, and he added eleven anti-Socinian letters to the second part of Fletcher's work.[144]

It remains only to add that towards the end of the eighteenth century there was a flurry of Baptist criticism of heterodox Christology. This is exemplified in a sermon of 1789 by Caleb Evans (1737–1791) of Bristol on 1 Corinthians 1:25–27. Socinianism and Arianism are clearly within Evans's sights and, in the published version Priestley is criticised in a footnote. Of Christ, Evans asserts, "That he was a man . . . we all allow. But if he were no more, if he had no other nature that he could call his own, if he had even no existence of any kind, as is now most peremptorily affirmed, till he was born into the world, and that in the course of ordinary generation as we are, as is also maintained; what becomes of his boasted condescension and grace?"[145] Evans cannot see that those who deny Christ's divinity have any fresh light to shed on the matter; nor do they have any new sources of information. On the contrary, the evidence for Christ's divinity is in the Bible, and it is plain for all to see. He proceeds to affirm Christ's pre-existence and his deity. When Jesus distinguishes between himself and his Father—as in the claim "I speak not of myself, but the Father which dwelleth in me, he doeth the works," it is not, as the heterodox say, because he was a mere man, but because he was the God-man. He was in the Father and the Father in him.[146] For this reason the Arian claim that the Father is superior to the Son is groundless. Further, when a Socinian writer (Priestley) argues that Jesus would have been a blasphemer if he claimed to be God, and therefore he made no such claim, Evans retorts, Why, then, did the Jewish High Priest charge him with blasphemy? With numerous other biblical references Evans bolsters his case.

It is interesting to note in passing that anti-heterodox sentiments could find their way to the grass roots of the churches, as in the covenant of 1790 of the Stony Stratford Baptist Church. This includes the clear declaration of commitment to "the infinite dignity of the Son of God in his original character as a divine person, possessed of all the perfections of Deity, and his all-sufficiency for the office of Mediator between God and Man, in consequence of the union of the divine and human natures

---

144. See further, Streiff, *Reluctant Saint?*, 276–80; Wood, *Revelation and Reason*, chs. 3–4.

145. C. Evans, *Christ Crucified*, 18. For Evans, see DEB, DWB, ODNB.

146. Ibid., 31–32.

in one person."[147] But the biggest Baptist challenge to the heterodox at the turn of the eighteenth century came from Andrew Fuller.[148]

In 1793 Fuller published *The Calvinistic and Socinian Systems Examined and Compared, as to their Moral Tendency*. The concluding clause is significant, for the Socinians/Unitarians were strong advocates of morality on the one hand, and highly suspicious of the antinomian tendencies of hyper-Calvinism on the other.[149] (It is, of course, important to distinguish between doctrinal antinomianism, of which John Brine, for example, was accused, and practical antinomianism, in which connection "David Crosley reigned supreme in Baptist demonology (though he did manage—or, rather, was enabled—to end his days as a 'trophy of grace.'"[150] Fuller touches on many points of dispute between evangelical Calvinism and Socinianism; Lindsey, Priestley and Belsham are rebuked, and the Baptist Robert Robinson's fall from Calvinistic grace is referred to on a number of occasions; but it is Christology that concerns us here. In the Preface to the second edition of his book (1802) Fuller explains that he persists in using the term "Socinianism" even though Unitarians object to it, on the ground that Trinitarians, no less than Unitarians, profess belief in one God only. When Socinians protest that "in proportion as we adore [Christ] we detract from the essential glory of the Father" whereas "they reckon themselves to exercise a greater veneration for God than we," Fuller explains that the earliest Christians worshipped Christ, and that "in worshipping the Son of God, we worship him not on account of that wherein he differs from the Father, but on account of those perfections which we believe him to possess in common with him."[151] Fuller grants that Priestley affirms that

---

147. Deweese, *Baptist Church Covenants*, 128.

148. For a detailed account of the matter, see Sell, *Testimony and Tradition*, ch. 6.

149. Although the question of morality is not paramount in this book, I may perhaps be permitted to observe that when I remark (Sell, *Testimony and Tradition*, 135) that whereas Fuller's opponents "clearly point out that to seek to judge the moral tendency of an entire denomination is a hazardous epistemological undertaking," Tom Nettles thinks that I misunderstand, for Fuller did no such thing. Rather, his intention was "to judge the moral tendency of the theological *principles*, not the 'entire denomination.'" See his paper, "Christianity pure and simple," in Haykin, ed., *"At the Pure Fountain of Thy* Word," 169. I, however, persist in thinking that Fuller made his view clear, namely, that Socinianism at large was founded upon theological principles the moral tendency of which was disastrous (exceptions in individual cases notwithstanding).

150. Sell, *Testimony and Tradition*, 58. Cf. Sell, *The Great Debate*, 46–47.

151. Fuller, *Works*, 73.

Christianity teaches great truths, but he reduces their number, and leaves some of the most important ones out of account. It is clear to Fuller that "The difference between Socinians and Calvinists is not about the mere circumstantials of religion. It respects nothing less than the *rule* of faith, the *ground* of hope, and the *object* of worship. If the Socinians be right, we are not only superstitious devotees . . . but habitual idolaters. On the other hand, if we be right, they are guilty of refusing to subject their faith to the decisions of heaven, of rejecting the only way of salvation, and of sacrilegiously depriving the Son of God of his essential glory."[152]

Fuller proceeds to beg a number of important questions:

> If the proper Deity of Christ be a Divine truth, it is a great and fundamental truth of Christianity. . . .
>
> If the Deity of Christ be a Divine truth, it must be the Father's will that all men should honour the Son in the same sense, and to the same degree, as they honour the Father . . . If the Deity of Christ be a Divine truth, he is the object of *trust*; and that not merely in the character of a witness, but as *Jehovah, in whom is everlasting strength*.[153]

The close alliance in Fuller's mind between Christology and practical Christianity is nowhere more manifest than in the following lyrical remarks: "Take away Christ; nay, take away the deity and atonement of Christ; and the whole ceremonial of the Old Testament appears to us little more than a dead mass on uninteresting matter: prophecy loses all this is interesting and endearing: the gospel is annihilated, . . . practical religion is divested of its most powerful motives; the evangelical dispensation of its peculiar glory; and heaven itself of its most transporting joys."[154]

It would seem that those Unitarian writers most likely to reply to Fuller bided their time in the hope that Priestley would speak for them all, but Priestley remained silent. Accordingly, in 1796 Joshua Toulmin (1740–1815) published, *The Practical Efficacy of the Unitarian Doctrine Considered, in a Series of Letters to the Rev. Andrew Fuller*, and on 6 July of the same year John Kentish (1768–1853) gave a lecture at the West of England Society of Unitarian Christians that was published two years later under the title, *The Moral Tendency of the Genuine Christian*

152. Ibid., 82.
153. Ibid., 82–83.
154. Ibid., 87.

Doctrine.[155] Toulmin sets out from the by now familiar Unitarian position: "there is but one God, the sole former, supporter, and governor of the universe, the only proper object of religious worship; and there is but one mediator between God and man, the Man Christ Jesus, who was commissioned by God to instruct men in their duty, and to reveal the doctrine of a future life." Appealing to the sufficiency of Scripture and rubbing salt into the wound he adds, "We think it, Sir, a just ground of boast over our fellow-christians who hold different tenets from us, that we can express our fundamental opinions in the *words* of Scripture."[156] Here is the non-worshippable, humanitarian Jesus, who came to instruct humanity in morality and to provide information concerning the future life. Kentish likewise begins with a declaration of the divine unity, Jesus being "simply of the human race, though greatly exalted above every former prophet."[157] Kentish insists that humanitarian belief does not diminish "the respect and obedience we render to [Jesus] as a moral instructor."[158]

It was not to be expected that Fuller would remain silent in face of what he regarded as Unitarian reductionism. He replied to Toulmin and Kentish in *Socinianism Indefensible on the Ground of its Moral Tendency* (1797), to which Toulmin responded in the 1801 edition of *The Practical Efficacy of Unitarian Doctrine*, and Kentish in *Strictures upon the Reply of Mr. A. Fuller to Mr. Kentish's Discourse* (1798). Points and arguments were repeated, and it is to be feared that in the exchanges under review no further light was shed upon Christological matters.

Elsewhere, however, Fuller, echoing other orthodox writers we have considered, does have more to say on the person of Christ. He considers the following objections:

> that sonship implies *inferiority*, and therefore cannot be attributed to the Divine person of Christ.—But whatever inferiority may be attached to the idea of sonship, it is not an inferiority of *nature* . . . and if any regard be paid to the Scriptures, the very contrary is true. Christ's claiming to be the Son of God was "making himself," not inferior, but *as God*, or "equal with God."

---

155. Toulmin was educated at Hoxton Academy, Kentish at Daventry Academy and then at Hackney (New) College. They are both in ODNB, SI.

156. Toulmin, *The Practical Efficacy of the Unitarian Doctrine*, 5.

157. Kentish, *The Moral Tendency of the Genuine Christian Doctrine*, 6.

158. Ibid., 27.

Once more, Sonship, it is said, implies *posteriority*, or that Christ as a Son could not have existed until after the Father. ... The truth is, the whole of this apparent difficulty arises from the want of distinguishing between the order of nature and the order of time. In the order of nature, the sun must have existed before it could shine; but in the order of time the sun and its rays are coeval; it never existed a single instant without them. ... And thus in the order of nature the Father must have existed before the Son; but, in that of duration, he never existed without the Son. The Father and the Son, therefore, are properly eternal.[159]

It remains to note two further controversies in the first of which Fuller was involved, from the second he remained aloof. William Vidler (1758-1816)[160] was raised a Particular Baptist, but he came to chafe under scholastic Calvinism, and found the doctrine of eternal punishment particularly offensive. In the 1790s he declared himself a Universalist, and took up his pen in the cause. In 1799 he published *God's Love to His Creatures Asserted and Vindicated*, and from 1797 onwards he edited *The Universalist's Miscellany; or, Philanthropist's Museum: Intended Chiefly as an Antidote against the Antichristian Doctrine of Endless Misery*. All of which drew eight letters from Fuller, of which the first was written in September 1795 and the last in July 1800.[161] In the early years of the nineteenth century Vidler espoused a humanitarian Christology and became a Unitarian.

In the mid-1790s another Baptist minister, Edward Sharman, who had succeeded William Carey (1671-1834)[162] at Moulton, became a Unitarian. In 1795 he published *A Letter on the Doctrine of the Trinity*. He explains that until about half a year ago he had accepted the doctrine on the authority of others, but when a labouring man asked him some questions that he could not answer, he examined the Bible on the matter and concluded that since the doctrine had no scriptural foundation, he could no longer, without hypocrisy, call himself a Trinitarian. Accordingly he now advocates the worship of the one God only, thereby, he is convinced, following the practice of Jesus himself and the early Christians. Writing from Northamptonshire, the heartland of Baptist

---

159. A. Fuller, *Works*, 944.
160. For whom, see ODNB.
161. Ibid., 133-49.
162. For whom, see DEB, ODCC, ODNB.

missionary endeavour, he supposes that modern missionaries must explain to their hearers that,

> though there be a few in our country we call *heretics*, who will worship the Father as the only true God, according to the Messiah's positive instructions, yet for our parts, we profess to worship gods *many*, and lords *many*; . . . Whenever you pray, you must address a compound person . . . But in such a perversion of a plain revealed truth, these ignorant Pagans as soon as they could read the scriptures, would have reason to suspect there must be something wrong . . .[163]

In a *Second Letter* (1796) Sharman reiterates his view and in 1799 he addressed *A Caution against Trinitarianism: Or, an Inquiry Whether Those Who Now Follow the Example of the Ancient Fathers, by Invoking God's Servant the Messiah as Supreme Deity, are the Only True Worshippers of the One Almighty God Revealed in the Bible; or Do Not Deserve the Name of Idolaters: in Five Letters Addressed to the Reverend Mr. Davis, of Wigston, Leicestershire, Containing Some Remarks upon His Late Publication, Stiled, A Caution against Socinianism, &c.* In 1800 he followed up with *A Second Caution against Trinitarianism; or, An Inquiry Whether that System Has Not Some Tendency to Lead People unto Deism and Atheism, in a Letter addressed to The Rev. Mr. Fuller, Kettering.* Both of his *Cautions* appeared under the authorship of "A Northamptonshire Farmer." He again declares that the one God alone is to be worshipped, and says, "I regard the Messiah as a finite dependant [sic] character, who derived his existence and all his powers from Jehovah, because he himself asserts it."[164] I cannot find that Fuller rose to Sharman's bait—perhaps because he thought it not worthwhile, or kind, to do so. As long ago as May 2, 1796 he had written thus to William Carey concerning Sharman's *First Letter*: "I reckon, though it be a blundering performance, it must be answered, and if it be we will send you the book & its answer together. He has lately lost his wife, and some think him touched with insanity."[165]

---

163. Sharman, *A Letter on the Doctrine of the Trinity*, 5–6.

164. Sharman, *A Second Caution against Trinitarianism*, 7.

165. Fuller Correspondence 1793–1815, MSS. BMS Vol. 1, Angus Library, Regent's Park College, Oxford.

4

Representative Ecclesial Repercussions in Eighteenth-Century England

Having elucidated the Christological excitements of the eighteenth century, it is now time to consider the ecclesial consequences; and here we need to keep our heads. I reiterate the point that it was perfectly possible for local churches to undergo doctrinal change without secession. Many examples might be given, but three from Yorkshire will suffice: the Presbyterian churches at Rotherham, at Westgate, Wakefield, and at St. Saviour's Gate, York, all became Unitarian by the end of the eighteenth century without disturbance. Let it also be granted that Dissenters were quite capable of seceding without any doctrinal encouragement, as when, in 1799, Zion (Presbyterian) Chapel, Wakefield, was enlarged. There followed dissention over the rearrangement and allocation of pews, and the disaffected departed and opened Salem Congregational Church in 1800.[1] The fact remains, however, that the long eighteenth century is characterized by a considerable number of secessions within Nonconformity, many of them inspired at least in part by Christological considerations. How is this concentration of secessions to be explained? It would seem to be a consequence of the freedom to worship granted under the Toleration Act of 1689. It is said that about one thousand meeting houses were licensed during the twenty years following 1689. Clearly, if one is legally free to worship, or not, in a building, one is legally free to secede from the fellowship gathered in it. Were it not anachronistic, we might say that the door was open to doctrinal consumerism. By the time we reach the early decades of the nineteenth century the several doctrinal tribes were settling down

---

1. Miall, *Yorkshire*, 341, 375, 388, 376.

behind more formal doctrine-*cum*-polity ramparts, and denominations as we have come to know them were being formed. New churches were being planted not so much as a consequence of doctrinal secession but, under the impetus of the Evangelical Revival, as the result of considerable home missionary effort.

As we proceed to examine the ecclesial situation on the ground we need not endorse the sometimes hysterical contemporary orthodox laments concerning a "Socinian blight" spreading across the land; still less should we fall for the claim that heterodoxy was the sole factor in the decline of many Dissenting churches as the century progressed. Social and personal factors were frequently involved, and it was hardly more likely that Arianism and Socinianism would cause churches to self-destruct than that high scholastic Calvinism would. Nor should we overlook the fact that the Unitarian cause in Exeter was strong at the end of the eighteenth century, as was the Particular Baptist church, Broadmead, Bristol; or the constituting of new (Unitarian) General Baptist churches at Cranbrook, (1807), Headcorn (1819) and Dover (1820).[2]

Furthermore, if heterodox preaching were often caricatured as cold and moralistic (and it was not all like that), hyper-Calvinistic preaching could equally be on the chilly side of cosy, not to mention boring: the obituary euphemism, "his gifts were not of the popular order" speaks volumes.[3] It is not difficult to find partisans on either side of the orthodox-heterodox divide who can make the point for us. Thus, we learn from Job Orton, Doddridge's student and friend, that the recently-deceased Paul Cardale of Evesham "hath written several pieces in favour of Socinianism, in a long and tedious way; but full of good sense and good temper. He had, I suppose, about twenty people to hear him at the last, having ruined a fine congregation by his very learned, and dry discourses, and extreme heaviness in the pulpit, and an almost total neglect of pastoral visits and private inspection."[4] W. T. Whitley cancels this out from the other side, with reference to the Baptist hyper-Calvinist: "Brine was at Currier's Hall exaggerating hyper-Calvinism till he had only thirty of the elect left."[5] To this Walter Wilson adds that Brine "was generally

---

2. See Packer, *The Unitarian Heritage in Kent*, 15.

3. See further, Powicke, "An apology for the Nonconformist Arians," 101–28.

4. Orton, *Letters*, I, 154. Cardale (1705–75) was educated under Ebenezer Latham at Findern Academy.

5. Whitley, *The Baptists of London*, 52. Though the late Dr. Kenneth Dix suggested

reputed a high Calvinist, but he went into all the unintelligible depths of the supra-lapsarian scheme, such as Calvin himself never allowed."[6]

For all that, C. H. Spurgeon was guilty of the fallacy of incomplete enumeration when he castigated "barren Socinianism", and observed:

> at the present time, certain ancient chapels shut up, with grass growing in front of them, and over the door there is the name *Unitarian Baptist Chapel*. Although it has been said that he is a benefactor of his race who makes two blades of grass grow where only one grew before, we have no desire to empty our pews in order to grow more grass. We have in our eye certain other chapels, not yet arrived at that consummation, where the spiders are dwelling in delightful quietude, in which the pews are more numerous than the people, and although an endowment keeps the minister's mouth open, there are but few open ears for him to address.[7]

The fact remains that many Presbyterian, and a handful of Congregational, churches had become Unitarian by the end of the eighteenth century (as had a number of General Baptist churches); but more Presbyterian causes had become Congregational—the body which, like the Baptist, was better able to benefit numerically from the Evangelical Revival,[8] albeit at some cost to the covenant idea of the Church (entry now often being perceived by many as being a matter of conversion and testimony, rather than baptism and nurture leading to profession of faith).[9] In addition, a New Connexion of more orthodox and evangelical Arminian General Baptist churches was formed in 1770 under the leadership of Dan Taylor (1738–1816).[10] The six articles of faith drawn up by this group emphasised the deity of Christ, thus: "We believe, that our

---

to me that this figure may refer to the number of those on the roll of members, not to the actual size of the congregation.

6. Wilson, *The History and Antiquities of Dissenting Churches*, II, 577.
7. Spurgeon, *An All-Round Ministry*, 94.
8. For my attempt at a county-by-county analysis of the situation in England at the end of the eighteenth century, see Sell, *Dissenting Thought*, 147–51. A general finding is that in 1718 there were some 637 English Presbyterian churches and some 203 Congregational churches. By 1772 there were 302 English Presbyterian churches and 400 Congregational churches. By 1800 the English Presbyterians had declined to 200 churches, while the number of Congregational churches had increased to 900.
9. See Sell, *Dissenting Thought*, 15–16, 64–67.
10. For whom, see DEB, ODNB.

Lord Jesus Christ is God and man, united in one person: or possessed of divine perfection united to human nature, in a way which we pretend not to explain, but think ourselves bound by God firmly to believe..."[11] Raymond Brown provides an example of dramatically contrasting Baptist attitudes: "By 1813 the New Connexion, disturbed about the spread of Socinian 'poison,' urged its churches not to allow any believers in 'that destructive system' to preach in their pulpits."[12] Unconcerned about anxieties of that kind, an 1815 General [Baptist] Assembly Committee reported on the "success of Unitarianism which, with the exception of baptism, may surely be called the cause of the General Baptists."[13]

As I review the doctrinal shifts of the long eighteenth-century, my preference is to think in terms of doctrinal change, rather than to use evaluative terms such as doctrinal "progress" or "declension."[14] With these caveats in mind let us now take some samples of the situation on the ground. In order to avoid the monotony of a succession of sentences beginning "In [plus date]" I have devised a chronology of events inspired by, or at least having some reference to, Christological considerations. It is not an exhaustive list, but it will at least suggest the geographical spread of doctrinal concern; the preponderance of strife from 1750 onwards; some instances in which doctrinal change in a local church did not result in secession; and the different ways in which secessions occurred: the orthodox on occasion leaving the heterodox behind, and *vice versa*. Some cases of local church discipline will also be noted. I shall refer to counties by their then current names,[15] and it will be convenient to deal first with England, and in the following chapter with Wales.

1710. In this year Samuel Hardman (d. 1761) became the minister at Mill Brow, Marple Bridge, Cheshire. Of him it is said that "his views of the plan of salvation were not very clear, as he had a leaning towards Arianism." He nevertheless remained there until 1741. His successor, Robert Harrop (1744–1831), trained at Daventry under Caleb

---

11. Lumpkin, *Baptist Confessions of Faith*, 343.

12. Brown, *The English Baptists*, 108, quoting the *General Baptist Repository*, V, no. xxviii, 183.

13. Ibid., quoting *The Monthly Repository of Theology and General Literature*, X, 1815, 320.

14. See further on this complicated matter, Sell, *Dissenting Thought*, ch. 5.

15. Thus, for example, Walsall will be located in Staffordshire, not in the West Midlands as at present.

Ashworth, arrived in 1765.[16] He had the joint pastorate of Mill Brow and Greenacres, Oldham. In 1769 he left for Hale, where he remained until he resigned in 1816. "His doctrinal leanings," we learn, "were Arian. On account of this, some of the more intelligent and respectable of his hearers attended the neighbouring chapels of Charlesworth and Hatherlow, where the gospel was still preached"[17]—an interesting remark, given that the "more intelligent and respectable" not infrequently flirted with heterodoxy.

1715. The Congregationalist Timothy Jollie (b. 1659/60), minister of New Meeting, Sheffield, died on Easter Sunday 1714.[18] Many church members hoped that his assistant, John de la Rose (d. 1723), the son of a French refugee and a high Calvinist trained under Jollie at Attercliffe Academy, would succeed him; but the trustees, some wealthy individuals, and adherents over-rode the wishes of the evangelical church members, locked de la Rose and his friends out of the chapel, and called John Wadsworth (1678–1745) of Rotherham—also an Attercliffe *alumnus*—to the pastorate. He had preceded de la Rose as assistant and was said to incline to Arianism. The evangelical Calvinists, led by Elias Wordsworth, seceded, and Nether Church was constituted with de la Rose as its minister.[19]

In the same year the Presbyterians seceded from the Broad Street, Reading, meeting, leaving behind the Congregationalists, Samuel Doolittle (1662–1727) the minister (whose education was at the Islington Academy of his father, the ejected Thomas Doolittle), and George Burnett, Doolittle's assistant and successor, who had subscribed at Salters' Hall. The inference is drawn by Summers that since the seceders called Richard Rigby, educated under John Chorlton (1666–1705) at Manchester and a non-subscriber at Salter's Hall, the Presbyterian party was of the heterodox sort.[20]

---

16. For Hardman and Harrop, see SI.

17. Urwick, ed., *Historical* Sketches, 334.

18. For Jollie, see ODNB, SI. He was educated at Richard Frankland's academy when it was located at Rathmell.

19. Miall, *Yorkshire*, 352–54. For de la Rose and Wadsworth see SI.

20. Summers, *History of the Congregational Churches in the Berks, etc.*, 162. Thomas Doolittle (d. 1707) was educated at Pembroke College, Cambridge, Rigby, under John Chorlton at Manchester Academy. They, together with Samuel Doolittle and George Burnett are in SI, and Chorlton is also in ODNB.

1719. A number of members of the Presbyterian Old Meeting at Warminster, Wiltshire, seceded to form a Congregational church. They alleged that the minister, Samuel Bates (d. 1761), assistant minister from 1705 and pastor from 1718, was an Arian. They also wished that "a Mr. Pike" had been appointed as assistant to Bates. Joseph Pike thus became their minister in 1719.[21] As for Bates, who remained at his post until his death in 1761, it does appear that some were determined to tar him with the Arian brush. The Church Book records the contrary opinion, dated 26 June 1719: "Whereas 'tis suggested that our minister favours the Arian notion, as we hear Mr. Butler told the Rev. Mr. Robinson, we can't but all readily declare this to be a vile slander, that he has been very free and full in speaking against that notion, in private and public, and this Mr. Butler heard but a few days before he went to London with his complaint."[22]

1727. Almost at the end of John Guyse's ministry at Hertford, the Church Book has the following entry for 10 May: "Whereas Mr. James Santeen and Mrs. Susanna Lob have been for sometime members with us, and after a 1st and 2nd solemn admonition do still persist in a denial of ye proper Godhead of Christ, we do in the Name of our Lord Jesus Christ, with a tender concern for His glory and their recovery and for the preservation of our own peace and purity, cut them off from all further relations to this church as if he or she were a heathen man and a publican."[23]

1734. James Ritchie (1698–1763), whose experience at Mixenden I have already recounted, became minister at the High Chapel, Ravenstonedale, in 1733. The following year the Presbyterian trustees ejected him and withheld his stipend on the ground that he had not "qualified himself to officiate in the congregation by subscribing to the Confession of Faith made in 1647, and agreeing to the doctrine of Calvin, so that they could not in conscience take the Lord's Supper at his hands." In January 1734 Ritchie applied to the Kendal Presbytery for ordination, but seven Ravenstonedale trustees wrote to oppose this. Ritchie launched a successful suit in Chancery against the trustees which lasted for fourteen years. He was awarded arrears of stipend and possession of the meeting

---

21. For Bates and Pike, see SI.
22. Quoted by Murch, *West of England*, 88.
23. Urwick, *Nonconformity in Herts*, 545.

house, but by then he had moved away. He and his supporters generously paid more than half the court costs of £820/0/0. It is not clear to which aspects of the *Westminster Confession* he took exception, but it is known that by 1753 he was an Arian.[24]

1736. Joseph Rawson, a member of Castle Gate Congregational Church, Nottingham, was accused by the co-pastor, James Sloss (1669–1772), of consorting with heretics. Charged with Arianism, Rawson was excluded from the Lord's Table and, when he announced that he would nevertheless present himself there, he was threatened with civil action. The Arian Presbyterian, John Taylor of Norwich, rose up in his defence.[25] Some church members who were sympathetic to Rawson left Castle Gate for High Pavement Presbyterian Church, which was moving in an heterodox direction. Indeed a Castle Gate resolution reads, "that no person be received from the High Pavement congregation as a member of this congregation without giving in their experience [as distinct from assenting to doctrinal statements], unless they have been received as members of that church before the Rev. Mr. Hewes left that congregation [Obadiah Hughes left in 1735]."[26]

1737. The Presbyterians of Bank Court meeting, Walsall, were coming under Arian influence, so their minister, the orthodox James Warner, had his house in Rushall Street licensed as an additional place of worship for Protestant Dissenters.

1742. In 1735 Thomas Collins (d. 1765), who had studied under Henry Grove at Taunton Academy, was called to the Old Meeting, Bridport, Dorset. Although he was not at all pugnacious, a number of members came to sense, more from what he did not say than from what he did,

---

24. Nicholson and Axon, *The Older Nonconformity of Kendal*, 289; Sell, *Church Planting*, 45; Woodger and Hunter, *The High Chapel*. For Ritchie, see SI.

25. See the Castle Gate Church Book, Dr. Williams's Library, London, MS. 201.33.8; Taylor, *A Narrative of Mr. Joseph Rawson's Case*, 2nd ed., 1742; Henderson, *History of Castle Gate*, 144–50; Whitehead, *History of the Dales Congregational Churches*, 95; Sell, *Dissenting Thought*, 230–32. Sloss also collided over the Trinity with Samuel Bourn of Coseley and Birmingham, ibid., 235–41. For Sloss, educated at Glasgow University, see also SI.

26. Castle Gate Church Book, quoted by Henderson, *History of Castle Gate*, 148. Hughes, educated at Kibworth Academy, was at High Pavement from 1728 to 1735. See SI.

that "the Saviour was not *exalted* in his sermons as formerly."[27] Collins gave ambiguous answers to a series of questions put to him at the suggestion of Isaac Watts; and his colleague, John Witty, proposed that he be asked directly, "do you believe that Jesus Christ was God equal with the father from all eternity?" Collins returned a negative answer. At this two hundred members withdrew, though three hundred remained; and none of those who left spoke ill of their former minister. On July 12, 1742 Daniel Taylor's house was licensed as the seceders' place of worship.[28]

1745. It would seem that the Cheshire Classis broke up following the announcement in its Minutes that the ordination of Richard Meanley (1717–1794)[29] would take place at Nantwich, for there are no further records. The church had had a reputation for Socinianism since the second decade of the century, and Meanley had been trained under the Arian Caleb Rotheram at Kendal. From the time of his departure in 1758 the church had a succession of decidedly Socinian/Unitarian ministers, of whom the first was Joseph Priestley (1758–1761).[30]

1746. The Presbyterian, Benjamin Mills, was minister at Maidstone, Kent, from 1726 to 1745. In 1736 the church opened a new meeting house in Earl Street. Mills, however, caused anxiety to some because of his Arian views, and on his departure the displeased were not inclined to acquiesce in the appointment of a successor of that ilk. But the trustees installed the General Baptist John Wiche (1718–1794),[31] who served from 1746 to 1794. He had impeccable liberal credentials, having been educated under Henry Grove at Taunton, Caleb Rotheram (1694–1752) at Kendal[32] and Ebenezer Latham at Findern. Wiche, like Priestley, had been converted to Socinianism by Nathaniel Lardner's *Letter on the Logos*. A section of the congregation objected to Wiche's appointment on the grounds that they had not had an opportunity to nominate a can-

---

27. Densham and Ogle, *Dorset*, 50. For Collins see SI.
28. Ibid., 50–51.
29. For whom, see SI.
30. F. J. Powicke, *Cheshire*, 11–12, 159.
31. Not W. Hazlett (*sic*) as given by Timpson, *Church History of Kent*, 335. Hazlitt was assistant minister there for an indeterminate period from 1770. For Wiche, see ODNB, SI.
32. For Rotheram, educated at Whitehaven Academy, see ODNB, SI; Sell, *Church Planting*, 39–41 and *passim*.

didate themselves, and that Wiche had been "arbitrarily imposed" upon them. Above all, "we had sufficient grounds to believe that the minister who has been chosen for a pastor was not sound in such doctrines as we esteem to be the fundamentals of Christianity, and upon which we desire to build our hopes of pardon and salvation."[33] They therefore departed, and established a church on the Congregational plan.

1748. In 1746 William Howell (1714-1776), an Arian trained under Thomas Perrot (d. 1733) at Carmarthen Academy, was called to Old Meeting, Birmingham.[34] A "considerable proportion" of the members seceded, and opened Carrs Lane Chapel in 1748. In November of that year they called their first pastor, Gervase Wilde, James Sloss's assistant at Nottingham.[35]

1753. William Cornish (d. 1763), an Arian educated under Henry Grove at Taunton Academy, was ordained to the Presbyterian ministry, together with Grove's nephew, Thomas Amory (1700/1-1774), on October 7, 1730.[36] Following a pastorate at Bishops Hull and West Hatch, Somerset, Cornish was called to Sherborne, Dorset, in 1744, and there he remained until his death. Following his arrival some evangelical church members left and joined others to form the Congregational church at Milborne Port. In 1753, Ridson Darracott (1717-1759),[37] the evangelical "Star of the West" came to Sherborne and stayed with Benjamin Vowell, a prominent member of Cornish's church. Cornish refused to open his pulpit to Darracott. This prompted a further secession, led by Benjamin and Thomas Vowell and Benjamin Whitehead, of members who had never been "satisfied with the mild morality of Mr. Cornish's preaching." The seceders met in homes at first, and then in 1756 they erected their own Congregational chapel.[38]

---

33. Ibid.

34. For Howell and Perrot, see SI. For Perrot, see DWB. He trained at Abergavenny under Roger Griffiths, and at Shrewsbury under James Owen.

35. Sibree and Caston, *Warwickshire*, 176-77.

36. Grove preached a sermon on the occasion, for which, see his *Works*, I, 467-542; Sell, *Dissenting Thought*, 181-82. For Cornish, see SI; for Amory, see ODNB, SI.

37. For whom, see ODNB, SI. He was educated under Philip Doddridge at Northampton Academy.

38. W. Densham and J. Ogle, *Dorset*, 256-57.

1755. Samuel Mercer (1733–1786),[39] who had been educated under Doddridge at Northampton and Ashworth at Daventry, followed James Scott (1710–1783), now removed to Heckmondwike, as minister at Tockholes, Lancashire. He resigned in the same year, having "developed Unitarian tendencies," and proceeded to Charlesworth, Derbyshire, where, owing to his theological position, he remained for under three years.[40]

1755 ONWARDS. The succession of ministers at Wem Congregational Church, Shropshire is of interest in that oscillating doctrinal views appear to have prompted no secessions. Thomas Harrop, who was educated under the liberal Ebenezer Latham at Findern Academy, arrived as minister in 1755, and remained until 1781. Since from 1741 to 1753 he had served as assistant at High Pavement, Nottingham, it comes as no surprise to learn that during his Wem ministry "Unitarian ideas were adopted."[41] He was followed by John Haughton (1730–1800), an alumnus of Northampton Academy and Glasgow University, "of whose ministry no particulars have been handed down."[42] Then came William Hazlitt (1737–1820), father of the man of letters, who served from 1787 to 1815. S. T. Coleridge, himself originally destined for the Unitarian ministry, was a frequent visitor to the Wem parsonage, "walking there from Shrewsbury, reading on his way."[43] There followed two ministers educated at Wymondley Academy: James Whitehead (1789–1859) and Thomas Toller (1796–1885). By Toller "the original doctrines were preached in the chapel."[44]

1756. The Socinian Presbyterian Benjamin Williams began his ministry at the Salt Lane Meeting, Salisbury, and almost at once some sixteen to twenty orthodox members seceded with their families. After a period of worshipping at Wilton Independent Church they opened their Congregational Chapel, also in Scotts Lane, in 1757.[45]

39. For whom, see SI.

40. Gibson, *A Brief History of* Tockholes, 5; Mansfield, *Charlesworth Independent Chapel*, 14.

41. Elliot, *Shropshire*, 64.

42. Ibid. For Haughton, see SI.

43. E. Elliott, *Shropshire*, 64.

44. Ibid., 66.

45. Abel, *A History of the Presbyterian Congregational United Reformed Church in Salisbury*, 1, 11.

In the same year John Wright (d. 1794) became minister at Tucker Street, Bristol.[46] He had studied under David Jennings (1691–1762)[47] at Hoxton, and Thomas Amory, Henry Grove's nephew and successor, at Taunton Academy. He was "inclined to Arianism"—a "matter of lamentation" to M. Caston.[48] Owing to vocal problems he resigned in 1765 and thereafter practised successfully as a physician in Bristol. His brother, Thomas (d. 1797), minister at Lewin's Mead Chapel, was in regular contact with him and "The intimacy which . . . existed between the respective congregations, and the frequent exchange of ministerial services, indicate an agreement where it could least be desired."[49] The "lamentable consequences begun now to appear, in the want of vital, active piety amongst the people, and the discontinuance of the ordinary privileges of church meetings, and meetings for social prayer . . ."[50] further distressed Caston. Things did not improve, from his point of view, when Dr. Edward Harwood (1729–1794) succeeded Wright in 1765.[51] He had been ordained on 16 October 1765 at Old Jewry, London, on which occasion the sermon was preached by Thomas Amory, and the charge was given by Samuel Chandler.[52] Later, Harwood composed a sermon on the occasion of the death of John Taylor.[53] All of which is indicative of Arian sympathies. An extract (only) from Caston's extensive adverse yet lyrical judgment reads, "The church of Tucker Street declined in numbers, piety, and energy. . . . The ways of Zion mourned. Few came to her solemn feasts; and 'Ichabod' had well nigh been inscribed on her walls."[54] Then, through "the favourable disposals of Divine Providence," Thomas Janes (d. 1775) succeeded to the pastorate, "the night of weeping gradually departed, and joy beamed in the morning."[55]

46. For John and Thomas Wright, see SI.

47. For whom, see SI. He was educated under Thomas Ridgley at Moorfields Academy, London.

48. Caston, *Independency in Bristol*, 96.

49. Ibid., 97.

50. Ibid.

51. For Harwood, see ODNB, SI.

52. *The Motives and Obligations to Love and Good Works, . . . To which is annexed the . . . Charge delivered by Samuel Chandler.*

53. Harwood, *A Sermon Occasioned by the Death of the Rev. John Taylor.*

54. Ibid., 97–98.

55. Ibid., 98. For Janes, see SI.

1758. In October Samuel Philipps (1702–75),[56] minister at Hill Street, Poole, since 1752, was dismissed because Arian subscribers, who seemed to have had more power than the church members, could not tolerate his evangelical opinions and manner. "The pastor," we learn, "had advanced doctrines not congenial with the opinions of the more moderate of his hearers, who also happened to be the majority, and he maintained them in a manner so disgusting that, after much indecorous altercation, he was locked out of the pulpit, and his adherents followed him."[57] The Arians were left in possession of the building, and a Unitarian chapel was later erected on the site.[58] Phillipps and his supporters established a meeting in Lag Lane, Poole, where he ministered from 1760 to 1766.

1763. In the wake of earlier secessions from Bank Top Presbyterian Church, Walsall, the evangelical Calvinists seceded, and constituted the first Congregational Church in Staffordshire at Dudley Street. The members,

> Mindful of the manner in which the Arian party in High Street had obtained possession of the pulpit and diverted the intention of the Presbyterian founders, the Dudley Street people were exceedingly careful in defining the purpose for which the new place was erected. By the wording of the Trust Deed the Minister must teach and instruct the people in the tenets, faith, and doctrine of the Larger and Smaller Catechisms, composed by the Westminster Assembly of Divines, and other parts of the doctrine relating to the faith of Protestant Dissenters, called Independents; that he should hold his office so long only as he does this, and so long also as he maintains a strictly moral and religious manner of life.[59]

On 21 September twelve Dudley Street members, led by Samuel Rooker, signed their Confession of Faith, which included the clauses: "We believe in One God . . . & that there are three persons in the Godhead, Father, Son, and Holy Ghost, the same in Substance, equal in power and Glory. . . . God of his free & undeserved mercy appointed his

---

56. For whom, see SI.
57. Murch, *West of England*, 292.
58. Densham and Ogle, *Dorset*, 195–96.
59. Willis, *A History of Bridge Street Chapel, Walsall*, 13. The chapel in Bridge Street succeeded that of Dudley Street in 1891 See further, Sell, *Dissenting Thought*, ch. 11.

Son Christ Jesus as God-man to be the Redeemer of all those that believe in him . . ."⁶⁰

1767. Rees Price (1762–96) arrived at Chalfont St. Giles *circa.* 1767, and was ordained there on 6 June 1770. An Arian, he served until 1808, by which time "the congregation had dwindled to about twenty."⁶¹

1768. A secession occurred at Crook Street Chapel, Chester. This chapel had been built for Matthew Henry in 1700. Henry was succeeded in 1713 by John Gardner, who remained until his death in 1765.⁶² It appears that he became Arian in his views from about 1750 onwards, while his assistant, John Chidlaw (1727–1800),⁶³ who arrived in 1751, was a Socinian. Chidlaw had been trained under David Jennings at Wellclose Square Academy, London, and was sole pastor at Crook Street from 1765 to 1798. The membership of the church had comprised both Presbyterians and Congregationalists but in 1768 the latter, in the interests of their favoured polity but urged on by Chidlaw's heterodoxy, seceded together with some orthodox Presbyterian members, and began to worship in Commonhall Street. Those who favoured orthodox doctrine and/or Congregational polity constituted a church in 1772 and opened a chapel in Queen Street in 1777, while those who were both congregational and believer baptist in their beliefs continued at Commonhall Street as a Baptist church.⁶⁴

1769. John Burnet (d. 1782),⁶⁵ the Congregational minister in Hull, was suspected of Arianism, and a secession occurred that led to the formation of the church at Blanket Row, afterwards Fish Street. George Lambert (1741–1816), trained at the evangelical Calvinist Heckmondwike Academy under James Scott, was called in the same year, and served there

---

60. For the full statement, and for the Rooker family, see Sell, *Dissenting Thought*, 349–50.

61. Summers, *Berks., etc.*, 36. For Price see SI. He was educated at Abergavenny Academy.

62. Gardner was educated at Oswestry Academy under J. Owen and at Shrewsbury, possibly under J. Benion. See SI.

63. For whom, see SI.

64. Urwick, ed., *Historical* Sketches, 37–39; Collis, *Baptist Churches of* Shropshire, 52–53.

65. For whom, see SI.

for forty-six years.[66] Scott, a Berwickshire man trained at Edinburgh, had come to England on hearing of the dearth of orthodox ministers. In the following year the Blanket Row Church adopted their *Covenant and Confession of Faith* which makes it clear that there is one God, and that "In the Godhead we believe there are Three Persons, the Father, the Son, and the Holy Spirit; none is before or after the other, being equal, possessing the same Name and Attributes, conjoining in the same Works, equal in Glory, Power, and Love."[67]

1773. Thomas Astley[68] arrived as minister at Elder Yard Chapel, Chesterfield in April. A Cumbrian, the son and father of ministers, he had been educated at Daventry under Caleb Ashworth, and at the liberal academy at Warrington. He had been ordained alongside Joseph Priestley and two others on 18 May 1762. Almost certainly because of Astley's heterodox views the Congregationalists seceded, the Presbyterians remained, and the church was in due course known as Unitarian. The seceders worshipped in a barn until in 1778 they opened the Blue Meeting House, to which their Soresby Street Church of 1823 was the successor.[69]

Also in 1773 Joseph Dawson (d. 1821), educated at Daventry Academy under Caleb Ashworth, and at Glasgow University, and minister at Upper Chapel, Idle, Yorkshire, signed the petition to Parliament for relief from subscription. Deemed an Arian, he eventually relinquished his pastorate and devoted himself to mining. He occasionally preached at the Unitarian Chapel in Bradford.[70]

1775. James Reed Harris (d. 1808), who was educated under the evangelical James Rooker at Bridport,[71] stunned all concerned when, at his

---

66. Miall, *Yorkshire*, 290, 292. See also SI. Among his assistants was George Payne, of whom more anon. See Sell, *Hinterland Theology*, 128-31.

67. Anon., "The Covenant and Confession of Faith of the Church of Christ meeting in Blanket-Row, Kingston-upon-Hull, 1770," 249.

68. For whom, see SI.

69. See Robson, *Origins and History of Elder Yard Chapel, Chesterfield*, 28-30. On p. 30 Robson says that the secession occurred in 1772, but this was before Astley's arrival, and is evidently a slip. Alternatively, Astley may have preached with a view to the pastorate in the year previous to his arrival and the Congregationalists disapproved of what they then heard, and left before he settled in the town.

70. See J. Horsfall Turner, *Nonconformity in Idle*, 46-49; Sell, "Caleb Ashworth," forthcoming.

71. For Rooker (1728/9-1780), see Sell, *Dissenting Thought*, ch. 11.

ordination he proclaimed himself an Arian. His sympathisers remained with him, but the evangelicals left and walked to Charmouth to worship. In 1798 Harris proceeded to the Socinian church at Ilminster, where he died on 23 January 1800.[72]

Edward Dewhirst (d. 1784), who was among the last students of Caleb Ashworth at Daventry, became minister at Cottingham, Yorkshire, in 1775. He was an Arian, and this caused a breach within the fellowship. George Lambert of Hull and George Gill (1752-1832)[73] of Swanland—both of whom had been educated at Heckmondwike Academy, preached to the disaffected as, later, did Richard Leggatt (d. 1806), who came from the Countess of Huntingdon's College at Trefeca, and succeeded Dewhirst in 1785. As for Dewhirst, "He lies buried in the churchyard; where, with a bigotry which deserves oblivion, his body and headstone lie in a reversed position. After his decease, the people became reunited. He was a man of superior classical attainments."[74]

1779. A secession of evangelical Calvinists from the Presbyterian cause in Warrington, Lancashire, led to the formation of the first Congregational church in that town. This occurred during the ministry (and tutorship at Warrington Academy) of William Enfield (1741-1797), who had trained at Daventry under Caleb Ashworth, and whose doctrines were tending towards Unitarianism.[75]

1782. After a period under Arian influence, the Presbyterian church at Leek, Staffordshire, called the Calvinist, James Evans, to be their minister. On his departure in July 1782 a majority of the trustees and subscribers called George Chadwick to succeed Evans.[76] Not all of the members were content, however, so at a further meeting in October thirty-six orthodox members, including two trustees, called Robert Scott (1749-1822), who had been educated at Heckmondwike Academy. Neither minister would give way, and the pair went to court. In 1783 the matter was determined in Chadwick's favour, but Scott appealed, and was likewise successful,

---

72. Densham and Ogle, *Dorset*, 151. See also SI.
73. For whom, see SI.
74. Miall, *Yorkshire*, 250.
75. See Nightingale, *Lancashire Nonconformity*, II.ii. 219-20; SI.
76. For Chadwick and Evans, see SI.

whereupon Chadwick and his supporters seceded, and thus "the meeting-house was permanently secured for the orthodox."[77]

1786. The Presbyterian Joseph Fawcett (1758–1804),[78] whose principal tutor at Daventry had been Thomas Robins, was minister of Marsh Street Church, Walthamstow, from 1780 to 1787. In 1786 a large number of members, disappointed by Fawcett's Socinian-Unitarian views on the one hand, and inspired by the Evangelical Revival on the other, seceded, constituted themselves as a Congregational church, and called the "fervent evangelical preacher" John Neal Lake (d. 1819),[79] who had been educated at Homerton College, to be their minister. Fawcett resigned from the ministry in 1787 and "is said to have devoted his leisure to the writing of poetry and the pursuit of agriculture."[80]

1788. The evangelical Calvinist Abraham Darby (d. 1782) became minister at Beaconsfield in 1767, but "Some of Mr. Darby's wealthy supporters . . . who were imbued with the Arian ideas then fashionable, are said to have treated him with great unkindness . . . he always appeared more happy in the pulpits of his brethren than in his own." But it was in his own that he was taken ill on 24 November 1782, and died. The Arian party replaced him with William Godwin (1756–1836). Godwin was the son of John Godwin, a dissenting minister who had lived among doctrinal tensions at Debenham, Suffolk (1758-60). Homerton College would not accept William for ministerial training, but Andrew Kippis (1725–1795) and Abraham Rees (1743–1825) at Hoxton Academy, London, admitted him.[81] Godwin passed through a Sandemanian phase, but it appears that during the few months to the summer of 1783 that he supplied Beaconsfield (he was not ordained[82]), he was of a deistic turn of mind. Whilst there he read Priestley's *Institutes*, with the result that "Socinianism appeared to relieve so many of the difficulties I

---

77. Matthews, *Staffordshire*, 151; Burgess, *The Story of Dean Row Chapel*, 50–51. For Scott, see SI.

78. For whom, see ODNB, SI.

79. For whom, see SI.

80. Budden, *The Story of Marsh Street Congregational Church*, 29–30, 38–40.

81. For Kippis, see ODNB, SI. For Rees, see DWB, ODNB, SI. Kippis was educated under Doddridge at Northampton Academy, Rees at Wellclose Square Academy under David Jennings.

82. *Pace* Locke, *A Fantasy of Reason*, 19; and on the same page read 1782 for 1872.

had hitherto sustained from Calvinistic theology, that my mind rested in that theory."[83] This was, however, merely a staging-post *en route* to scepticism.

1789/90. During his thirty-two year ministry at Bank Street, Bury, Lancashire, John Hughes (1748–1803), trained at Daventry under Caleb Ashworth, "became Arian, if not Unitarian."[84] This prompted a secession, and the founding of the first Congregational church in Bury.

1789. The Arian Robert Kell (1761–1842)[85] was educated under Thomas Belsham at Daventry Academy. In 1787 he opened a school in Wareham, Dorset, John Angell James, later of Carrs Lane Congregational Church, Birmingham, being among his pupils.[86] In 1789 he was imposed as minister upon the Wareham church by the Presbyterian trustees in succession to Simon Reader, one of Doddridge's Northampton students.[87] This caused considerable distress to the majority of the members, who objected to Kell's doctrine. They protested in the following terms: "Make choice of such an one (as the former pastor) and you may still hope to see the congregation united and flourishing; but, if not, be it known to you, be it known to all the world, we will not give up the gospel of Christ without a struggle to preserve it. . . . We wish not for separation, but cannot unite with you in the choice of Mr. Kell."[88] Their words fell on deaf ears, and the church was not consulted. Hence the evangelical secession, and the formation of the West Street Congregational church in the town. The seceders were encouraged by Thomas Reader (1725–94), Simon's younger brother, the minister at Paul's Meeting, Taunton.[89]

1791. The Arian, Richard Aubrey (1760–1836),[90] trained at Hoxton Academy under Abraham Rees, had arrived at Stand, Lancashire, in

---

83. Quoted by Summers, *Berks, etc.*, 23. For Godwin, see ODNB, SI.
84. Nightingale, *Lancashire Nonconformity*, II.i.181. For Hughes, see SI.
85. For whom, see SI.
86. For James (1785–1858), see DEB, ODNB. He went on to Gosport Academy.
87. For whom, see SI.
88. Densham and Ogle, *Dorset*, 344.
89. For Thomas Reader, see SI. He was educated at Bedworth Academy under J. Kirkpatrick. He combined the conduct of the Western Academy with his pastorate at Paul's Meeting, Taunton, from 1780–94.
90. For whom, see SI.

1787/8. By 1791 he seems to have embraced Unitarianism, for in that year a large minority of Calvinists seceded and, after a period during which they worshipped in a barn in Sheephey, they moved into their own Congregational chapel in Chapelfield. In August 1792 the seceders explained their position in a document, thus:

> We whose names are hereunto subscribed having been formerly connected with a religious society of Protestant Dissenters at Stand in Pilkington, judging it our duty to dissolve our religious connection with them on account of their attachment to Socinian errors, and having resolved to associate together for the purposes of enjoying divine ordinances, according to the dictates of our own consciences: we have unanimously called and invited the Rev. James Fordyce to discharge the duties of the pastoral office; and in consequence of his acquiescence in our call, We hereby, with his concurrence, voluntarily form and constitute ourselves into a regular Christian Church, and solemnly give ourselves to the Lord and to one another by the will of God.

They further "profess and resolve to maintain the fundamental doctrines and ordinances of the reformed Protestant Churches, particularly the Divinity of the person of our Lord Jesus Christ."[91] Despite the grounds of the secession Fordyce[92] became a Unitarian, and remained in pastoral charge until 1799. By that time the church was in serious decline, and it was re-formed in 1801, when twelve members signed a new covenant, which affirms that "the Lord Jesus Christ is truly God and man in one person."[93] A later Unitarian minister, Arthur Dean offered a complacent-*cum*-partisan observation on the episode: "Such disunion is rather to be expected than wondered at, when the ministers advance to a purer mode of faith, and arrive at more scriptural notions of Gospel truth, and their people remain in the same gloomy system of religion which the Nonconformists divines held in all the rigorous of the school of Calvin."[94]

91. An unattributed single sheet.

92. For whom, see SI.

93. These extracts (from an unattributed document) were used in a sermon of Richard Slate (1787–1867) delivered in 1852. He was educated at Hoxton, and was minister at Stand from 1809 to 1826. See also, Nightingale, *Lancashire Nonconformity*, II.i.226–27.

94. Herford, *Memorials of Stand Chapel*, 34. Cf., Gordon, *Historical Account of Dob Lane Chapel, Failsworth*, 43–44.

Representative Ecclesial Repercussions in Eighteenth-Century England 79

1793. At Stretton-under-Fosse, Warwickshire, there was

> for more than fifty years, and till about ten years ago [i.e. 1845], a Book Society, one of whose leading principles was, that books on both sides of any debatable theological subject should be introduced. Such a society, existing not thirty miles from Birmingham, was sure to catch some excitement from the fearful riots of 1793 in that town, when the house of Dr. Priestley was burnt to the ground, with all his valuable library and apparatus. Many sympathies were awakened for him at Stretton. His works were read; and his religious views took firm hold of many. These sentiments, however, were never those of the [Congregational] congregation generally; and are not held by any at the present time [1855].[95]

1794. Jabez Hirons (1728–1812),[96] a Presbyterian educated under Philip Doddridge at Northampton, was minister at Dagnal Street, St. Albans, from 1750 until his death in 1815. He embraced Arian views, and among his congregation were the founders of the Martineau Unitarian family. Some members began to sit under John Gill (1730–1809), the nephew of the London high Calvinist of the same name, at the Baptist Church. However, in 1794 those members who favoured the Congregational way and were of an evangelical disposition, and who regretted that they had been deprived of the sacraments of baptism and the Lord's Supper, seceded. They worshipped first in a cotton mill, then in a renovated barn. They constituted themselves as a church on 1 February 1796. Eventually, after Samuel Burder's ministry (which ended with his seeking and gaining Episcopal ordination in the Church of England), and during that of his successor, John Hayter Cox, they opened Spicer Street Chapel on June 10, 1812.[97]

1798. On September 5th the Devonian Richard Fry (1759–1842),[98] educated at the evangelical academies at Homerton and Bridport, preached a sermon to his flock at Billericay Congregational Church, Essex. The text of the sermon is written out in the Church Book, and it was published in 1800 under the title, *The Exercise of Reason and Liberty of Conscience the Sacred Right of all Men in Examining and Professing the*

---

95. Sibree and Caston, *Warwickshire*, 229.
96. For whom, see SI.
97. Urwick, *Herts*, 202–6; 229–32; 842. For Cox, see SI.
98. For whom, see SI.

Christian Truth. Taking Romans 14:5 as his text, Fry declared that he had now rejected Trinitarianism and embraced Socinianism. At a subsequent church meeting twenty-six members voted against the minister, two for him, while of the "subscribing non-members" fifty-one favoured dismissal against twenty-one who wished Fry to remain. The church, as well as individual families within it, was thus grievously fractured. Among various ensuing steps was a suggestion from Fry that his opponents might call a minister of their choice who would lead worship prior to a later service to be conducted by himself. He thought that in time harmony might be restored. But it was to no avail, and a new meeting house was built by Fry's supporters, with the minister himself contributing £48.19.0 towards the total cost of £140.19.0. Not all of those who had supported him at the church meeting followed him into the new chapel. A Baptist church was formed in Fry's meeting house in 1815.[99] Meanwhile Fry had removed to Cirencester (1803–1807),[100] where his two predecessor ministers had been Habakkuk Crabb (1776–1787),[101] who had been educated under Caleb Ashworth at Daventry academy, and the Carmarthen-trained Thomas Rees (1777–1864).[102] Fry's subsequent pastorates are also doctrinally significant: Coseley (1807–1812), where Samuel Bourn the Younger was among his predecessors, High Pavement, Nottingham (1812–1813), and New Meeting, Kidderminster (1813–1855). The New Meeting Unitarian Chapel was opened on 18 October 1782, following the secession from the Old Meeting of those Arians who did not wish to sit under the evangelical ministry of the Homerton-educated John Barrett (1751/2–1798), whose call "was signed by 112 persons—46 refusing to sign it—though some of them were not unfavourable to it."[103]

In the wake of this catalogue of doctrinal turmoil and ecclesial unrest the case of William Buckley (1731–1797)[104] comes as something

---

99. See Taylor, *Calling the Generations*, 27–29.

100. Not immediately to Staffordshire as stated by Taylor, *Calling the Generations*, 29.

101. For whom, see ODNB, SI.

102. For whom, see DWB, ODNB, SI.

103. Hunsworth, *Baxter's Nonconformist Descendants*, 46. Hunsworth takes issue with Thomas Wright Hill, who had branded Barrett's predecessor, the highly-regarded Benjamin Fawcett, a crypto-Arian. See ibid., 40–41. For Barrett, see SI.

104. For whom, see SI.

of an antidote. The son of a minister, also William, he was educated at Daventry under Caleb Ashworth and ministered at Atherstone, Warwickshire from 1760 to 1762. He then returned to the place of his birth and succeeded his father at Dukinfield, Cheshire. He remained until 1791, notwithstanding that he was "not only an Arian but also a clerical dandy." It was this last characteristic that led to a secession, when a church member expostulated, "Where silk gowns and powdered wigs come, there cometh no gospel."[105] His case serves to remind us that the causes of secessions were multifarious, and that Christological considerations were not always in view when they occurred. For an example of a secession prompted by questions of doctrine and polity combined is that of Swan Hill Church, Shrewsbury. The secession occurred in 1766, and it was unusual in that the majority of the congregation seceded, presumably because the trustees owned the building. The seceders opened a new chapel opened in the following year, and they proclaimed the cause of the disruption in the stonework on the front wall: "This building was erected in the year 1767, For the public worship of God, And in defence of the right of majorities in Protestant Dissenting Congregations To choose their own ministers."[106] The trustees of the Presbyterian Meeting had installed Benjamin Stapp (1743–1767),[107] trained at the liberal Warrington Academy, as assistant to Joseph Fownes (1715–1789),[108] in preference to Robert Gentleman (1746–1795),[109] a student of Caleb Ashworth's at Daventry. The latter became the first minister at Swan Hill. Something of the acrimony aroused by the incident emerges in a letter of 7 March 1767 from Cheney Hart to John Seddon (1725–1770) of Warrington. Siding with the trustees, Hart both abuses Gentleman and libels Job Orton, who had just left the church for retirement in Kidderminster: "The dictator [that is, Orton] remains inflexible, for any other person to be chosen here than *Gentleman*, a boy whom three years ago we all saw an apprentice beyond a counter in the town, but possest of the spirit of *Methodism* and pride to be the mouth of a worshipping society cloaked under the cant term of desire of saving souls. . . . [T]his is the man our

105. See Nightingale, *Lancashire*, I, 293–94.
106. Elliot, *Shropshire*, 23.
107. For whom, see SI.
108. For whom, see SI. He was educated under Ebenezer Lathan at Findern Academy.
109. For whom, see ODNB, SI.

bigots have modestly offered to impose upon us; for him they secede still from us . . ."[110] In a previous letter, of March 7, Hart, committing the fallacy of the false cause, had declared that "The seceders, bigoted and narrow-minded with their desertion, have caused the death of Mr. Stapp."[111] In fact Stapp died of a fever.

The above chronology, though necessarily selective, has gone some way towards showing that Christological considerations were implicated in numerous ecclesial adjustments on the ground during the eighteenth century, and that secessions in which divergent views of the person of Christ played their part led to the formation of new churches in many parts of England. The chronology also suggests that the Particular Baptists did not suffer as many secessions motivated by disagreements over the person of Christ as did the Presbyterians and, to a lesser extent, the Congregationalists. They were, however, susceptible to a variety of "in-house" issues on which they could cut their doctrinal teeth, among them the question of close *versus* open communion, hyper- *versus* high and evangelical Calvinism, the propriety of hymn-singing at the Lord's Table, and the appropriate day of the week—the first or the seventh—on which Christians should gather for public worship. Suppressing a sigh of relief, I rule these matters beyond our current purview.

---

110. Waddington, *Congregational History, 1700–1800*, 509.
111. Ibid.

5

Representative Ecclesial Repercussions in Eighteenth-Century Wales

I SHALL NOW ADDUCE evidence to show that during the eighteenth century Wales was not immune to Christological change with consequent ecclesial repercussions. The early eighteenth-century Baptists in Wales were of the Particular sort. They made the 1689 *Confession* their own, and it was translated into Welsh by Rees David in 1721. As T. M. Bassett has observed, "it was only a very small minority of the denomination's ministers who had received any formal education in the eighteenth century and it is not strange therefore that they produced very little by way of literature."[1] This deficiency did not, however, prevent the discussion of doctrinal matters at the meetings of the Baptist Association. At the Association meeting held at Swansea on 23 and 24 May 1727 there was "some debate about the eternal filiation of the Son of God: but it was advised, that ministers should preach the plain, clear gospel, and not puzzle the people with inexplicable mysteries."[2]

In 1727 Jenkin Jones (1700?–42), who spent two years at Carmarthen Academy (1720–22),[3] and was said to have been a Congregationalist at Pantycreuddan, seceded from that church and began to proclaim Arianism. In 1733 he built the first Arian chapel in Wales, at Llwynrhydowen, Cardiganshire. He was influential in the district, and brought other ministers around to his views. His successor in the pastor-

---

1. Bassett, *The Welsh Baptists*, 69–70.
2. Joshua Thomas, *A History of the Baptist Association in Wales*, 43.
3. There is a discrepancy here as between DWB and ODNB on the one hand and SI on the other. The former have Jones at Carmarthen, SI suggests Brynllywarch Academy under Samuel Jones, but notes the Carmarthen alternative, which would seem to be correct.

ate, Dafydd Llwyd (1724–1779), was an Arian by 1767, and he, too, drew many towards heterodoxy: "One proof of his influence was that three of Phylip Pugh's congregations, Caeronnen, Cilgwyn and Ciliau Aeron,[4] swiftly moved towards Arianism after Pugh's death in 1760. In the same spirit, the congregation of Crug-y-maen invited Llwyd to act as their minister after the death of their old minister, David Jenkins, in 1758. Despite these incidents, the Independents as a whole showed no desire to turn to Arminianism and Arianism."[5]

Llwyd was joined in ministry in 1763 by the Arian David Davis (1745–1827).[6] A scholar and poet, he was ordained at Llwynrhydowen, and as well as serving in the pastorate, from 1783 he kept a school at his farm, Castell Hywel. This "Athens of Ceredigion," we learn, "prepared students for the English Universities, the Presbyterian College at Carmarthen, and even trained men for Holy Orders."[7] Having served Llwynrhydowen and neighbouring churches for fifty-two years, Davis retired in 1820. Meanwhile in 1801 and 1802 some church members, favouring a more decided Unitarian position, had seceded to form churches to their liking at Pant-y-defaid and Capel-y-groes. Their leader was Charles Lloyd (1766–1829), who had trained at Carmarthen Academy during its sojourn in Swansea.[8] He had been an Arian, but by now was Unitarian in his beliefs. He had hoped to serve as assistant to Davis, but the latter would not have his Arian doctrines compromised, and refused the overture. Hence the secession, and the founding of the first two strictly Unitarian churches in Cardiganshire.[9]

In 1745 there was strife at Albany Presbyterian (later Congregational) Church, Haverfordwest, where the minister, Jenkin Jones,[10] educated under Philip Doddridge at Northampton, was suspected of holding

---

4. See D. Elwyn Davies, *"They Thought for Themselves,"* 55.

5. R. Tudur Jones, *Congregationalism in Wales*, ed. Robert Pope, 107. For Pugh, a Congregationalist, see DWB, ODNB, SI. He was educated at Brynllywarch Academy under Samuel Jones and then under Roger Griffiths at Abergavenny.

6. For whom, see DWB, ODNB, SI. He was educated at Carmarthen Academy under Samuel Thomas.

7. D. E. Davies, *They Thought for Themselves*, 35.

8. His tutors were Solomon Harries and others. See DWB, ODNB, SI.

9. See D. E. Davies, *They Thought for Themselves*, 168.

10. For whom, see SI.

Arian views. There is reason to suspect that in the view of some of his members this was the most respectable of his faults, for:

> his conversation was . . . destitute of that gravity and of those marks of seriousness and spirituality which dissenters were accustomed to expect of their ministers. Mr. Jones, being the fine gentleman and disposed to indulge in the amusements of gentlemen, took his gun and went into the fields as a sportsman, and while thus imprudently, and therefore improperly, spending a portion of his time for exercise and health, and attempting to force his way through a hedge, a thorn is said to have pierced his eye and the injury he sustained was such that it terminated in his death.[11]

James Davies (d. 1760) was a Congregational minister, educated at Carmarthen Academy.[12] In 1724 he became minister of the mixed Calvinist-Arminian church at Cwm-y-glo. He was a Calvinist of the evangelical sort, who not only maintained his pastorate, but preached widely in north Glamorganshire and Monmouthshire, and enthusiastically welcomed the Calvinistic Methodist Revival—to the extent of inviting Howell Harris (1714-1773)[13] to preach in the neighbourhood. In 1738 the Arminians within the Cwm-y-glo church called Richard Rees (1707-1749) of Gwernllwyn Uchaf as Davies's co-pastor, but the two men could not work harmoniously together. This resulted in the secession in 1747 of the Rees party, who formed the Cefn-coed-cymer church, which became avowedly Unitarian and came to be known as the Old Meeting.[14] The Presbyterian Edward Evans (1716-1798)[15] was among those who left the Cwm-y-glo church with Richard Rees. He was Arian in his beliefs, as is suggested by his 1757 translation of one of Samuel Bourn's catechisms into Welsh. On 1 July 1772 he was ordained pastor at the Old Meeting, where he served until 1796.

---

11. G. Bernard Williams, *Albany United Reformed Church Harverfordwest*, unpaginated/6.

12. See DWB, SI.

13. For whom, see DEB, DWB, ODCC, ODNB.

14. For Rees, see DWB, SI. He was educated at Carmarthen Academy under Thomas Perrot.

15. For whom, see DWB, ODNB, SI.

In 1756 the Congregationalist Owen Rees (1717–1768)[16] became minister of the Old Meeting, Trecynon (Aberdare), a branch of the Cwm-y-glo church. When called he was orthodox, but he passed through Arminianism to Arianism, and his son, Josiah (1744–1804), of the Presbyterian church, Gellionnen, Glamorganshire, led his people on to Unitarianism. By 1802 he was on the committee of the South Wales Unitarian Association.[17] In the year of Josiah's death the Association published a tract of his, which does not survive, to which the orthodox Baptist, Joseph Harris (1773–1825) responded in the same year with *Bwyall Crist yng Nghoed Anghrist* (*Christ's Axe in Satan's Trees*).[18] Josiah's son, Thomas (1777–1864) who, like his father, was educated at Carmarthen Academy and was a Unitarian, served at Gellionnen for one year (1805–1806), but otherwise in England. He was made LL.D of Glasgow University in 1819.

In 1757[19] the Congregational Fund Board insisted upon the removal of the ministerial training it supported from Carmarthen to Abergavenny. This was in response to the perceived and actual heterodoxy of the tutors Samuel Thomas (1692–1766) and Jenkin Jenkins (d. 1780), both of whom were Arians and Congregationalists. The former had assumed his tutorial duties in 1743, the latter in 1759.

Nathaniel Williams (1742–1826) was raised a Congregationalist, but became first a Particular, and then a General Baptist. He caused a stir in 1778 when, in his *Dialogus*, he published a critique of the Athanasian doctrine of the Trinity, at the same time maintaining that Jesus Christ was Son of the Father and God incarnate. The Baptist Assembly of 1779 repudiated his views.[20] He left the Particular Baptists at the time of the Baptist schism of 1799.

This schism, which resulted in the departure of the General Baptists from the Baptist Association, was a multi-faceted incident, one strand of which was Christological. On the General Baptist side, for example,

---

16. For whom, see DWB, SI.

17. D. Elwyn Davies, *They Thought for Themselves*, 82. For Josiah Rees, see DWB, ODNB, SI. He was educated at Carmarthen Academy.

18. For Harris, see DWB. He sojourned for just four months at Bristol Baptist College.

19. H. P. Roberts notes that 1755 is often given as the date of the opening of the Abergavenny Academy, but states that the minutes of the Congregational Board have 1757. See "Nonconformist academies in Wales (1662–1862)," 21.

20. J. Thomas, *A History of the Baptist Association of Wales*, 68.

was William Richards (1749–1818). He repudiated first Calvinism, then Athanasianism, but was also opposed to the "Methodistical" revivalist emphasis by which some Particular Baptists were becoming, as he thought, tainted. He did not, however, land in Unitarianism. William Thomas (d. 1813) was ordained at Pant Teg church in Carmarthenshire, and retained it for the Unitarian General Baptists. The churches at Wick and Nottage, Glamorganshire also continued as General Baptist, and by 1808 Evan Lloyd (1764–1847), who had earlier refused to assent to the Particular Baptist *Confession*, was in pastoral charge. He was apparently an Arian until the age of sixty, when he embraced Unitarianism. Joshua Watkins (1769/70–1841) and his church members at Penuel, Carmarthen, had a more fluctuating experience. They seceded from the Particular Baptists and went over to the General Baptists. But Watkins would not forsake Arianism, and stoutly opposed Unitarianism. Hence in 1805 he and his church were restored to the Particular Baptist fold, to the great pleasure of all concerned. A similar course was followed by Moses Williams (d. 1819) and his churches at Llandyfân and Pontbrenaraeth—except that they remained orthodox—who found the sometimes aggressive Unitarianism of the General Baptists more than they could stomach. The personal pilgrimage of David Oliver (fl. 1785–1814) was somewhat unusual. A Particular Baptist, he became a General Baptist at the time of the 1799 schism, advanced towards Unitarianism, but in 1814 was received by the Congregationalists at Llangefelach. The debate rumbled on among the Baptists for some years, but Joseph Harris's defence of Trinitarianism in *Priodol Dduwdod Ein Harglwydd Iesu Grist* (The True Divinity of our Lord Jesus Christ) (1816–1818) did much to bring it to an end, and was well received beyond Baptist circles.[21]

The first minister in Wales never to have been anything other than Unitarian was Thomas Evans (1764–1833). Theophilus Lindsey encouraged his studies and sent him books, and he became known as "little Priestley." In 1811 he became minister at the Old Meeting, Aberdare, and his Christological views are clearly expressed in the following affirmation from his 1794 "Declaration of Faith": "I believe, according to the testimony of the Scriptures, that Jesus Christ was a Man like ourselves . . . of the same nature as the rest of mankind, being different only in the remarkable power and honour given to him by God, and his own excellent virtue and piety . . ."[22]

21. See further, Bassett, *Welsh Baptists*, 115–24.
22. Quoted by D. E. Davies, *They Thought for Themselves*, 179

As with England, so with Wales: the Dissenters found a number of other matters on which to disagree. For example, the Baptists took up sides over the extent of the atonement, with John Jenkins (1779–1853) and others insisting on limited atonement, and Micah Thomas (1778–1853), influenced by Andrew Fuller, espousing an evangelical Calvinism that did not forbid the "free offer of the Gospel";[23] the Nonconformists divided into two camps over the question how far high Calvinism should be modified, with the Congregationalist John Roberts (1767–1834), a follower of Edward Williams (1750–1813) taking the revisionist side, and the Calvinistic Methodist Thomas Jones of Denbigh (1756–1820) the conservative—not least in opposition to Owen Davies (1752–1830), the superintendent of the Wesleyan mission based at Ruthin.[24] But, as in England, such disputes were not normally productive of secessions on the ground. Granting the influence of "non-theological" issues, on both sides of Offa's Dyke the shape of ecclesial life in both Wales and England had more to do with differing views of the person of Christ within the broader context of Trinitarian debate than with any other Christian doctrine. The experience of both England and Wales makes it clear that there was no necessary progression from Arianism to Unitarianism. On the contrary, there was on occasion not simply disagreement but hostility between the proponents of these diverse sentiments. With hindsight, however, we can see that the days of Arianism—ever an unstable halfway house—were numbered, though it lingered longer in Wales than in England. What Alexander Gordon wrote with respect to Cross Street Chapel, Manchester, could be applied to many districts of England and Wales: "In [1810] the preaching of an evangelical Arianism at Cross Street ceased with the death of Thomas Barnes (1747–1810). The introduction of a positive type of Unitarianism by his successor, John Grundy (1782–1843) was hailed, or deplored, in many quarters as marking a new departure. After 1810, the Lancashire Arianism either melted away very rapidly, or drifted off to other denominational conditions."[25]

23. See further T. M. Bassett, *Welsh Baptists*, 124–25. For Jenkins and Thomas, see DWB. The latter attended Bristol Baptist College.

24. For Roberts, see DWB, ODNB, SI. For Williams, educated at Abergavenny Academy, see DEB, DWB, ODNB, SI. For Jones, see DEB, DWB, ODNB. For Davies, see DMBI, DWB, ODNB.

25. Gordon, *Addresses Biographical and Historical*, 329. For Barnes, see ODNB, SI. He was educated at Warrington Academy. For Grundy, see SI. He was educated in Bristol and at Manchester Academy.

6

Christological Contributions and Ecclesial Developments 1800–1891

IT GOES WITHOUT SAYING, ideas knowing no centennial termini, that Nonconformist disagreements over the person of Christ spilled over into the nineteenth century. In general, however, they were not as numerous or as ecclesially disruptive as they had been in the eighteenth century. The denominational doctrinal lines had more or less been set, and what followed was the establishing of denominational structures as we have come to know them. Numerous projects and issues claimed the attention of Nonconformists. They were by now increasingly involved in both overseas and home mission. The removal of most of the remaining disabilities imposed by law upon the Dissenters consumed some energy, as did the question of the disestablishment of the Church of England. Catholic emancipation, the Oxford Movement and ritualism provided further grist to the mills of Nonconformist pamphleteers. The youthful Arminian Methodists, as if emulating the older Dissenting traditions, began to secede from one another—albeit not generally on Christological grounds, while the Unitarians had to decide whether or not to make the transition from the biblical Unitarianism of Priestley and others to the Free Christian ideals of Martineau, underpinned as they were by his view that the individual conscience, not the biblical text as such, was the seat of authority in religion. The Calvinistic Methodists of Wales left the Church of England in 1811 and organized themselves into a churchly body with mission at its heart, so that by the end of the nineteenth century the Presbyterian Church of Wales had the largest membership of any Nonconformist denomination in the Principality.[1]

---

1. Baptists: 106,566; Congregationalists: 147,513; Presbyterians: 158,114.

A further denominational ingredient was added when expatriate Scots, together with some Presbyterian exiles from Ireland and Wales, joined with the minority of orthodox English Presbyterians of Old Dissent who had not become Congregational or Unitarian in constituting the Presbyterian Church *in* England in 1842. In the following year the Disruption occurred in Scotland, largely over the issue of the intrusion by patrons of non-evangelical ministers into churches that did not wish to receive them. Thus the Free Church of Scotland was constituted under the leadership of Thomas Chalmers. In 1844 the Presbyterian Church in England formally declared independence from the Church of Scotland, urged that Church to repent, and embraced the Free Church as a sister Church. Churches of the United Presbyterian Church of Scotland (1847) became established in England, and these united with the Presbyterian Church *in* England to form the Presbyterian Church *of* England in 1876. Thus a denomination of 46,540 members, many of them nurtured in voluntarism, threw its lot in with the longer established English Free Churches.

As if all of this were not enough, the rise of modern biblical criticism had to be reckoned with, as did evolutionary thought and the increasingly vocal atheism, agnosticism, materialism, and secularism: there was more than enough for Nonconformist apologists to do. Again, socio-political issues began to press upon the denominations, and anyone who has attended some of the more politicized church assemblies of the present day cannot but have a certain sympathy with Joseph Parker (1830–1902) who, at the Annual Assembly of the Congregational Union of England and Wales in 1876 declared, "What an amazing amount of so-called 'business' we have to do! We have to disestablish the Church [of England], modernize the Universities, rectify the policy of School Boards, clear the way to burial grounds, subsidize magazines, sell hymn-books, place the hose upon [the Anglican] Convocation, and generally give everybody to understand that if we have not yet assailed or defended them, it is not for want of will, but merely for want of time."[2]

On occasion there was a Christological dimension to social questions, notably those concerning education. For example, Peter Dean (1849–1905), the Unitarian minister at Walsall who crusaded for non-

---

2. Quoted by Peel, *These Hundred Years. A History of the Congregational Union of England and Wales*, London: Congregational Union of England and Wales, 1931, 264. For Parker, see ODCC, ODNB, SI. He was educated at University College, London.

sectarian education, was convinced that his denomination was being discriminated against by the local School Board. On January 17, 1880 the *Walsall Observer* published one of his letters in which he complained that his children were made to sing,

> He came down to earth from heaven, *Who is Lord and God of all.*
> [Dean reverses the two nouns].

"And I am made to pay for that which is the entire opposite of that which I believe and preach," he expostulated. He acknowledged that by a conscience clause his children were not legally bound to sing the hymns, but he would still be contributing money through the rates in support of a system of education that he abominated. Dean, himself a journalist, had a way with words, but there were occasions when words were not permitted. Eventually elected to the Board of Education he was forbidden to speak, and so took off his boot and banged it on the table.[3]

All of which is to say that nineteenth-century Nonconformists had many themes to occupy their minds and pens in addition to Christology and that, with the denominational lines more or less settled (or with Athanasians and Unitarians safe from one another in their relatively protective denominational bunkers), there was less writing on that subject than hitherto. We are not, however, confronted by a Christological *tabula rasa* and we shall do well now to continue the story (for a reason that will become clear) to 1891. It will be convenient now to take England and Wales together, and to consider first some further secessions, then some wider-than-local concerns, and finally some doctrinal publications.

I

Throughout the nineteenth century, secessions, wholly, partly, or ostensibly on Christological grounds, continued to occur in both England and Wales, albeit there were fewer of them than in the preceding century.[4] Thus, for example, Joseph Bealey (1756–1813), an alumnus of Daventry Academy who had trained under Caleb Ashworth and his successor, Thomas Robins (1732–1810), was an Arian friend of Thomas Barnes

---

3. For more on this lively character, see Sell, *Dissenting Thought*, ch. 16.

4. There were also secessions (in some cases oscillations there and back again) to the Irvingites and (Plymouth) Brethren, but these were not Christologically inspired, and therefore fall outside our purview.

(1747–1810), his predecessor at Cockey Moor, Ainsworth, Lancashire. After five years there Bealey succeeded William Enfield at Warrington Academy, but in 1791 he returned to Cockey Moor. He read Belsham's work, *A Calm Inquiry into the Scripture Doctrine concerning the Person of Christ*, on its appearance in 1811, and was persuaded by it. On April 4, 1813, in the course of a sermon on "Jesus, the Man of Sorrows, and acquainted with grief," he declared his commitment to Unitarianism. This engendered "heated discussions, and family divisions," and "several withdrew from his ministry, and joined themselves to Mawdsley Street Chapel, Bolton." On August 9 in the same year, Bealey died, and was buried on 13th. So many crowded into the gallery of the chapel on the Sunday following, that "the gallery was found to be giving way, and the service had to be concluded in the graveyard."[5]

William Howell (1740–1822), like his father, William Howell of Birmingham, an Arian, was educated at Warrington and Carmarthen Academies. From 1786 he was minister of the Presbyterian church, Swansea, but in 1813 he resigned on account of blindness.[6] When the church offered to seek an assistant he withdrew his resignation, but when agreement could not be reached as to who should be appointed, Howell and his supporters seceded and formed Castle Street Congregational Church, which opened in 1814. We learn that "The real cause of the trouble was that [Howell] refused to adopt the Unitarian doctrine, which was accepted by his successor, Richard Aubrey."[7] The posts held by Aubrey (1760–1836) sufficiently indicate his heterodox leanings: Cranbrook; Librarian at Dr. Williams's Library; Dob Lane, Failsworth; Stand, Lancashire (1787–1797), during which time orthodox members seceded to form Stand Congregational Church; and Gloucester. He served at Swansea from 1814 until his death.[8]

John Horsey (1754–1827), who had been educated at Homerton Academy, accepted the call to the pastorate of Doddridge's church, Castle Hill, Northampton, in 1777, and remained there until his death fifty years later. Of him it is written, "it must be allowed ... that there was a certain vagueness in his statements respecting the person and work of the Redeemer, which showed either that the mind of the preacher was

---

5. Nightingale, *Lancashire*, II.i.125. For Bealey, see SI.
6. For Howell, see DWB, SI.
7. DWB, 369.
8. For Aubrey, see SI. He was educated at Hoxton Academy.

not earnestly intent on discovering and grasping the truth, . . . or that it had formed opinions to which it was unwilling to give a clear and distinct utterance. . . ."⁹ When in 1789 Belsham resigned from Daventry Academy on embracing Unitarian views, Horsey was appointed in his stead, combining his tutorial role with his continuing pastoral duties at Castle Hill. Some ten years later David Saville, a stalwart Calvinistic Scot, was appointed classical tutor. He secretly reported to the Coward Trustees that the Academy was "tinctured not a little with Socinian principles." The Trustees informed Horsey by a letter of June 15, 1798 that his services as tutor were no longer required, and that they were closing the Academy forthwith. This they did, and a fresh start was made at Wymondley.¹⁰ Thirty years later Horsey referred to the "exceedingly uncomfortable" ninth year of his tutorial tenure, made so "by the introduction of a very unsuitable classical tutor," who had brought "unmerited censure" upon him.¹¹

Horsey was succeeded at Castle Hill by Charles James Hyatt (1805–47),¹² but not long after his ordination on September 25, 1827 some friends of Horsey's seceded and formed a Unitarian church in the town. On November 27, 1827 they held their first church meeting, from which they sent a letter to the Castle Hill church which reveals both their conscientiousness and their tendentiousness: "having, in obedience to our consciences, united in the formation of a society of Christians, whose worship is directed solely to the one God the Father, agreeably to the express injunctions of our Saviour, [we] deem it proper to withdraw . . . from the worship and communion of the Church to which we have hitherto belonged."¹³

In 1782 John Ingham (d. 1833) began his ministry at Rawtenstall, Lancashire, remaining there until his death in 1833.¹⁴ The church's trust deed was drawn up in 1760. The cause was founded by those who had

---

9. Coleman, *Northamptonshire*, 32. For Horsey, see SI; Sell, *Philosophy, Dissent and Nonconformity*, 53–54.

10. That not all was sweetness and light at Wymondley may be seen in John Waddington, *Congregational History: Continuation to 1850*, 255–73. The Homerton-trained principal, William Parry (1754–1819) was accused of Socinianism, a charge he strenuously repudiated. See *The Evangelical Magazine*, 1818, 172.

11. Horsey, *Lectures to Young Persons*, xiii–xiv.

12. For whom, see SI. He was educated at Wymondley Academy.

13. Coleman, *Northamptonshire*, 33.

14. For Ingham, see SI.

been impressed by the preaching of William Allt of Hinckley, a follower of George Whitefield. We learn that "Both minister and congregation at the beginning were staunch High Calvinists; but in the year 1818 they agreed in adopting Unitarianism."[15] This bland statement is suggestive of "sweetness and light," but it stands in stark contrast with the following information on the same page: "This was a period full of the greatest anxiety. It is recorded that on one occasion 'Mr. John Hopkinson locked the chapel doors and was missing at the time announced for the meeting, for he feared for the consequences had the contending parties met that day.'"[16]

Two Daventry educated ministers served at Old Meeting, Wareham, Dorset, in the last decade of the eighteenth century and the first two decades of the nineteenth century. As we saw, Robert Kell, educated under Belsham, became minister in 1789. He left in 1800 following his marriage to Mary Bythewood Delacourt—a match that, for an unspecified reason, caused offence to some of his "leading people."[17] That he was an Arian would seem to be confirmed by his subsequent pastorates: High Pavement, Nottingham and Old Meeting, Birmingham. His successor, Thomas Thomas (d. 1823),[18] began his Wareham ministry in 1800. He was similarly inclined towards Arianism. He would sing Isaac Watts's hymns, but only after he had amended them to his doctrinal satisfaction. During his ministry John Brown, a wine merchant, arrived in the town and married into the church. He was an ardent Calvinist who became the leader of those members of the church "who held the Divine Nature and mission of Jesus Christ."[19] After some strife, Brown secured election as a trustee in 1819. Thomas retired in 1822, to be succeeded in the same year by Joseph Dobson (1801–85), "an attractive preacher of great ability, and holding evangelical opinions,"[20] who had been educated at Wymondley Academy. Dobson later worked for the infant Evangelical Alliance. The Unitarians in his congregation hoped that the Calvinists would secede and join another church of their persuasion in the town,

---

15. Herford and Evans, eds, *Historical Sketch of the North and East Lancashire Unitarian Mission*, 118.

16. Ibid.

17. Densham and Ogle, *Dorset*, 349.

18. For whom, see SI.

19. Densham and Ogle, *Dorset*, 349.

20. Ibid. For Dobson, see SI.

but they did not. Hence they "were compelled to withdraw and form themselves into a distinct society; and on the first Sunday in the month of February 1828, though but a small flock and without a pastor, they commenced assembling together in a temporary place of worship."[21] In due course they opened a chapel in South Street.

II

For a sample of some wider-than-local concerns we may turn first to Dan Taylor and the New Connexion of General Baptists. We recall that he had founded the New Connexion in 1770, but he had also sought to maintain fellowship with the original body. By 1803 he felt that on doctrinal grounds he could no longer do this. In 1813 the New Connexion denounced "the baneful poison of Socinianism."[22] From the opposite pole came the not untypical comment of John Burgess, a General Baptist who emigrated from the heartland of Ditchling, Sussex, to America: "I think the doctrine of the Trinity one of the greatest corruptions in the Christian Church. The doctrine of the pre-existence of Christ I have entirely given up."[23] Some among the Old General Baptists, Joseph Calrow Means (1801–1879),[24] Secretary of the General Baptist Assembly, among them, opposed the Unitarianism in their midst and strove to maintain fellowship with the New Connexion. Relations fluctuated for some years, but ceased with the union in 1891 of the New Connexion with the Particular Baptists to form the Baptist Union, into which the Old Connexion churches at Headcorn, Winchmore Hill, London, Long Sutton, and Saffron Walden were afterwards received.[25]

We further recall that in 1739 the Edinburgh-educated James Scott had come down to England to assist in the dispersal of Socinian clouds. After ministries at Stainton, Hinton and Tockholes, he had removed to Heckmondwike, Yorkshire, where he was pastor from 1754 and, in

---

21. Murch, *West of England*, 281.

22. Quoted by Briggs, *The English Baptists of the Nineteenth Century*, 126.

23. Anon., "A Sussex lay preacher seeing camp meetings in America," 324–25.

24. For whom see ODNB. He was educated at University College, London, and at the General Baptist Academy under Benjamin Mardon. The latter held his tutorial post from 1828 to 1855, combining this work with that of pastor at Worship Street Chapel, London. Means succeeded him in the latter role in 1855.

25. See Briggs, *The English Baptists of the Nineteenth Century*, 126–27; Sellers, "The Old General Baptists, 1811–1915," 30–41.

addition, academy tutor from 1756 to 1783. Further Congregational academies had been established at Rotherham (1795) and Idle/Airedale (1800), but there had been no orthodox Dissenting academy in Lancashire since 1712. This point was not lost upon those Lancashire Congregationalists who were eager to establish an Academy, and to this lack the Committee of Blackburn Academy, established in 1816, attributed the fact that whereas while there were but twenty Unitarian chapels in Yorkshire there were thirty-nine in Lancashire (a rare occasion on which the Lancastrians did not wish to outdo their rivals over the Pennines). When the Committee further committed the fallacy of the false cause by declaring that "This circumstance speaks volumes as to the efficiency of Academical Institutions, in diffusing the principles of those communities by which they are established,"[26] they were almost using fear of Unitarianism as a fund-raising ploy—as well as conveniently overlooking the fact that, for example, many Arians and some Socinians had issued forth from the Congregationalist Caleb Ashworth's academy at Daventry, and even from that of his predecessor, Philip Doddridge, in Northampton. Undeniably, the Lancastrian Congregationalists were spurred on by a brand of Unitarianism that was more evangelistic, and more inclined to reach out to the less "genteel," than that found in most other parts of the country.[27]

The founders of Spring Hill College, Birmingham, the predecessor of Mansfield College, Oxford, had no intention of permitting their institution to stray from orthodox paths. In the trust deed of 1838 it is provided that "No person shall ... be deemed eligible to be a member of the Committee unless he profess and declare, by writing under his hand, that he believes the unity of the Godhead, the divinity of Christ ... the

---

26. Slate, *A Brief History of the Rise and Progress of the Lancashire Congregational Union*, 130. See also Sell, *Hinterland Theology*, 136.

27. It is not without significance that the first body in Lancashire responsible for Unitarian ministerial training was the Unitarian Home Missionary Board, established by John Relly Beard in 1854, with the support of William Gaskell. The objective was "to take men with limited educational background and train them for a new kind of ministry—a ministry to speak to working men and women and their families, to foster new Unitarian causes and indeed to help fill the pulpits of congregations of English Presbyterian origin still suffering in the aftermath of the Lady Hewley court case which had threatened to deprive them of their ancient buildings and endowments." So Geoffrey Head in Leonard Smith, ed., *Unitarian to the Core*, 41. Beard served as Principal from 1854–74, Gaskell from 1874–84.

divinity and personality of the Holy Spirit . . . and the plenary inspiration of the Holy Scriptures."[28]

During the first three decades of the nineteenth century two of the Nonconformist bodies set down the things commonly believed among them. The *Confession of Faith of the Calvinistic Methodists, or the Presbyterians of Wales* was adopted at the Associations of Aberystwyth and Bala in 1823. Not surprisingly in view of the history of Arianism, Socinianism and Unitarianism in Wales, there is a statement on the doctrine of the Trinity that is full to the point of repetitive, and a clear affirmation concerning the person of Christ, albeit the latter is separated from the former by ten clauses on the divine decrees and the covenants of works and of grace:

> Though there is but one God, and though there cannot be more than one true God, still it is the clear testimony of Holy Scripture that there are in the Godhead THREE persons, the Father, the Son, and the Holy Ghost; that these three are co-eternal and co-equal, not one before or after another, nor greater or less than another, but one God. Every one of these Persons is true God, and the one Person is not the other Person; nevertheless, there is only one God. The Father, the Son, and the Holy Ghost are not names, offices, or attributes, but divine Persons; the Father an eternal Person, the Son an eternal Person; the Holy Ghost an eternal Person; but the three Persons one eternal God. . . . And, though we cannot comprehend the doctrine of the Trinity, we ought to believe it, because God so testifies concerning himself. . . .
>
> In the fullness of time, God's own Son, eternally begotten, an infinite Person in the Godhead, equal with the Father, the express image of his Person, true God, took upon him human nature, in the Virgin's womb,—true, entire humanity, but holy and free from its defilement. A body was prepared him by the Father, and formed by the Holy Ghost, of the substance of the Virgin, free from all taint of impurity; and this body the Son assumed into union with his own Person. Thus a divine Person and human nature have been indivisibly united in the one Mediator, without conversion or confusion of the Divine and human natures. The infinite Person, Christ Jesus, is true God and true man; yet, one Mediator, between God and man. . . .[29]

28. Quoted by Waddington, *Congregational History: Continuation to 1850*, 518–19.
29. *Confession of Faith of the Calvinistic Methodists*, 43–45, 62–63.

In 1831 the Congregationalists decided to form a national union, and concurrently a draft *Declaration of the Faith, Church Order, and Discipline of the Congregational, or Independent Dissenters*, drawn up at the request of "several brethren" by George Redford (1785–1860) of Angel Street Church, Worcester, was read out.[30] It was afterwards circulated with a covering letter from the Secretaries, in which they explained that the document was not so much for the information of Congregationalists themselves, but rather as a dissuasive against "a very large proportion of our countrymen [who] take us to be either SOCINIANS or METHODISTS."[31] Furthermore, the Savoy Declaration was now scarce, so a new document was required. It was unanimously adopted on May 10, 1833.[32] The *Declaration* exemplifies moderate Calvinism, but to note the dilution or exclusion of typically Calvinistic emphases is not our purpose here.[33] We must, however, advert to a certain Christological modification, which becomes clear when the document is placed alongside the *Savoy Declaration*. According to the new *Declaration*, Congregationalists:

> believe in one God . . . They believe that God is revealed in the Scriptures, as the Father, the Son, and the Holy Spirit, and that to each are attributable the same Divine properties and perfections . . . They believe that, in the fullness of the time, the Son of God was manifest in the flesh, being born of the Virgin Mary, but conceived by the power of the Holy Spirit; and that our Lord Jesus Christ was both the Son of Man and the Son of God; partaking fully and truly of human nature though without sin—equal with the Father and "the express image of His person."[34]

What is omitted here, but present in *Savoy*, is a reference to the eternal generation of the Son; and whereas Jesus is said to partake fully and truly of human nature, he is not said to partake fully and truly of the

---

30. For Redford see DEB, ODNB, SI. He was educated at Hoxton Academy and Glasgow University. Interestingly, when the Baptist Union, now comprising the evangelical General Baptists and the Particular Baptists, made a fresh start, its members did not venture a fresh declaration of their faith.

31. See Peel, *These Hundred Years*, 68.

32. See further Sell, *Dissenting Thought*, 51–53; Sell, *Saints: Visible, Orderly and Catholic*, 67–60.

33. Though see Sell, *Enlightenment, Ecumenism, Evangel*, 152–54.

34. The most recent reprint of the *Declaration* is in Bebbington, Dix, and Ruston, eds., *Protestant Nonconformist Texts III: The Nineteenth Century*, 39–44.

divine nature, on which point *Savoy*, more robustly, declares that "two whole perfect and distinct natures, the Godhead and the manhood, were inseparably joined in one person, without conversion, composition, or confusion; which person is very God and very man, yet one Christ..."[35] Interestingly, in the heyday of liberal theology, when the centenary of the Congregational Union was celebrated, Robert Mackintosh remarked, "A most staggering note is appended in Preliminary Note 7. Unless for personal peculiarities of expression, the framers of the declaration "believe that there is no minister or church among them that would deny any one" of the doctrinal and ecclesiastical "Principles" which follow. How unlike present-day [1933] conditions!"[36]

In his address of 1864 to the Congregational Union, Henry Allon (1818–1892)[37] spoke on "The Christ, the Book and the Church." The authority of all of these, he declared, is under attack. In relation to Christ, the question "is no longer, what does the Christ say? but who is the Christ that He should speak at all?"[38] Those who worship Christ as the incarnate God are now told that Jesus was less than a mere good man. Hence Allon's expostulation:

> This is the apotheosis of infidelity!... [However] When argument thus degenerates into absurdity and impossibility, a cause is lost. We are not, therefore, troubled concerning the Christ. ... Strauss and Renan simply prove that counter-theories are exhausted.... Even the sober and reverent theory of English Unitarianism makes no impression upon our religious and social life. It continues traditionally, *but it has no living assimilating power*; and when now and then, under the relentless exigencies of logic, some venturesome writer impugns the perfect human sanctity of the Christ, he excites only a passionate resentment, or an apologetic pity. It is manifest that he is arguing from *a priori* principles rather than from the constraint

---

35. Matthews, *The Savoy Declaration*, VIII.ii.

36. Mackintosh, "The genius of Congregationalism," in Peel, ed., *Essays Congregational and Catholic*, 111. For Mackintosh (1858–1933) see DNCBP, DTCBP, ODNB, SI (but note, not New College *London*); Sell, *Robert Mackintosh*. He was educated at Glasgow University, New College Edinburgh, and the universities of Jena and Marburg.

37. For whom, see ODNB, SI; Argent, "Henry Allon." He was educated at Cheshunt College.

38. In this paragraph my quotations are from John Waddington's extensive transcriptions of Allon's address in *Congregational History 1850–1880*, 426–30.

of resistless evidence. The controversy concerning the Christ, then, does not disquiet us.[39]

If the Congregationalists were not disquieted in 1864, by 1877 many of them—not least Henry Allon himself—were; for on October 16 of that year the Leicester Conference on Religious Communion was held at Wycliffe Congregational Church, Leicester, during the week of the autumn meetings of the national Union. The leader of the "advanced" thinkers was James Allanson Picton (1832–1910),[40] whose views Waddington accurately epitomized thus: "Christ was a mere man, who performed no miracles, who shared at least *some* of the prejudices and errors of His time and nation, and who wrought the great revolution traced to Him by appealing to and revealing the eternal element in man."[41] However, the main thrust of the conference was not technically Christological. Rather, the objective was to advance the view of Picton and others that doctrinal agreement was not a *sine qua non* of religious communion. Picton made no bones about declaring himself a pantheist, and at a time when an immanentist form of spirituality was in the air, he and others sought a general unity with the divine and eschewed attempts at doctrinal definition as divisive. On the opposing side of the argument, alongside Allon, was—not surprisingly in view of his crusade against theological paucity—David Worthington Simon (1830–1909),[42] who had been two years ahead of Picton as a student at Lancashire Independent College. In the event, in 1878 the Congregational Union reaffirmed its commitment to its *Declaration of Faith* of 1833. I need not pursue the details of the debate because, to repeat, technical questions concerning the person of Christ were not central to it. I mention it solely because, although A. J. Grieve (1874–1952) later referred to it as "a small theological breeze,"[43] it was indicative of the rise of theological liberalism in Congregationalism in the wake of modern biblical criticism, and in

---

39. Ibid., 428.

40. For whom, see ODNB, SI. He was educated at Lancashire Independent College, and at Halle, Heidelberg and Leipzig universities.

41. Ibid., 532.

42. For whom, see SI, WTW; Sell, *Hinterland Theology*, ch. 7 and *passim*.

43. A. J. Grieve, "The nineteenth century," in Various, *Congregationalism through the Centuries*, 98. For Grieve see SI; Surman, *Alexander James Grieve*. He was educated at University College Aberystwyth, Mansfield College Oxford, and at the University of Berlin.

the context of Romantic intuitionalism and post-Hegelian pantheizing immanentism.[44] The Downgrade Controversy, which agitated Baptist Union waters in 1887–1888, at the heart of which was C. H. Spurgeon (1834–1892), likewise made no substantial contribution to our understanding of the person of Christ.[45]

In view of these Baptist and Congregational skirmishes, it is as pleasant as it is well nigh miraculous to record that in 1899 the National Council of Evangelical Free Churches managed to publish *An Evangelical Free Church Catechism for Use in Home and School*, the objective of which was, positively, to state commonly held doctrines in a non-technical way for wide consumption and, negatively, to distinguish the doctrinal position of the National Council from that of the Unitarians, whose request to join the body had been declined.[46] The document was drafted by the Presbyterian, J. Oswald Dykes (1835–1912), Principal of the Presbyterian Theological College, London.[47] A sizeable committee chaired by the Wesleyan, Hugh Price Hughes (1847–1902) revised the document, and it sold for one penny. Clauses 5 and 19, which do not dwell on the two natures in Christ, or upon the eternal Sonship, are of interest to us:

> 5. *What does Jesus say about Himself?*
>
> That He is the Son of God, Whom the Father in His great love sent into the world to be our Saviour from sin.
>
> 19. *What is the mystery of the blessed Trinity?*
>
> That the Father, the Son, and the Holy Spirit, into Whose Name we are baptized, are one God.[48]

---

44. For a detailed and competent discussion of the Leicester Conference, see Hopkins, *Nonconformity's Romantic Generation*, ch. 4. See also Peel, *These Hundred Years*, 266–72. For Simon's part in the proceedings, see Sell, *Hinterland Theology*, 268–70. For a discussion of immanentism in the nineteenth century, see Sell, *Theology in Turmoil*, ch. 1.

45. See Briggs, *The English Baptists of the Nineteenth Century*, 175–98; Hopkins, *Nonconformity's Romantic Generation*, ch. 7.

46. See Jordan, *Free Church Unity*, 50, 61.

47. In the same year, 1899, the Presbyterian Theological College removed to Cambridge and was renamed Westminster College. For Dykes, see *Who Was Who, 1897–1916*; Sell, *Nonconformist Theology in the Twentieth Century*, 19, 130.

48. With the exception of clause 27 (the ten commandments) the *Catechism* is found in Bebbington, Dix, and Ruston, *Protestant Nonconformist Texts. III The Nineteenth Century*, 52–58. See further, Jordan, *Free Church Unity*, 61–64.

III

We shall look to Nonconformity in vain for significant original literary contributions to the discussion of the person of Christ in the first eight decades of the nineteenth century. There is a novelty of a different kind, however, namely, the arrival on the scene of the first significant Arminian Methodist theologian—and this before the founding of the first Wesleyan Theological Institute at Hoxton in 1834. Richard Watson (1781–1833),[49] had been raised among the Calvinistic Methodists of the Countess of Huntingdon's Connexion. He was converted from the latter brand of Methodism to the Arminian in 1794, and in 1801 was enrolled as a Wesleyan minister. In the same year, however, word informally spread that he had denied the divinity of Christ. This so irritated him that he resigned from the ministry, went into business, but was eventually received as a minister in the Methodist New Connexion in 1807. He swiftly rose to high office in the Connexion, but became increasingly irked by the influence of laypersons over ministers in that tradition. Jabez Bunting (1779–1858),[50] who would never have allowed such a thing to happen in Wesleyanism, became Watson's friend, and eventually, in 1812, Watson was reinstated as a Wesleyan minister. Meanwhile his older Wesleyan contemporary, Adam Clarke (1762–1832),[51] an able polymath, was depositing the bulky volumes of his *Commentary on the Whole of Scripture* (1810–1824) on the Bible-reading public, 11,800 of whom purchased the initial print run.[52] Since Clarke's account of the eternal Sonship of Christ provoked Watson's reply I shall first present Clarke's view of the matter.

At the end of his commentary on Proverbs 8, Clarke professes to find his beliefs in the word of God alone, and denies that the Protestant creed is determined by the decisions Church fathers and Councils. There follows his most succinct statement on the eternal Sonship *vis à vis* the Trinity:

---

49. For whom, see DEB, DMBI, ODNB.
50. For whom, see DEB, DMBI, ODCC, ODNB.
51. For whom, see DEB, DBMI, ODNB.
52. See Maldwyn Edwards, "Adam Clarke the Man," 146–53. Edwards writes: "Adam Clarke was the greatest name in Methodism in the generation which succeeded Wesley. He had not the tireless missionary zeal of Coke, nor the statesmanship of Jabez Bunting. He had not the sparkling eloquence of Samuel Bradburn nor the theological acumen of Richard Watson, but in combination of gifts he surpassed them all" (ibid., 150).

> I believe Jehovah, Jesus, the Holy Ghost to be one infinite, eternal Godhead subsisting ineffably in three persons. I believe Jesus the Christ to be, as to his Divine nature, as unoriginated and eternal as Jehovah himself; and with the Holy Ghost to be one infinite Godhead, neither person being created, begotten, nor proceeding, more than another: as to its essence, but one Trinity, in an infinite, eternal and inseparable unity. . . . But I believe not in an eternal sonship or generation of the Divine nature of Jesus Christ. Here I have long stood, here I now stand, and here I trust to stand in the hour of death, in the day of judgment, and to all eternity.[53]

He proceeds to observe that supporters of eternal generation who challenge its deniers to show how they avoid tritheism or Sabellianism might in their turn be asked how they avoid Arianism. But he would not raise such objections, or query the faith of another whose verbal interpretation differed from his own: "I have passed through the waters of strife, and do not wish to recross them . . . I will have nothing to do with ill-tempered, abusive men; I wish them more light and better manners."

Elsewhere in his *Commentary* Clarke returns to the theme. Commenting on the words, "Therefore also that holy thing (or person)—shall be called the Son of God" (Luke 1:35), he contends that the angel does not refer the term "Son of God" to Christ's divine nature, but to the one born of the virgin Mary. The divine nature, he explains, could not be born of Mary, for it had no beginning and was afterwards made flesh. He can find no place in the Bible where "it is plainly said that the Divine nature of Jesus was the Son of God." For this reason the doctrine of the eternal Sonship of Christ is "anti-scriptural, and highly dangerous." He rejects it for five reasons: (a) A repetition of the claim just quoted; (b) "If Christ be the Son of God as to his divine nature, he cannot be eternal; for son implies a father; and father implies, in reference to son, precedency in time, if not in nature too. . . ." (c) "If Christ be the Son of God, as to his Divine nature, then the Father is of necessity prior, consequently superior to him." (d) "If this Divine nature were begotten of the Father, then it must be in time; i.e., there was a period in which it did not exist, and a period when it began to exist. This destroys the eternity of our blessed Lord, and robs him at once of his Godhead." (e) ". . . Son supposes time, generation, and father; and time also an-

---

53. Adam Clarke, *The Holy Bible containing the Old and New Testament*, upaginated.

tecedent to such generation. Therefore the conjunction of these two terms, Son and eternity is absolutely impossible, as they imply essential different and opposite ideas." Supporters of eternal generation destroy the Son's deity and vitiate the entire gospel scheme of redemption, he declares.[54]

Yet again, when commenting on the phrase "this day have I begotten thee" (Heb 1:3), Clarke refers the words to Christ's incarnation or, preferably, to his resurrection (and hence some accused him of adoptionism). It is, he insists, the resurrection which "declares [Jesus] to be the Son of God with power." He supplements his comments on Hebrews 1:8 with a long appended note. He argues that God is the father of the human nature of Jesus in the special sense that this nature was produced in the womb of Mary by divine energy. There follows the repetition of his view that "I know not any scripture, fairly interpreted, that states the Divine nature of our Lord to be *begotten* of God, or to be the *Son of God*." Indeed, he thinks that the doctrine of eternal Sonship produced Arianism, Arianism produced Socinianism, and Socinianism "produces a kind of general infidelity" *vis à vis* the sacred writings. He reports that three years before John Wesley's death, the two of them discussed Clarke's remarks on eternal generation as at Luke 1:35. Wesley thought Clarke's argument conclusive on his own presuppositions, but he himself stood by the classical view of eternal generation. Clarke concludes his note on Hebrews 1:8 thus: "The proper essential Godhead of Christ lies deep at the foundation of my Christian creed; and I must sacrifice ten thousand *forms of speech* rather than sacrifice the thing. My opinion has not been formed on slight examination."[55]

It seems clear to me that Clarke, by insisting that the Son was "unoriginated" was intending to hold Arianism at bay in a manner not entirely distinct from that of Thomas Ridgley. This allowance was not, however, made by all, and Watson rose in defence of eternal generation with his *Remarks on the Eternal Sonship of Christ and Use of Reason in Matters of Religion*. This was published in 1818 at a time when Wesleyans were nervous of creeping Unitarianism in their midst. Indeed, in the same year some of the followers of the late Joseph Cooke (1775–1811),[56] a Wesleyan minister whose thought had moved from evangelical

54. Ibid., V.
55. Ibid., VI.
56. For whom, see DMBI, ODNB.

Arminianism through Socinianism to Unitarianism, held the first annual meeting of the Methodist Unitarian Association in Rochdale.[57]

Watson does not succumb to name-calling. Unlike others, he refrains from branding Clarke an Arian or a Socinian, and he does not question his commitment to belief in the divinity of Christ. In fact the two men remained on good terms, to the surprise of some partisans on both sides of the argument. Watson urges the following points against Clarke. He denies Clarke's claim that the scriptures reserve the term "Son of God" to Christ's humanity, by noting a number of biblical texts in which the term clearly refers to Christ's divinity, among them John 1:18: "No man hath seen God at any time; the only begotten Son, which is in the bosom of the Father, he hath declared him." He observes that the contrast here between what (all other) men might have seen, and what "the only begotten Son" knew shows that the reference of term "Son of God" is not restricted to Christ's humanity. In his own words, "Between the term 'only begotten' and the nature of man there is an obvious opposition."[58] Again, when in his confession of faith, "Thou art the Christ, the Son of the living God" (Matt 16:16) Peter calls Jesus "Messiah=Christ," Watson takes this as further evidence that "Son of God" refers to Christ's divinity, for Jews did not normally think of the Messiah as a divine person.[59]

Adam Clarke was no fan of systematic theology, but Watson emerged as the first Wesleyan systematician with his *Theological Institutes* (1823-28). The work follows the familiar pattern of such scholastic treatises, albeit its atmosphere is evangelical Arminian. It combines with this an eighteenth-century apologetic flavour insofar its first part is concerned with the place of reason, the biblical evidences, and the like. Throughout

---

57. See McLachlan, *The Methodist Unitarian Movement*.

58. Watson, *Remarks on the Eternal Sonship of Christ*, 9.

59. In another line of argument Watson charges Clarke, who averred that doctrines that cannot withstand rational scrutiny cannot be true, with elevating reason above revelation and making the former the judge of the latter. See ibid., 51–52. I cannot here pursue this charge, but see Hamilton, "The 'eternal Sonship' controversy in early British Methodism," though note that the article refers only to Arminian Methodism. I would simply observe (a) that Watson's objection is one that was regularly levelled against Locke's view that "we can never receive for a truth any thing, that is directly contrary to our clear and distinct Knowledge," see his *Essay Concerning Human Understanding*, IV.xvi.14; (b) Any who think that only the heterodox, or those tending in that direction, could be rationalists have never opened a book by Gill or Brine. See further, Sell, *John Locke and the Eighteenth-Century Divines*, 62–74.

it is argumentative, not simply declamatory, though its arguments are characterized by circularity at crucial points. Thus when launching into the doctrine of Christ's pre-existence, Watson writes, "By establishing, on Scriptural authority, the pre-existence of our Lord, we take the first step in the demonstration of his absolute Divinity."[60] He thinks that while Christ's pre-existence does not refute the Arians because it does not evince his Godhead, it does scupper Socinian humanitarianism. In this connection he refutes Belsham to his own satisfaction. Six chapters on he comes to the humanity and divinity of Christ. He affirms the Chalcedonian Formula, and rebukes the Congregationalist, John Pye Smith (1774–1851),[61] trained at Rotherham and theological tutor at Homerton, for undue zealousness in seeking to appropriate respective properties to Christ's humanity and divinity in a way that the New Testament scarcely does.[62]

It would seem that following Watson's critique of Clarke the dust settled in Wesleyanism as far as eternal generation was concerned. But the topic was pursued elsewhere. Thus the Congregational theological tutor, George Payne (1781–1848), who trained at Hoxton Academy and Glasgow University, regularly pursued Unitarians, and declared of Socinians that they "have made many attempts to nibble away those texts which directly assert the divinity of the Saviour; but till they can, not only do this, but expunge from the book of God that numerous class of passages to which we have referred . . . they will accomplish next to nothing after all."[63] Against Arians in general he contends that the attribution of power to Christ means much more than that he was an instrument empowered by God; it means that Christ sustains all things, and hence is divine. Against low Arians in particular he insists that worship is properly ascribed to Christ. Against high orthodox scholasticism he urges that the point of revelation is "not to show what God is in himself, but what he is in relation to us,"[64] and he regrets that orthodox divines tend "either to degrade the Lord Jesus Christ, or to throw impenetrable obscurity over all our statements concerning the Trinity."[65] In his view

60. Watson, *Theological Institutes*, in *The Works of Richard Watson*, X, 149.
61. For whom, see DEB, ODNB, SI.
62. The reference is to John Pye Smith, *The Scripture Testimony to the Messiah*.
63. Payne, *Lectures on Christian Theology*, II, 39.
64. Ibid., I, 248.
65. Ibid., 249.

it cannot be denied that in ordinary usage "son" implies "posteriority, derivation, inferiority."[66] He thus concludes, that "as a divine subsistent [the second person of the Trinity] does not bear the name of Son . . . that title is given to him on account of the office he assumed as Emmanuel, or God with us."[67] Consistently with this Payne cannot assent to the doctrine of the eternal generation of the Son. He, like Ridgley—and also Adam Clarke—adduces arguments to show that Hebrews 1:3 and John 1:26 are not supportive of the doctrine. He reviews five objections to his position, of which the most important is the charge that Christ is referred to as "Son" before his incarnation. Payne replies that "he was so in intention and appointment, though not in act and accomplishment; . . . He became actually the Son of God by his miraculous incarnation."[68] As I have elsewhere explained, "This is not to deny the eternal existence of the second person of the Trinity (with which claim Payne avoids adoptionism), but it is to claim that Christ did not eternally exist as Son."[69] Throughout, Payne's concern, like that of Ridgley, was to hold Arianism at bay by closing the door to any suggestion of posteriority, derivation, and inferiority.

In the middle decades of the nineteenth century the question of eternal generation became a church-dividing issue among Strict and Particular Baptists. At the fountainhead of this dispute was John Stevens (1776–1847),[70] who managed to raise the eyebrows of his co-religionists over his double-barrelled claim that the Son of God was not eternally generate, and that Christ's human soul predated his incarnation. The latter was the pre-existarian view associated with Isaac Watts. It was "possibly introduced into Particular Baptist circles by John Allen, pastor of the Petticoat Lane Church, London, 1764–7."[71] Not surprisingly, Allen was trounced by John Gill. Stevens proclaimed his newly-embraced doctrine in 1811, and reaffirmed it in two publications: *Verses on the Sonship of Christ and the Pre-existence of His Human Soul* (1812), and *A Scriptural*

---

66. Ibid.

67. Ibid., 251.

68. Ibid., 268.

69. Sell, *Hinterland Theology*, 180. For Payne see ibid., ch. 5 and *passim*. In the above paragraph I summarize what is there written.

70. For whom, see Dix, *Strict and* Particular, 170–72.

71. So Oliver, *History of the English Calvinistic* Baptists, 214. For Allen, see Wilson, *History and Antiquities*, IV, 426–28. Allen ended in disgrace—and in America.

Display of the Triune God and the Early Existence of Jesus's Human Soul (1813). He insisted that he could maintain the unity of the three persons of the Trinity, notwithstanding his denial of the doctrine of the Son's eternal generation; and that by virtue of his pre-existarianism, he upheld the eternity of the Son.[72] His pre-existarian views were also propagated in *The Gospel Herald, or Poor Christian's Magazine*, the first issue of which appeared in January 1833 under the editorship of its founder, Samuel Collins. Thus, for example, in 1837, under the title, "The man Christ Jesus personally God," Stevens gathers biblical texts by way of showing that

> Peter, Paul, and Jude, as three inspired witnesses, unitedly declare the eternal Godhead of the Lord Jesus Christ. On this stable foundation rests the saving worth of his obedience and sacrifice. . . . He is both God, and the only begotten Son of God: the former by nature as a person of the eternal essence; the latter by the sovereign will of God, as a complex person of two infinitely different natures, united, but not blended. It is easy to perceive that all arguments, proceeding on a separation of the two natures in our Lord's person, must be of a misguiding tendency. On the other hand, whosoever maintains that the Man Christ Jesus is *personally* God, at the same time, maintains the hypostatical union of divinity and humanity in his one complex person, as the Son of God, and the Saviour of guilty men. He who so believes concerning him, may be learned, or he may be illiterate; he may be public, or he may be obscure; but he evidently is not hereby entitled to the name of an heretic.[73]

It would seem that such views stimulated John Gadsby to launch *The Gospel Standard* in 1835.[74]

More serious were the repercussions of Stevens's repudiation of eternal generation. In this he was not alone. Kenneth Dix notes

---

72. Stevens, *A Scriptural Display*, 212.

73. Stevens, "The Man Christ Jesus is Personally God," 158–59.

74. See Paul, *Historical Sketch of the Gospel Standard Baptists*, 21. The proliferation of magazines, for children as well as adults, sponsored by this relatively small constituency of Baptist churches at least in part in order to advocate certain interpretations of doctrine and to repudiate others, prompts the thought, "By their magazines ye shall know them." For Gadsby (1808–93) see Various; Ramsbottom, *The History of the Gospel Standard* Magazine, 114–29. Gadsby edited *The Gospel Standard* from 1870 to 1877, and the June 1879 issue.

that Samuel Collins (1799–1881) of Grundisburgh,[75] William Palmer (1799–1873) of Homerton Row, London,[76] George Murrell (1784–1871) of St. Neots,[77] and James Wells (1803–72)[78] of London, all opposed the doctrine,[79] and men like these were in *The Gospel Standard's* sights. Their most powerful *Gospel Standard* opponent was Joseph Charles Philpot (1802–1869),[80] a Fellow of Worcester College, Oxford, who resigned his Church of England curacy in 1835 and joined the Strict Baptists. In 1844 a letter by Philpot was published in *The Gospel Standard*, in which he declared that "To my feelings, the real, true, and proper Sonship of Christ shines with such a ray of light through the New Testament, that I could no more give it up than I could His blood and righteousness. Nay, I consider the denial of it to be a serious and dangerous error, and not very far removed from that passage, "Whosoever denieth the Son, the same hath not the Father" (I John 2: 23).[81] The doctrine was fairly frequently defended in *The Gospel Standard*, and I cannot here recount all of the particulars.[82] The important thing is to indicate the position of the main proponent, Philpot, and I shall draw this from the reprint of material first published in *The Gospel Standard*, of which Philpot became the third editor (1849–69).

Philpot affirms (like orthodox *and* heterodox divines before him) that "Our first rule must be that *the Scriptures* shall be the *only standard of appeal*, and these taken in their plain, literal meaning, without perverting or mystifying their evident signification."[83] Natural reasoning as distinct from Scripture, and carnal conclusions opposed to Scripture

---

75. For whom, see Bland, "Samuel Collins, of Grundisburgh," 257–60, 321–25, 353–56.

76. For whom, see Anon., Obituaries. *The Earthen Vessel* was founded by Charles Walter Banks and edited by him. For Banks (1808–93) see Various. He held to eternal generation himself, but permitted the expression of other views in his magazine.

77. For whom see Chambers, *The Strict Baptist Chapels of England, IV: The Industrial Midlands*, 98–99.

78. For whom, see *The Baptist Handbook*, 1873, 209.

79. Dix, *Strict and Particular. English Strict and Particular Baptists*, 175, and see further on Stevens's writings, ibid., 173–77.

80. For whom, see DEB, ODNB; Ramsbottom, *The History of the Gospel Standard Magazine*, 102–13.

81. *The Gospel Standard*, X no. 94, January 1844, 38–39.

82. For these, see Paul's *Historical Sketch*, ch. 3.

83. Philpot, *The True, Proper, and Eternal* Sonship, 18.

must be discarded, and the teaching of the Holy Spirit sought. He compiles a collection of biblical verses that, in his view, affirm the eternal generation of the Son, and then turns to views deemed mistaken. First, Christ did not become Son at his incarnation, as if he were not Son previously. Secondly (as if *contra* Adam Clarke), he is not the Son of God because of his resurrection from the dead or, thirdly, because of his exaltation to the right hand of God. He proceeds to argue that it is an "undeniable scripture truth that the Lord Jesus Christ is the *Son of God as God*," and that "when the Scripture speaks of Jesus as *the only-begotten* Son of God, it speaks of Him as such in His divine nature."[84] He opposes those who say that Jesus is the only-begotten Son because of the everlasting covenant, for "Begetting implies a being, not a compact; and to be begotten implies a nature, a mode of existence, not a covenant."[85] There follows a defence of the view that Jesus is "*God's own, proper, true and eternal Son.*"[86] He is not Son "merely by office or covenant title, or by virtue of His complex Person."[87]

Philpot turns finally to some objections. In holding to eternal generation we do not make a begotten God, for we are Trinitarians, and God is one in thee persons. It is thus "in His *Person*, not in His *Essence*, that [Christ] is the only-begotten Son of God."[88] To the objection that the doctrine of eternal generation denies Christ's co-eternity and co-equality with the Father because the latter must be prior to the former, Philpot answers that we must not "weigh and measure the nature and being of God by the nature and being of man," and that to call Jesus the eternal Son is already to declare his co-eternity with the Father.[89] Others, again, object to the term "eternal generation." Gathering epithets from an article entitled, "A little one," published in the *Earthen Vessel* in November 1860, he says that the term "has been called even lately "a piece of twaddle," "a metaphysical conceit," "a self-contradiction," "carnal and contrary to the Scriptures," "a fable," "a figment," "an error which has seen its day, which is now dying out, becoming effete, waxing old

---

84. Ibid., 49.
85. Ibid., 51.
86. Ibid., 53.
87. Ibid., 59.
88. Ibid., 82.
89. Ibid., 84.

and vanishing away."[90] Philpot declares that although objectors cavil at the term as being unscriptural, it is the doctrine that they really loathe. In any case there are numerous terms that are used—"Trinity," "particular redemption" among them, that are not in the Bible. Moreover, the term "eternal generation of the Son" was introduced "to distinguish the proper and eternal filiation of Jesus from His generation in the sense of Arius, who admitted the generation of the Son, but not his eternal generation, and craftily used generation in the sense of making or forming, not begetting. He thus denied that the Son was co-equal, co-eternal and con-substantial . . . with the Father."[91]

That not all Strict Baptists were persuaded by Philpot is clear from the fact that the controversy continued for some time. James Wells, for example, took up cudgels in the *Earthen Vessel*, while Thomas Row (1786–1868) of Little Gransden revived the pre-existarian case. In 1852 Row criticised some sermons by Philpot in *The Gospel Herald*, and he contributed two further articles to *The Earthen Vessel*. Replies to the latter two were forthcoming from one "Naphtali."[92]

Doctrinal differences caused local ecclesial upset in some places, as at Gower Street Strict and Particular Baptist Chapel, London, where, on 20 February 1860 a special meeting was convened with a view to settling the matter. The following statement was agreed by the majority present: "We, the members of this church, believe the Second Person in the ever-blessed Trinity to be the only-begotten Son of God, and that He was such in his Divine Person before all worlds. Because opponents of the doctrine had remained in the church and caused trouble, it was 'Resolved, . . . that within three months from the passing of this resolution, each deacon and member is required to sign the foregoing declaration of faith in the Eternal Sonship of our Lord and Saviour Jesus Christ. And every member refusing to do so is, by this resolution, deprived of membership.'"[93]

---

90. Ibid., 85.

91. Ibid., 88.

92. See T. Row, "Remarks on a second and third sermon by Mr. Philpot," 9–11; "True freedom by the Son of God," 152–54; "The soul and sympathy of Christ," 258–59. For Row see Anon, Obituary. For "Naphtali's" replies see *The Earthen Vessel*, XI, 1855, 207–10, and ibid., XIII, 1857, 268–70.

93. Marriott, *A History of Gower Street Chapel*, 27–28.

As late as 1926, James Kidwell Popham (1847–1937),[94] editor of *The Gospel Standard* from 1905 to 1935, could say with regard to the events of 1860, "From that day to this the breach has remained open, and the two parties have been known as the *"Gospel Standard"* Churches and the *"Earthen Vessel"* Churches, respectively, and as holding the exact opposite views on that fundamental doctrine [i.e. the eternal generation of the Son]."[95] In the same year the Gospel Standard churches resolved that in order to preserve the purity of their proclamation, only those preachers who upheld the agreed doctrines should be permitted to preach in Gospel Standard churches—a decision of which some of their preachers took a dim view.[96]

Needless to say, the activities of orthodox writers did nothing to stem the flow of heterodox ideas and publications. Unitarianism was advancing, sometimes in crusading style. As it did so, the fault line between the older biblical, or Priestleyan, Unitarianism and the later Romantic Unitarianism, was more clearly revealed, and this notwithstanding the fact the latter did not banish the former overnight, any more than Arianism had been immediately swept aside by Socinianism. Thus, for example, in 1824 John James (1779–1864)[97] published a Welsh translation of Belsham's *A Calm Inquiry into the Scripture Doctrine Concerning the Person of Christ; Including a Brief Review of the Controversy between Dr. Horsley, and Dr. Priestley, and a Summary of the Various Opinions entertained by Christians on this Subject* (1811) (*Ymofyniad tawel I'r Athrawiaeth Ysgrythurol am Berson Crist*); in 1840 the Wesleyan minister David Evans (1814–1847),[98] concerned by the spread of Unitarianism in Swansea, published *The Proper Deity of our Lord Jesus Christ* (*Duwdod Priodol ein Harglwydd Iesu Grist*). But by the time Robert Spears (1825–1899)[99] published his "Six hundred scriptural

---

94. For whom, see Gosden, *Memoir and Letters of James Kidwell Popham*; Ramsbottom, *The History of the Gospel Standard Magazine*, 191–204.

95. Popham, "An opening word," 13. He here defends the view that the Gospel Standard Baptists "are a definite, distinct, and separate body, or denomination," ibid., 9. They also appear to be a formally doctrinally subscribing body, in contrast to their Particular Baptist forebears.

96. For one example, see Sell, *Alfred Dye, Minister of the Gospel*, 34–35.

97. For whom, see DWB. He was refused admission to Carmarthen Academy—in his view on account of his Unitarianism—but was admitted by Timothy Kenrick at the third Exeter Academy.

98. For whom, see DWB.

99. For whom, see ODNB.

illustrations of Christian Unitarianism" in 1861, and declared that "Our faith in the offices, teaching, life, and death of Jesus Christ is scriptural, rational, and practical"[100] the tide was already with the newer Unitarian thought. As Herbert McLachlan pointed out,

> With the rejection by the teachers and pupils of Manchester College of the principle of "the sufficiency of Scripture," and their recognition of the essential relation of Christian doctrine to religious philosophy and the new science of comparative religion, the Unitarian study of Christian Doctrine took a new and decisive turn. The leaders of this movement were John James Tayler [1797–1869], James Martineau [1805–1900], James Drummond [1835–1918], Joseph Estlin Carpenter [1844–1927], and Philip Henry Wicksteed [1844–1927].[101]

This "new and decisive turn" was more than an institutional or an insular matter: the influence of exotic ideas, notably those of William Ellery Channing (1780–1842) and Theodore Parker (1810–1860) should not be underestimated. With hindsight, J. H. Muirhead summed up the situation thus:

> Under [Martineau's] leadership Unitarianism had recently been emancipated from belief in the miraculous element in Christian doctrine, including the resurrection and the authenticity of the Messianic claims as we have them in the Fourth Gospel. Jesus of Nazareth was a fellow man and an elder brother, only knowing the mind of the common Father more intimately and profoundly than any other before or since, and in that sense the captain of our salvation. To be worthy followers constituted man's highest task, believing *with* him rather than *in* him. Religion was to be directed *by* Jesus rather than *to* him.[102]

I note in passing that the change of emphasis here detected was by no means confined to Unitarianism. It was to be found in ostensibly more orthodox circles as liberal theology developed in the wake of modern

---

100. R. Spears, *The Unitarian Handbook of Scriptural Illustrations & Expositions*, 17. Spears edited *Christian Life*, an organ of biblical Unitarianism.

101. McLachlan, *The Unitarian Movement*, 232–33. For Tayler, Drummond, Carpenter, and Wicksteed, see ODNB. Tayler was educated at Manchester College York, and Glasgow University; Drummond at Trinity College Dublin and Manchester New College under Tayler and Martineau; Carpenter and Wicksteed at University College London and Manchester New College.

102. Muirhead, *Reflections of a Journeyman in* Philosophy, 64–65.

biblical criticism, evolutionary thought, and the immanentism propagated by post-Hegelian idealists. It would seem that for some the use with reference to Jesus of the terms "master," "leader," "elder brother," and the like, was a way of avoiding the terms "Lord" and "Saviour."

What W. G. Tarrant wrote of more recent Unitarian hymnals applies to much Unitarian writing:

> The "miraculous" is dropped; the "official" position formerly assigned to Jesus Christ is minimized or wholly effaced; the bases of religious verity are sought in the experiences of the soul. To use the title of Dr. Martineau's own book . . . "The Seat of Authority" is no longer sought by Unitarians without—whether in a book, a church, or an historical character—but within, where the moral conflict attests a Righteousness Eternal, and where the "love, joy, peace" which are the "fruit of the spirit" bear witness to the indwelling God.[103]

Although the bulk of Martineau's major writings appeared following his retirement in 1885, the main lines of his thought had long before been widely disseminated—not least through controversies. Thus, for example, in his *Endeavours after the Christian Life* (1843) he encapsulates much of his general stance on the first page, in two sentences that have almost the character of a manifesto: "All that we believe without us, we first feel within us; and it is the one sufficient proof of the grandeur and awfulness of our nature, that we have faith in God; for no merely finite being can possibly believe the infinite. The universe of which each man conceives, exists primarily in his own mind."[104] This was too much for David Lloyd (1805–1863),[105] as it was for others. Lloyd, educated at Carmarthen Academy and Glasgow University, and now principal of the Academy, was staunchly "old school" Unitarian. Undeterred, Martineau continued to propagate his belief in the immanence of God as witnessed to by inward spiritual experience. He went further, and in 1861 declared that "The Incarnation is true, not of Christ exclusively, but of Man universally, and God everlastingly."[106] This sentiment caused great flutter-

---

103. Tarrant, *The Story and Significance of the Unitarian Movement*, 71–72. This may suggest undue subjectivism, and Martineau was, indeed, charged with this. I have elsewhere sought to defend him on this matter. See Sell, *Commemorations*, 22. See also ibid., ch. 10.

104. Martineau, *Endeavours after the Christian Life*, 1.

105. For whom, see DWB.

106. Martineau, *Essays, Reviews and Addresses*, III, 51.

ings in some orthodox dovecotes on the ground of its perceived radical doctrinal reductionism, and for one of its homelier consequences we may recall the experience of the philosopher Henry Jones (1852–1922).[107] He had preached a sermon at Llanfair PG, but had not been invited to return. He enquired of John Morris Jones why this was, and, having consulted the deacons of the church, Jones replied, "'They are told . . . that you deny the divinity of Christ.' 'I!' said Henry, 'I deny the divinity of Christ! I do not deny the divinity of any man!'"[108] Martineau caused further distress when he advised Christians to refrain from thinking in Jewish terms of Jesus as the Messiah—advice which prompted the Priestleyans to remind him that no less a person than Locke had specified the belief that "Jesus is the Messiah" as that which qualifies a person as a Christian. But if some took exception to Martineau's views, others propagated them with enthusiasm, among them William James (1848–1907),[109] who held the prominent post of secretary of the Unitarian Association.

We may gauge the tone of more popular presentations of Unitarian Christology towards the end of the nineteenth century by citing J. C. Perry (1852–1883). In a paper entitled, "Unitarianism an affirmative faith," he asks, "what shall we say about our belief in Jesus Christ? We deny his deity? Yes; because we make the far greater affirmation of his humanity. I do not want now to discuss the whole doctrine of the deity of Jesus. Suffice it to say that it is both unscriptural and unintelligible. The Gospels know nothing of the Godhead of Christ."[110] Far from discussing the doctrine, he simply gathers steam—or, rather, lets off steam; and he waxes apoplectic when Unitarians are charged with denying Christ: it "makes my blood boil in my veins," he cries. "Deny Jesus Christ! . . . He is my teacher, my guide, my friend."[111] There we are, then. Perry's co-contributor, Charles Beard (1827–1888), writing (more temperately) on "Jesus Christ," explains that "I have not advanced the doctrine of Christ's sinlessness. I do not know what sinlessness means as applied to human nature; . . . Imperfection is of the very essence of humanity. . . . From any true apprehension of the humanity of Christ the idea of progress cannot be excluded . . . And growth implies at least relative imperfection:

---

107. For whom, see DWB, ODNB; Sell, *Philosophical Idealism and Christian Belief*.
108. Hetherington, *The Life and Letters of Sir Henry Jones*, 43.
109. For whom, see DWB.
110. Perry, "Unitarianism an affirmative faith," 95.
111. Ibid., 97.

a present stronger than the past, a future completer than the present. ... But then it will be evident, from all that I have already said, that I find no fault in Jesus."[112]

Sufficiently relieved, we may direct our thoughts elsewhere—in fact to three Welsh ministers. The first, in both chronological order and distinction is the Presbyterian, Lewis Edwards (1809–87),[113] Principal for fifty years of Bala Calvinistic Methodist College. His book on *The Atonement* was published in 1860 in Welsh, and it appeared in English in 1887 in a translation by his son, Thomas Charles Edwards (1837–1900).[114] The book is in the form of a dialogue between a teacher and a disciple and, as dialogues do, and as the author admits in his Preface, it does not adhere strictly to the title, but meanders into other aspects of Christian doctrine, the person of Christ among them. Some snatches of the conversation will make the point and indicate Edwards' emphasis in Christology. The teacher puts his finger on the problem:

> The union of divinity and humanity in the person of Christ is of so exalted a nature that it is difficult for us to believe that the man Christ Jesus felt as we do, possessed a human will like ours, partook of our weaknesses, and was exposed to the same temptations. On the other hand, it is still more difficult to realize the conception that He was, when suffering and dying, a Divine Person co-equal with the Father. . . . [W]e are prone to think . . . that Christ is in a position intermediate between God and men, not only in respect to His mediatorial office, which it true, but also as a Being, which is not true. . . . [A]n opposite difficulty to this arises from our inability to comprehend the closeness of the union between divinity and humanity in the person of the Mediator. . . . If we ought to believe, on the one hand, that the two natures remained unchanged, we ought to believe as firmly, on the other hand, that the person of the Mediator, as He is God and man, entered into all the humiliation, and that this person, as God and man, is now highly exalted.[115]

---

112. C. Beard, "Jesus Christ," 112–13. For Beard, see ODNB. He was educated at Manchester New College, and in Berlin.

113. For whom, see DWB, ODNB.

114. For whom, see DWB, ODNB. He was educated at Bala College and Lincoln College, Oxford.

115. Edwards, *The Doctrine of the Atonement*, 106–8.

Christological Contributions and Ecclesial Developments 1800-1891   117

The second of the three Welshmen is the Congregationalist James Rhys Kilsby Jones (1813-1889) [116]—an "original"; the third, the Presbyterian William James (1848-1907)[117] was Moderator of the General Assembly in 1895. As if to show that one could emphasise the humanity of Christ without falling for the humanitarianism of the Unitarians, both men elaborated on the theme. In a sermon of Hebrews 2:14-16, Jones spoke as follows:

> If [Christ] was a mere man—necessarily, not voluntarily—subject to the laws of our being, one does not see much condescension in calling His brethren equals. There is no room for the exercise of condescension where there is equality. But if Christ became a man, and was a man from choice—assumed human, rather than angelic, nature from preference, and not by necessity—then there is room for condescension. The conclusion to which even this hasty, cursory examination of the passage has conducted us seems to be the utter impossibility of interpreting it fairly and intelligibly except on the assumption of Christ's pre-existence and superiority to our nature.[118]

For his part, in 1889 James delivered a paper at the first English Conference of the Presbyterian Church of Wales in which he argued that Christ's human nature was not absorbed into the divine, but was made "more truly human by the indwelling of the divine." Jesus struggled as we do, but not from the imperfect to the perfect; he grew in knowledge; and a genuine *kenosis* was implicit in the incarnation.[119] We shall return to the term *kenosis* shortly.

At the beginning of the nineteenth century we found two Wesleyans, Clarke and Watson; in the seventh and eighth decades of the century a number of thorough works were published by another Wesleyan, William Burt Pope (1822-1903),[120] who trained at the Wesleyan Theological Institution at Hoxton. The books that concern us are *The Person of Christ* (1871), which was translated into German; his three-volume *Compendium of Christian Theology* (1880); and the *Higher*

---

116. He added this name—that of Kilsby, Northamptonshire, where he was minister from 1840-49). See DWB, ODNB, SI.
117. For whom, see DWB.
118. Quoted in Vyrnwy Morgan, *The Life and Sayings of the Late Kilsby Jones*, 140.
119. See Knox, *Voices from the Past*, 40-41.
120. For whom, see DMBI, ODCC, ODNB; Sell, *Dissenting Thought*, ch. 19.

Catechism of Theology (1883). In Pope's opinion, "The Divine-human Person of our Lord is the mystery and the glory of the Christian faith."[121] This leads us to expect a high Christology, and this is precisely what we are given. Far from being simply a moral exemplar, "It is in the Person of His Son that God unites again our race to Himself."[122] Pope draws a distinction between Christ's personality, which ever remains divine, and the Divine-human Person who became incarnate. In answer to the question, "Is not this notion of a human nature apart from a distinct human personality an unreality?" he replies, "In human philosophy it may be; but not in the Divine philosophy of Scripture, which assumes this without explaining it. Our Lord was the Son incarnate; not a man united to God in any manner however pre-eminent."[123] It is not difficult to see what Pope is ruling out here. He further explains that

> The Person of Christ is the result of the indivisible and abiding union of the Divine and human natures. This is perhaps the most wonderful proposition that theology has to affirm: a stumbling-block to the unbeliever, it is a sore offence to a certain philosophy, but the very rejoicing of the heart to Christian faith. . . . The four leading terms or watchwords, which like a quaternion guard the sacred Person of the Lord, are simply the plain teaching of Scripture classified and condensed into single defensive terms: Christ is "truly" God, "perfectly" man, "indivisibly" one Person, "unconfusedly" two natures.[124]

The practical importance of all of this, for human beings, is that "as Divine [Christ] represents God to man; as human He represents mankind to God."[125]

Jesus is called "the only-begotten Son, the Son of God, the Son absolutely, and the Son of man."[126] Of these, the first three assert or imply the eternal Sonship, which Sonship is related to the incarnation thus:

> (1) As to the Holy Trinity: only the Son, in the unfathomable mystery of the Godhead, could be and was sent; not the Father nor the Holy Ghost.

---

121. Pope, *The Person of Christ*, 31.
122. Ibid., 7.
123. Pope, *A Higher Catechism of Theology*, 160.
124. Pope, *The Person of Christ*, 16, 27.
125. Pope, *A Higher Catechism*, 156.
126. Ibid., 159.

> (2) This shows, as to man himself, that between the Son, the eternal Image of God, and man, the human image of that Image, there is some mysterious and blessed bond.[127]

There may be a "mysterious and blessed bond" between the Son and the rest of humanity, but in one respect in particular Christ differs from us: "His human nature was conceived of the virgin by the Holy Ghost, and thus saved from the taint of original sin as well as its condemnation. . . . He was impeccable, or for ever incapable of sin, because His only personality was never other than that of the Eternal Son."[128] These words bristle with exegetical, philosophical and theological difficulties, and it must be said that while he was alive to many new intellectual departures—he pondered kenotic theories, for example, and repudiated them on the ground that they threatened God's immutability—Pope's works mark the end of a line of biblical exposition that could not with integrity be further pursued. For all that, his writings are characterized by reverence and spiritual depth, so that after I had compared his published legacy with that of the Congregationalist A. M. Fairbairn (1838–1912)[129] and the Irish Presbyterian Robert Watts (1820–95), I concluded that of them all, "it is Pope who can still *feed* us most."[130]

I earlier observed that we should look in vain for substantial original Nonconformist contributions to Christology during the first eight decades of the nineteenth century, and I can now invoke David Worthington Simon in support. In an address delivered at the first International Congregational Council in 1891 he despaired over the state of systematic theology at large in his own, Congregational, denomination: "during the last thirty-five years only one "Systematic Theology" has been published by British Congregationalists; . . . of out of some 600 registered Congregational publications during, say, twenty-five years, scarcely 50 are scientifically theological; . . . out of upwards of 450 discourses by Congregational ministers printed during the last five years or thereabouts in *The Christian World Pulpit*, scarcely thirty were properly

---

127. Ibid.

128. Ibid., 160.

129. For whom, see DHT, ODCC, ODNB, SI, WTW; Sell, *Dissenting Thought*, ch. 19. Largely self-taught, he studied under James Morison of the Evangelical Union, and attended classes at Edinburgh University but, like some other able students of his generation, did not graduate.

130. Sell, *Dissenting Thought*, 575.

doctrinal."[131] He did concede that some had shown interest in inspiration, the atonement and future punishment, though with "decided signs of unreasoned sentimental conviction which is styled 'finding' or 'being found by' a truth."[132]

What Simon could not foresee (and what may give hope to any present-day Nonconformists who lament the state of Nonconformist theology), was that during the next sixty years there was an proliferation of Nonconformist theological publication the like of which had not been seen since the seventeenth century. Perhaps this is not surprising, for although early warning signs of Nonconformity's subsequent numerical decline can, with hindsight, be detected, psychologically Nonconformity was on the crest of a wave. More particularly, this was the period of its largest and most securely established theological colleges, with their attendant opportunities for academic employment. I shall introduce samples of Christological writings published during this period in the chronological order of their authors' births.

---

131. Simon, "The present direction of theological thought in the Congregational churches," 78.

132. Ibid.

7

The Proliferation of Nonconformist Christology 1891–1950

THE BAPTIST SAMUEL G. Green (1822–1905),[1] who was educated at Stepney College, became a tutor at Horton College, Bradford, and removed with the College when it became Rawdon College, Leeds. He contributed an essay on the "Deity and humanity of Christ" to the volume, *The Ancient Faith in Modern Light* (1897), which is interesting not only because he is alive to the then current issue of *kenosis*, but also because of the way in which he appeals not only to the New Testament but also, in "modern" fashion, to the way in which the truth of the Gospel is confirmed in the believer's religious experience.[2] He opens by observing that "The most significant fact in connection with modern theological study is the growing concentration of thought upon our Lord's human character and life. . . . Religious teaching, which, within the memory of some, concerned itself chiefly with what He has done for us, now dwells upon the antecedent question, Who and what He was."[3] There follows a brief investigation of the New Testament witness to Christ's divinity and humanity which reaches the conclusion that "The truths are kindred . . . standing not in mysterious and inexplicable contrast, but in perfect and glorious harmony."[4] Important though the testimony of the New Testament is, Green insists that this is not "a mere theory. We read it

---

1. For whom, see ODNB. He was educated at Stepney College and graduated in the University of London.

2. He does not, of course, make the forlorn apologetic move of suggesting that the believer's experience constitutes evidence that would or should suffice to convince a sceptic.

3. Various, *The Ancient Faith in Modern Light*, 157.

4. Ibid., 158.

... in the great volume of Christian experience everywhere. For surely the history of the Church and the records of missions are sufficient to prove that wherever the living Christ is preached in fellowship with men's souls, demanding faith, obedience, consecration, there is spiritual life. We must go to him as to our God, else we sadly miss the way."[5] In the light of this claim Green at once weighs Unitarianism and finds it wanting:

> One fact, uniformly and mournfully apparent in the annals of Unitarianism, is its absence of transforming and vitalising power. It *does not convert*. This is simply the testimony of its adherents,—their constant, sorrowful conclusion. ... A brilliant author of our own day[6] has raised the question anew—Why is it that Unitarianism makes so little progress? And part of the explanation, alas! is found in the remains of *Puritanism* that cling to it. "Unitarianism wants more beauty and more enthusiasm." ... [But] unless we have read amiss the experience of all the Christian ages, no splendour of adornment or pomp of ritual will give life to a Church when Christ as the divine and only Master is not the object of worship, the centre of trust and love.[7]

The upshot is that "Testimony and experience alike reveal to us His humanity and Deity as correlated truths."[8] He finds these truths properly presented in the Chalcedonian Formula, the Athanasian Creed, and the Westminster Confession, and then comes to a discussion of Christ's emptying of himself—"a phrase which perhaps more than any other in Scripture engages the best and deepest thought of our time."[9]

Green needs no persuading that "Plainly, our Lord laid something aside,"[10] and he proceeds to review the possibilities pondered by kenoticists. He considers the proposed division of Christ's attributes into immanent and relative ones, with holiness, veracity and love being immanent, and omniscience and omnipotence being relative. He grants that this accords with some historical facts concerning Jesus, but he is concerned that the division is arbitrary. Others suggest that Christ chose

---

5. Ibid., 163.
6. Green refers to Mrs. Humphry Ward, *Unitarians and the Future*, 1894.
7. Ibid., 163–65.
8. Ibid., 165.
9. Ibid., 173.
10. Ibid.

not to exercise some of his attributes, and that this self-renunciation both proves his love and displays his omnipotence—in which latter connection Green quotes Gregory of Nyssa: "That the omnipotence of the divine nature should have had *strength to descend* to the lowliness of humanity, furnishes a more manifest proof of power than even the greatness and supernatural character of the miracles."[11] Jesus advanced in wisdom and knowledge, and, eschewing both Nestorianism and docetism, Green arrives by a process of induction from the New Testament at the conclusion that Jesus "retained what was needful for man's salvation; of the rest He 'emptied Himself.'"[12]

Again, Jesus was not ignorant as man and knowledgeable as Son of God—Nestorianism again; rather, "That knowledge, which it was no part of His saving purpose to reveal, did not, in fact, lie within the sphere of His present consciousness. Not to possess it was a part of His voluntary renunciation."[13] Above all, Jesus was perfected through his sufferings, which are not to be explained away in docetic fashion by focussing upon the physical and outward aspects rather than upon the "travail of his soul."[14] Green concludes that while the term *"kenosis"* is convenient, it must not be pressed too far and, in face of kenotic theorizing, he concurs with James Denney that Paul does not propose a metaphysical kenotic theory, but "impresses the heart and touches the imagination rather than aids the intelligence."[15] Green's last thought on *kenosis* construed as renunciation is this: "From pondering the *Kenosis* of which Paul speaks, it is good to turn to the proem of John's Gospel, and to read the open secret of the Incarnation there. To reveal the Infinite Holiness, translated into human life, to manifest the Eternal Love and the Eternal Righteousness, as in reality and essence One, and thus to become the Light and Life of men, was the great intent of [Christ's] mission."[16]

Robert William Dale (1829–95)[17] is widely regarded as the most distinguished Congregationalist of the nineteenth century. He was edu-

---

11. Ibid., 174, quoting Gregory *via* R. L. Ottley, *The Doctrine of the* Incarnation, II, 287.
12. Ibid., 179.
13. Ibid., 180.
14. Ibid., 182.
15. Ibid., 185, quoting Denney, *Studies in Theology*, 57.
16. Ibid., 187.
17. For whom, see DHT, ODCC, ODNB, SI.

cated at Spring Hill College, Birmingham, under Henry Rogers (1806–1877).[18] There followed a long and distinguished ministry at Carrs Lane, Birmingham, during which time Dale became a noted preacher, a man of affairs, and a widely-read author. He touched on all of the major Christian doctrines, and his Congregational Lecture on *The Atonement* (1875) reached its twenty-first edition in 1900, and was reprinted in 2003. For all his considerable abilities, we do not go to Dale for detailed technical discussions of doctrine. The verdict of W. B. Selbie (1862–1944)[19] is not unjust: "The remarkable thing about [Dale's] theology is the entire absence from it of anything like mere academic argumentation. . . . His Christology was as practical and energetic as his theology."[20] Indeed his understanding of Christ as a living reality with whom one has personal relations pervaded all his writings, and with this emphasis he did much to redirect Nonconformist theology (at least) from more traditional and pre-critical approaches to doctrine. Moreover—with indebtedness to F. D. Maurice—Dale's Christ is the cosmic Christ. "The supreme fact in the history of the world," he declares, "perhaps[21] in the history of the universe—is that God had become man in the Person of the Lord Jesus Christ."[22] In the midst of theological confusion, attacks on the Christian faith and historical criticism of the biblical text, Dale feels that the real challenge is not adequately grasped:

> The storm has moved around the whole horizon; but it is rapidly concentrating its strength and fury above one sacred Head. This, this is the real issue of the fight—Is Christendom to believe in Christ any longer or no? It is a battle in which everything is to be lost or won. It is not a theory of ecclesiastical polity which is in danger, it is not a theological system, it is not a creed, it is not the Old Testament or the New, but the claim of Christ Himself to be the Son of God and the Saviour of mankind.[23]

Here is the conviction that fuelled Dale's Christocentrism. What, then, did he make of the person of Christ?

---

18. For whom, see ODNB, SI; Sell, *Dissenting Thought*, chs. 17, 18.
19. For whom, see ODNB, SI, WTW. He was educated at Brasenose and Mansfield Colleges, Oxford.
20. Selbie, *Congregationalism*, 171.
21. Henry Rogers would not have wanted him to go beyond the evidence.
22. Dale, *Essays and Addresses*, 89.
23. Ibid., 5.

In a discourse on Christian doctrine he tackles the humanity of Christ. Our understanding of the incarnation, he insists, must be governed by the experiences of those who knew Jesus during his earthly life. From these we learn that Jesus developed as we do, that he was hungry, thirsty and susceptible to pain; that he had human affections and emotions, that he could be indignant, and that he was tempted. He prayed to his Father, and was sustained by him in his supreme conflict. Thus "The proof is complete. Christ was truly man."[24] Similarly, it was by experience that the first apostles came by their faith in Christ's divinity, and so it is with us (as his Baptist contemporary, Green, also realised): "In these last days, our own faith in the Lord Jesus Christ as Son of God and Saviour of men—however we may have first come by it—derives its life and vigour from our own knowledge of His power and glory. Experience, not mere authority,—experience, not mere theological demonstration—is the surest ground of our belief that He is the Son of the Eternal."[25]

The divinity of Christ is presupposed by all of the earliest Christian preaching: for example, the apostles urged people to repent, and they offered remission of sins in Christ's name; and the divinity of Christ is likewise taken for granted in the epistles. Throughout the world Jesus Christ is acknowledged as God's Son, and worshipped as such. Although the humanity of Jesus is unquestioned, Dale admits that Jesus is not exactly like ourselves. He was free of the consciousness of sin, he prayed alone, his knowledge of his Father was in the highest degree intimate, and his personal authority over the moral and religious life of people was "native to him."[26] Jesus did not need salvation, everyone else does. He offers eternal life, he gives assurances concerning it to his friends; he says that he will send the Spirit after he has left them; and he shares his Father's sovereignty: "All things whatsoever the Father hath are mine" (John 16: 15). Dale sums matters up in a manner that is as homiletic as it is interrogative: "Who can this be through whom the sins of the race are forgiven, through whose death we ourselves have received the forgiveness of sins? We know that He is man; but surely He is more than man. Who is He? To Him the saved of all generations owe their eternal salvation. Who is He? Who? If you shrink from calling Him God, what other title adequate to the greatness of His work will you attribute to Him?"[27]

24. Dale, *Christian Doctrine*, 72.
25. Ibid., 77.
26. ibid., 107.
27. Ibid., 114.

Before we leave Dale, two further points remain to be added. First, Dale was writing at a time when the incarnation of Christ was coming increasingly into vogue, especially among Church of England theologians. It is noticeable, however, that whereas the latter frequently expounded incarnation in terms of weaker or stronger varieties of post-Hegelian immanentism,[28] Dale remained biblically rooted and historically aware. Secondly, notwithstanding that his most significant work was on the atonement, Dale came to distance himself from the older evangelicalism by giving the incarnation precedence over the atonement: "The incarnation, with all that it reveals concerning God, man, and the universe, concerning this life and the life to come, stands first; with the early Evangelicals the Death of Christ for human sin stood first. . . . In theology the Incarnation lies deeper than the Atonement; and the great and august mystery of the Trinity lies deeper than the Incarnation."[29] No doubt Dale felt moral revulsion concerning some of the more grotesque ways in which evangelical doctrine had been (and, sadly, still is) proclaimed. The fact remains that it was not the incarnation as such that gave the early apostles and New Testament writers the experiences on which Dale rested his understanding of the person of Christ; it was what Christ had done, supremely at the Cross; and this was all of grace. Of course, as I explained at the outset, temporally the incarnation is prior to the atonement because Bethlehem comes before Calvary; logically the incarnation is prior to the atonement because Christ can do what he does only because he is who he is; but all of Dale's questions that I have just quoted, and that are summed up in the question, Who is he?, can be fully answered adequately (I do not say fully) only by those who have seen first, not just that he came, but who have experienced the results of what he did through what Calvin called "the whole course of his obedience,"[30] and supremely at the Cross—Dale among them. How else could he have written that Christ's "sufferings and death are the ground of the actual relations between all men and God. We are born—not into a lost world—but into a world that has been redeemed by the death of

---

28. As, for example, in the position of J. R. Illingworth, for which see Sell, *Philosophical Idealism and Christian Belief*, 195-97.

29. Dale, *The Old Evangelicalism and the New*, 48-49.

30. Calvin, *Institutes*, II.xvi.5.

the Son of man, who is also the Son of God. We are not under Law, but under Grace."[31]

D. W. Simon, who was appointed Resident Tutor and Professor of Theology at Spring Hill College, Birmingham in 1869, and who remained there until he removed to become Principal of the Scottish Congregational College, Edinburgh, in 1884, had Dale as the Chairman of the College Committee, and the two men could hardly have been more different in type: Simon self-effacing and shrinking from public gaze, Dale the Nonconformist man of affairs *par excellence*. If Dale's thought seems to flow from his pen, Simon's seems to struggle to get out of his mind, and this for temperamental reasons and not simply because his writing is more technical than Dale's. The result is that Simon sometimes leaves hostages to fortune, not least when he is discussing the person of Christ. Thus, for example, he thinks of the eternally manlike Logos as being enfleshed, but elsewhere denies that the second person of the Trinity, who emptied himself at the incarnation was man: "He was essentially akin to man, He differed from man in nature, in powers, in sub-consciousness, and in intermittent consciousness, no less than in His moral and spiritual character."[32] But if "akin to" here means "similar to," and not "related to," do we not hear echoes of the ancient view that the Logos took the place of the human soul of Jesus? Again, Simon denies the eternal generation of the Son, and maintains that Jesus was designated "Son of God" from the incarnation onwards, and that the designations of God and Father and Jesus as Son are modal or economic: "they refer to the relation which arose in consequence of the incarnation of the Logos."[33] As I have elsewhere written,

> All of this is asserted without argument, and it does seem to imply that to Simon the ontological Trinity comprises "three personal or personific factors, each eternally co-existent,"[34] but none of which are Father or Son. I am uncertain whether it is fair to say that adoptionism beckons because even that would seem

---

31. Dale, *Fellowship with Christ*, 64. This is from the Annual Sermon of the Baptist Missionary Society, preached on 1 May 1889—the same year in which Dale distanced himself from the older evangelicalism. As compared with Spurgeon, Dale was the epitome of consistency on the person of Christ. See Mark Hopkins, *Nonconformity's Romantic Generation*, 144–46.

32. Simon, *Reconciliation by Incarnation*, 327.

33. Ibid., 328.

34. Ibid. 327.

to require more than "personific factors"; but it is to say the least, all very puzzling, not least because elsewhere... Simon does not hesitate to speak of the eternal Father, the co-equal Son and the Holy Spirit.[35]

Robert Mackintosh (1858–1933), theological professor at Simon's *alma mater*, Lancashire Independent College, from 1898 to 1930, judged that Simon was "a shirt-sleeved and carpet-slippered philosopher,"[36] and there is some justification for this; but Simon's attractiveness resides in his wrestling both intellectually and spiritually, and in the fact that he sought to broaden the minds of students at a time when many thought that a highly dangerous thing to do.

If doctrinal technicalities are to the fore in Simon's Christology, in that of James Drummond (1835–1918) religious experience is central. Drummond was educated at Manchester New College, London, where Martineau was Professor of Philosophy and J. J. Tayler (1797–1869)[37] was principal. He served as assistant to William Gaskell (1805–1884)[38] at Cross Street Unitarian Church, Manchester from 1860, and in 1869 was appointed Professor of Biblical and Historical Theology at his *alma mater*, in succession to Tayler. In 1885 he followed Martineau as Principal, and in 1889 he removed with the college to Oxford, and retired in 1906. He delivered his Hibbert Lectures in Oxford and London in 1894, and these were published in the same year under the title, *Via, Veritas, Vita: Lectures on Christianity in its most Simple and Intelligible Form*. The subtitle is revelatory of Drummond's desire to cut through doctrinal technicalities and metaphysical subtleties with a view to exposing the heart of the Christian message. Throughout he has "the great mass of believers" in mind, and of them he writes,

> a Christianity without Christ would be something fundamentally different from that by which they have lived. He is bound up in their religious affections, and his is the quickening breath which turns into living creatures the cold forms of truth. He is more to them than all his teaching; his love has taken captive of

---

35. Sell, *Hinterland Theology*, 299. Simon is the subject of pp. 227–302 of this book, and *passim*.

36. Mackintosh, *Historic Theories of Atonement*, 274.

37. For whom, see ODNB; SI.

38. For whom, see ODNB. He was educated at Glasgow University and Manchester College York.

their hearts, and led them to the throne of God, and constrained them to all that is not unworthy and selfish in their conduct. Nor have they seen in him only Man ascending to the pinnacle of human goodness, but the grace and love of God coming down to reconcile and save and estranged and sorrowful world.[39]

We are at once aware of being in a very different atmosphere from that of the earlier biblical Unitarianism. In asserting that Jesus is not only "Man ascending to the pinnacle of human goodness" there is an implied rebuke to the balder humanitarianism espoused by some of his fellow Unitarians. This is clearly Christ-centred Unitarianism—which is not to say that it is altogether orthodox. We see this in Drummond's Essex Hall Lecture of 1902, in which he offers *Some Thoughts on Christology*. He turns his back upon classical, technical Christological terms, but equally upon the notions that Jesus is a random product of evolution, and, at the other extreme, that the Bible comprises a corpus of infallible truths. As before, he appeals to the Christian consciousness in which resides the unity to be found among Christians throughout the ages. Christ is central to this consciousness, but he "is not so much a model, which we are to look at and copy, as a spirit of life which may diffuse itself, like a purifying atmosphere, through every variety of human vocation."[40] Christ is the universal spirit to whom all Christians look, and he brings the love of God close. Jesus is fully and completely a man, and he may be called *the* Son of God, for he founded the spiritual brotherhood of such sons. Jesus was neither pre-existent nor a mere man, because "The Spirit which was manifested in him was "the eternal Life," which weaves together the ages, which has ever dwelt in holy souls . . ."[41]

From 1890 onwards the Fourth General Council's Chalcedonian Formula (451) was subjected to criticism, both positive and negative, by a number of Nonconformist writers, among them the Presbyterian James Oswald Dykes (1835–1912). He was educated at Edinburgh, Heidelberg and Erlangen,[42] and became Principal of the Presbyterian Theological College in London, moving with it in 1899 to Cambridge,

---

39. Drummond, *Via, Veritas, Vita*, 291–92.
40. Idem, *Some Thoughts on Christology*, 33.
41. Ibid., 56. See further Sell, *Nonconformist Theology*, 49–50.
42. Dykes was one of a number of Nonconformist scholars of the period who studied in Germany. Others included D. W. Simon, A. M. Fairbairn, Robert Mackintosh, and P. T. Forsyth.

where it assumed its present name, Westminster College. In 1905–1906 Dykes contributed a substantial four-part article on "The Person of Our Lord" to *The Expository Times*. It is one of the most careful and balanced appraisals of the Formula of the period, and it will serve as a canon against which to measure the reflections of others on the subject.

In his opening sentence Dykes declares that the Formula "has proved to be the high-water mark of confessional Christology," and then proceeds to the caution that "It would be a mistake to ask of any creed what it cannot give—an explanation either of the Person or of the Work of our Saviour."[43] Rather, creeds "were an attempt to stake off the limits of that area which the Church had come to claim as reserved for faith and sacred to it."[44] The Formula makes two positive claims. First, against Arianism and docetism "culminating in its most seductive shape of Apollinarism", it affirms "the true Deity and the complete Humanity of our Lord."[45] Secondly, it declares that in Christ these comprise "a unity of Personal Life." Hence, "no solution which divines may put forward by way of explanation or solution can be acceptable to faith, which either (1) denies to our Lord essential divinity, or (2) mutilates the completeness and invades the reality of His humanity, or (3) takes away the singleness of Christ's Person, or (4) merges into one His Deity and Humanity."[46] Dykes regards it as unfortunate that in stating their position the framers of the Formula employed terms borrowed from their familiar philosophy and thereby conferred confessional sanction upon them (though one might wonder what else they could done if communication were their objective). The Council of Nicaea (325) "took the first step on a questionable road" when it employed the term *ousia* by way of securing the deity of the second person in the Godhead, while *homoousia* was invoked in order to hold manifold varieties of semi-Arianism at bay. But the Formula extended the application of *homoousia* from Christ's deity to his humanity, so that he is like us in all respects, sin excepted. However, "this is not at all the sense in which the Church affirms the Three Distinctions in the Holy Trinity to be "of one substance." The *ousia*, or essence of Godhead—that which makes God to be what He

---

43. J. O. Dykes, "The person of our Lord," 7.
44. Ibid.
45. Ibid.
46. Ibid., 8.

is—is not *specifically* identical only in all the Three Blessed Persons, but is *numerically* identical, one and the same: a single essence."[47]

A further complication is the use of "*nature*," as in "the two-nature" doctrine, for this term "connotes something which has come to be, a derived or originated thing, the life or activity of which is straitly determined for it by its mode of origin and the laws under which it has come into existence";[48] and it is doubly unfortunate when, as at the present time, nature is used of the physical universe. The word suitably denotes human nature as an element within the physical order, "But it did not so well suit the simple, unbeginning, and unchanging Being of God. . . . At the very least, the word means one thing when you speak of the human nature of Jesus, and a very different thing when you speak of His Divine nature."[49] Similarly, the Council's use of the terms *prosopon* and *hupostasis*, also borrowed from earlier Trinitarian doctrine, undergo a change of reference in the process, for "Personality is not ascribed to the Sacred Three Distinctions within the Godhead in the same sense in which we are conscious of ourselves as Human Persons."[50]

The upshot is that:

> The few fixed points laid down in 451, valuable as they are to faith, offer us nothing better than hard and meagre outlines of a *doctrine*. A Being who combines in an inscrutable fashion Divine with Human properties, and of whom consequently contradictory assertions may be made, whose single Person is Divine, while His dual natures hold an undefined relation to one another: this is not a scheme to satisfy either head or heart. It is but a bare skeleton of a dogma, in which one cannot readily recognize either the Jesus of the Gospels or the Christ of the Church's worship. It needs to be filled up with the details of our Saviour's earthly life, and with the meaning of His saving work as Revealer of the Father and Redeemer of man, before we can see in Him the Person whom Christians trust and love.[51]

Dykes proceeds to discuss the subsequent history of Christological debate, concluding that "When night fell on Oriental Christendom, the

---

47. Ibid.
48. Ibid., 9.
49. Ibid.
50. Ibid.
51. Ibid., 10.

Roman West settled down contentedly into that acceptance of dualism [exemplified by Anselm]: Christ's Deity loosely attached to His human nature, yet overbearing it, and reducing to little better than a phantasm the moral victories and pathetic conflicts of His earthly career."[52] For all the insights to be gleaned from Reformed theology—and especially from Luther—Dykes considers that the basic Christological problem of the relation of the human and the divine to the one person remained unsolved; for what Luther bequeathed us, namely,

> a Human Nature semi-deified to begin with, but then stripped once more of its divineness and depotentiated; which on earth at least emptied itself of its Divine Majesty in order to lead our impoverished life from cradle to grave, gives us no help at all for the understanding of the life of Jesus among men. He might as well, for our problem, have received no such share in Divine attributes at all. . . . [We are not] one step nearer to that unity of incarnate experience . . . that unifying of the conscious life-experience of our Lord on earth as at one Divine and Human, yet single.[53]

Dykes's verdict on the course of Christological debate up to the middle of the nineteenth century is thus as follows:

> Twice over . . . had theologians endeavoured to secure of the Incarnate One a single theanthropic life by potentiating the feebler created factor till it approximated to the level of the divine: first at Alexandria by a merging of two natures into one; next at Wittenberg by a communication of divine properties to the human nature. Both times without success. What remained save to assail the problem from a new direction—that is, by depotentiating the nobler uncreated factor till it shrunk within the limits and lived upon the level of the humanity it had assumed?[54]

Hence the kenotic theology as worked out in 1845 by Thomasius, Dykes's teacher at Erlangen, who fully appreciated that his move entailed the reversal of Lutheran Christology at certain points—a reversal taken to its extreme by Gess in 1856. Dykes questions whether kenoticism, even in a moderate form, would have been so easily accepted by A. M. Fairbairn and others had there not been a mass of textual work on the life of Jesus inspired by the hope of approaching the secret of his person

52. Ibid., 59.
53. Ibid., 105.
54. Ibid., 106.

through the facts of his life. Dykes goes so far as to declare that "The subtle tendency to a docetic interpretation of Jesus which had beset theology ever since the Church formulated the doctrine of her Lord's divinity has been overcome."[55] Kenotic theories require the repudiation of older notions concerning a double will in Christ, as well as the theory that whereas as divine he might know something, as human he does not know it; but, constructively, they do not all follow exactly the same line: "Either Kenoticists suppose a suspension by the loving will of the Son of His divine activities (*all* His activities, save the will so to suspend them) which may be described as *total*, because it extends even to His universal activity as Lord of all worlds. Or they limit this surrender of His Divine ability to the sphere of His incarnate life as Man upon earth—leaving His cosmical and universal action as God otherwise unaffected."[56] Along the former path we reach a truly human life, but a human life only. Not surprisingly most English kenoticists have taken the latter route, and understand the cosmic life and activity of the Second Person as occurring prior to the incarnation. This yields "a human consciousness which fairly well answers to the requirements of the evangelical narrative. What it does not give us . . . is unity of consciousness in one Person. Our problem, therefore, is not solved by it."[57]

Dykes thinks that at bottom the difficulty is a psychological one, "the answer to which lies hid somewhere in the mysterious subject of personality."[58] (Psychological considerations were becoming increasingly prominent at the time of Dykes' writing, with even some theologians dabbling in mesmerism and the like). He grants that some will prefer the Ritschlian response of "declining the difficulty of a dogmatic solution by reposing in a practical religious certainty . . . I grudge no man his right to take shelter, if he can go no farther . . ."[59] For his part, Dykes cannot rest, and he ends by treating us to some psychological speculation: "Within Christ's complex and wonderful constitution, room might be found for a life-activity verily His own, yet of which He had on earth no human consciousness, or at most, it may be, an intermittent and imperfect knowledge; and, if it were so, the psychology of human personality has

55. Ibid., 151.
56. Ibid., 154.
57. Ibid., 155.
58. Ibid.
59. Ibid., 155–56.

nothing to say against it."[60] Perhaps not; but is the old doctrinal dualism really overcome by intermittent epistemological intimations?

Thomas Charles Edwards (1837–1900) was educated at his father's college in Bala, and at Lincoln College, Oxford, where he came under the influence of Mark Pattison and Benjamin Jowett. In 1872, following pastoral experience, he became Principal of the University College of Wales, Aberystwyth—the first college of the University of Wales. In 1891 he succeeded his father as principal of the Bala College, which he transformed into a theological college. He published biblical commentaries, but the work that concerns us is his Davies Lecture of 1895, *The God-Man*. In relatively brief compass he considers a number of Christological topics, among them the Logos, eternal generation and *kenosis*; and he does this with reference to authors ancient and modern, including Origen, Augustine, Richard of St. Victor, Luther, Dorner, John Caird, and Westcott.

Edwards does not shrink from speaking of the Son's subordination to the Father. This, he thinks, is indicated by the Son's willingness to obey the Father, even at the cost of suffering. Indeed, "subordination, rightly understood, contains a great truth, and Origen's happy phrase, "eternal generation," implies subordination, without sacrificing equality."[61] Moreover, this subordination pertains to the sphere of the Trinity, not, as Augustine wrongly thought, to the Son's humanity only. Whereas "man is the image of God because he has received his life from God, and has it only in God; . . . the Son, who likewise has received his life from God, inasmuch as He is Son, has that life, inasmuch as he is God, 'in himself'" [John 5:26].[62]

Edwards holds that "the Incarnation is a special form of God's immanence."[63] At the same time he emphasises the distinction between immanence and incarnation, namely, that immanence can be construed polytheistically as well as monotheistically. Hence the need of the transcendent corrective supplied by Athanasius and Luther, according to whom God is "transcendent, that He may be immanent; Christ *for* us, that He may become Christ *within* us."[64]

60. Ibid., 156.
61. Edwards, *The God-Man*, 8–9.
62. Ibid., 20.
63. Ibid., 26.
64. Ibid., 28.

In Christ "we recognise ideally what is highest and divinest in man," Edwards declares. However,

> The doctrine of the Logos, as eternal Man, may be stated in such a way that it becomes a dangerous error. But it is true and innocent (1) if it be distinguished from the theory of a eternal creation, which is pantheistic; (2) if the Divine Logos be preserved intact as existing actually within the Trinity; (3) if the eternal Man be understood only as an idea of what the Logos incarnate will be; (4) if care be taken not to destroy any element of humiliation or suffering in the new condition into which the Logos will enter through incarnation, or any element of a contingent character that may arise because of sin and the resulting gracious redemption.[65]

The Logos is active both as the second person of the Trinity, and as the Logos incarnate, the God-Man: "it is the same divine Person that occupies both positions. The whole personality of the Son became incarnate, and, at the same time, the whole personality of the Son continued to exist and act without incarnation, as sustainer of the universe."[66] The incarnation, Edwards continues, results from the initiative of the Logos, and "that initiative is an ethical act, a 'becoming poor' [2 Cor 8:9], based upon a change of metaphysical condition. The Apostle calls it a self-emptying, which is a word so extreme and emphatic that we must beware of making the fact that it is unique a reason for refining it away."[67] We should not go to Gess's extreme of supposing that the Logos divested himself of all divine attributes in becoming incarnate, nor did the Logos as incarnate inhibit Christ's humanity. It is by *kenosis* that Christ's humanity acts freely. Edwards concludes that "the God-Man was a Divine Person, who had a human as well as a Divine personality.... The human personality of the Incarnate Logos supplied what would otherwise have been lacking to the Son of God during the days of His flesh."[68] There was an evolution as his character was formed. As to the sinlessness of Christ, Edwards argues that the laying aside of Christ's metaphysical omnipotence did not imply the weakening of his moral omnipotence. We must

---

65. Ibid., 17–18.
66. Ibid., 108–9.
67. Ibid., 125. In n. 1 on p. 116 Edwards surmises that his father was the first to teach kenotic doctrine in Wales. He takes A. B. Bruce, Martensen and Gess to task on pp. 128–32.
68. Ibid., 148–49.

remember that "the *kenosis* was itself an act of moral omnipotence . . . and that the indwelling of the Spirit was enough to enable Christ to overcome any such possible weakening effects of His self-emptying."[69] Edwards concludes his lecture thus: Christ "was in idea from eternity God-Man. He is and will be to eternity actual God-Man."[70]

The response in Wales to Edwards's lecture was not altogether favourable, and controversy bubbled up in the religious magazines of the day, with Edwards's view of the subordination of the Son causing considerable disquiet in some quarters.[71] His reticence on the inspiration of Scripture caused similar concerns: "With Lewis Edwards and Principal David Charles Davies, the practical inerrancy of Scripture had been a postulate. . . . Without any theory on the subject, Thomas Charles Edwards broke thought this constraint. Thus it was that the very same thing made him a subject of anxious concern to conservative minds and a tower of refuge to the young."[72]

Sympathetic to a modified kenoticism, eager, like Edwards, to identify the Logos with the Son of God, and with a psychological thrust similar to that of Dykes, the Congregationalist[73] A. M. Fairbairn (1838–1912), the first principal of Mansfield College, Oxford, made the consciousness of Christ the pervading theme of his theology. Not, indeed, that his writings are ideologically or sentimentally ahistorical. On the contrary, he published his *Studies in the Life of Christ* in 1880; and in the Preface to his major work, *The Place of Christ in Modern Theology* (1893), he welcomed the fact that modern criticism "has placed constructive thought in a more advantageous position than it has ever before occupied in the history of the Christian Church . . . by making our knowledge more historical and real, and so bringing our thought face to face with fact."[74] Above all, the Christian theologian "can now stand face to face with the historical Christ, and conceive God as He conceived Him"[75] (two claims, the first of which seems with hindsight to be boldly optimistic

---

69. Ibid., 153.

70. Ibid., 154.

71. See J. M. Davies, "The Present-Day Theology of Wales," 38.

72. J. Puleston Jones, "Principal Thomas Charles Edwards," 372.

73. Formerly Evangelical Union of Scotland, by whose James Morison he was initially trained.

74. Fairbairn, *The Place of Christ in Modern Theology*, viii.

75. Ibid.

now that we are in the midst of the third—or is it the fourth?—quest of the historical Jesus; the second of which seems a little immodest). Fairbairn further announces that his interpretative standpoint will be "the consciousness of Jesus Christ, and this consciousness where it is clearest and most defined, in the belief as to God's Fatherhood and His own Sonship."[76] Why? Because "What was most distinctive of [Christ] was His consciousness of God, the kind of God He was conscious of, and the relation He sustained to Him. God was His Father; He was God's Son. What God was to Him He desired Him to be to all men; what He was to God all men ought to be . . . Men are God's sons; filial love is their primary duty, fraternal love their common and equal obligation."[77]

Fairbairn cautions us against speaking of the incarnation of God, for "Jesus Christ is neither God nor the Godhead incarnate, but He is the incarnate Son of God."[78] Some things were possible to the Son that were not possible to the Godhead, notably identification with human beings in the world. As Fairbairn elsewhere puts it, Christ's humanity "is of a character so universal that He can only be described as the Man, of a nature so human that He is to us as realized humanity."[79] To effect this identification, however "a supreme renunciation was necessary; He had to stoop from the form of God to the form of a servant."[80] In a word, there was a *kenosis*, a self-emptying in order to the assumption of the status of created Son. Thus,

> the Incarnation, while it was not of the whole Godhead, only of the Son, yet concerned the Godhead as a whole. And this carried with it an important consequence:– Physical attributes are essential to God, but ethical terms and relations to the Godhead.

---

76. Ibid. In view of the emphasis upon consciousness, it is somewhat surprising that his first student—and later his successor—at Mansfield College, W. B. Selbie (1862–1944) should say that Fairbairn's "metaphysical bent" was the main factor in causing him "to overlook the importance of psychology for the interpretation of religion." I also think that the description, "metaphysical bent" requires qualification, for to me it seems that Fairbairn excelled in the depiction of vistas, rather than in close metaphysical analysis or construction. See Selbie, *Congregationalism*, 174. See further, Franks, "The Theology of Andrew Martin Fairbairn," 140–50; Hinchliff, *God and History*, ch. 8.

77. Fairbairn, *The Place of Christ in Modern Theology*, 48. The Irish Presbyterian, Robert Watts, objected that human beings are not sons of God *qua* human. See further Sell, *Dissenting Thought*, 563–6 for this and other criticisms levelled by Watts.

78. Fairbairn, *The Place of Christ*, 475.

79. Fairbairn, *Studies in the Life of Christ*, 57.

80. Fairbairn, *The Place of Christ*, 476.

> In other words, the external attributes of God are omnipotence, omniscience, omnipresence; but the internal are truth and love. But the external are under the command of the internal; God acts as the Godhead is. The external alone might constitute a Creator, but not a Deity; the internal would make out of a Deity the Creator. Whatever, then, could be surrendered, the ethical attributes and qualities could not. . . . So conceived . . . the Incarnation may be described as the most illustrious example of the supremacy of God's moral over His physical attributes. . . .[81]

This would seem to suggest that in Fairbairn's view that in the incarnation the metaphysical attributes of divinity were, if not relinquished, at least held in abeyance, whereas the moral ones were not (though his description of metaphysical attributes as "external" seems problematic).

Be that as it may, Fairbairn, conscious that "as to Christ Himself as the incarnate Person little has been said," sums up his position on the person of Christ thus:

> The person, to be real, must be a unity, for two wills or two minds were two persons. But the natures, if He is to be qualified for His work, must be distinct. Only their integrity must not be developed into antagonism or incompatibility. The union within the Person is not a work of mere omnipotence, but expresses a real affinity, ethically mediated, though personally realized. And the natures in their union condition each other; because of their kinship a real and reciprocal *communicatio idiomatum* is possible. Hence by its union with the Deity the humanity is not superseded or diminished, but rather exercised, realized, and enlarged; and by its union with the humanity the Deity is not discharged or lessened, but rather actualized, personalized, made articulate. . . . And so He was, in a sense, a double incarnation—of manhood and Godhood. In Him humanity was realized before God and revealed to man; in Him God was revealed to man by Godhood being realized before him.[82]

The Congregationalist Walter Frederic Adeney (1849–1920)[83] was educated at New College, London, where, following a pastorate at Acton, London, he held the Chair of New Testament Exegesis, History, and Criticism (1889–1903). He then became Principal of Lancashire

---

81. Ibid., 476, 477.
82. Ibid., 478–79.
83. For whom, see SI, WTW; Sell, *Hinterland Theology*, ch. 9 and *passim*.

Independent College (1903–1913). Adeney was highly regarded by biblical scholars—he was the General Editor of the well-known *Century Bible Commentaries*, and he published widely on biblical themes at both the scholarly and the popular levels. Whilst holding his New College Chair he also taught Church History at Hackney College, and published volumes on the early Church, and a massive work on *The Greek and Eastern Churches* (1908). He contributed articles to the religious and daily press, and worked tirelessly for the Sunday School Union. As if all this were not enough, he published a number of works on then current theological trends, as in *A Century's Progress in Religious Life and Thought* (1901).[84]

When combined with his historical and theological interests, Adeney's expertise in New Testament studies found him particularly well placed to ponder Christological questions, and this he did in a faithful yet critical way, believing that biblical theology should precede systematic theology, for "Here we have the stream at its fountain-head."[85] In 1894 he published *The Theology of the New Testament*. A second edition followed in 1895, and the book was translated into Japanese. He reviews the New Testament witness on many doctrinal topics, but I here concentrate on Christology. He finds, for example, that "Jesus Christ, the personal, living Redeemer and Lord, was the centre of St. Paul's religious life and thought, and the inspiring subject of all his preaching."[86] Paul's thought is, however, marked by a certain subordinationism, but,

> It is not the Arian subordination of the creature who has a beginning in time. Christ is the Son, not a creature. . . . Still, Christ is in a degree subject to His Father. God *sent* His Son, and the Sender must be superior to the sent. . . . Moreover, St. Paul never distinguished between the human and the Divine in our Lord in such a way that anything like personality could be ascribed to the former exclusively. He thinks of one person throughout as the Son of God, who was "formed in fashion as a man", and afterwards exalted to the highest glory.[87]

---

84. For the views on various Christian doctrines of Nonconformist theologians to be mentioned from this point onwards, see Sell, *Nonconformist Theology*.

85. Adeney, *The Theology of the New Testament*, 2.

86. Ibid., 175.

87. Ibid., 182–83. Cf. Adeney, "The Trinity," 134.

Adeney finds the humanity and divinity of Christ held together all through the New Testament, notably in Hebrews, the Johannine writings and Revelation.

In 1909 Adeney returned to the theme in *The New Testament Doctrine of Christ*. He here adumbrates a view of the Virgin Birth that was becoming ever more widely received in his day by those Christians who, in the wake of modern biblical criticism, were neither myopic nor aggressively reductionist:

> There are theologians who regard the virgin birth of Jesus as an essential condition of His divinity.... There is nothing in the New Testament to warrant us in giving that central and all-important position to a belief which, by the very nature of the case, is and always was incapable of proof. None of the apostolic writers ... make any reference to it.... [T]he virgin birth appears as explaining the way in which One whose whole life was marked with superhuman traits came into the world.... [Even so] it is not by means of this mystery that we shall come to an understanding of the nature of Christ. There were Unitarians in the second century who accepted the virgin birth, but denied the divinity of Christ.[88]

Adeney is, we might say, on the side of cautious kenoticism. He contrasts kenoticism with the position of Irenaeus and Dorner, who thought in terms of a gradualism such that more and more of divinity was found in Jesus as he progressed through his earthly life. I italicize the operative words in Adeney's uncharacteristically elusive verdict on this suggestion: "*Possibly* some of us *may* think this view more acceptable than the Kenotic theory."[89] Be that as it may, regarding Philippians 2, Adeney reminds us that Paul was not writing a systematic treatise or drawing up a legal document, but writing a letter. He did not speculate upon what Christ's self-emptying might imply, and he certainly did not distinguish, as some later theologians have done (and as "we may well believe"), between retained moral attributes and abandoned metaphysical ones: "All that [Paul] suggests is the great general truth that Christ did not come in divine majesty, but came in a humble serving life; that His dazzling glory of divinity was not simply veiled, that it was abandoned."[90] The upshot is that Paul's writings

---

88. Adeney, *The New Testament Doctrine of Christ*, 2–4.
89. Adeney, *The Christian Conception of God*, 183.
90. Adeney, *The New Testament Doctrine of Christ*, 107.

do not justify the virtual tritheism of three actual equal persons to be found in some clauses of the Athanasian Creed—although it is repudiated by other clauses of the same creed—not the Sabellianism of Schleiermacher and Horace Bushnell, not the Swedenborgian simple identification of Jesus with God. But they teach that Jesus Christ is in a unique way God's own Son, who existed in the past eternity and appeared by a great act of condescension as a man; who now lives and reigns in heaven; who, while sharing the nature of God, is in some respects subordinate to his Father; who together with God is the source of redeeming grace; and who is to be trusted, served and worshipped as our Lord and Saviour.[91]

In Adeney's opinion, "One of the happiest products of recent theological thought has been its recovery of the genuine humanity of Jesus."[92] This should in no way prompt us to sit loose to Christ's divinity, for the humanity and the divinity are inseparable. As he elsewhere cautions, "Unitarianism—or the denial of the trinity in theology—always goes with humanitarianism, or the denial of the divinity of Christ in Christology."[93] Again, he distinguishes strongly between the incarnation of Christ and the inspiration of Christ as commended by those who espouse ahistorical immanentism. Above all, Adeney elevates the resurrection of Christ—"one of the best attested facts of history"—in support of Christ's divinity.[94]

Peter Taylor Forsyth was a graduate of Aberdeen University and an alumnus of Hackney College, London. He also sat under Albrecht Ritschl in Göttingen. He served five pastorates before becoming Principal of Hackney College, London, in 1901. Without question Forsyth was Nonconformity's twentieth-century theologian of the Cross *par excel-*

---

91. Ibid., 115. Elsewhere he is even more sternly opposed to some of the assertions in the Athanasian Creed: he find the idea of the equality of the Persons "simply unintelligible, a collection of phrases, each marvellously clear in itself; a triumph of concise statements; but in its totality hopelessly self-contradictory." See "The Trinity," 133. Adeney is less blunt concerning the Nicene Creed: "It is so metaphysical, so antique, and at the same time so crisp and clear and positive, where some of us must confess to great wonderment and a sense of profound mystery. But I am convinced that most of the theologies that deny its central ideas are further from the truth of God revealed to us by Christ." See *The Christian Conception of God*, 272–73.

92. Adeney, *The Christian Conception of God*, 156.

93. Adeney, "The Trinity," 126.

94. Adeney, *The Christian Conception of God*, 160.

lence. Not surprisingly, therefore, the Cross was never far from his mind even when he writing what some consider to be his greatest book, *The Person and Place of Jesus Christ* (1909).

Like others of his period, Forsyth adjusts himself to the Chalcedonian Formula, though his criticisms are more swingeing than most. His starting-point is that "If we ask *how* Eternal Godhead could make the actual condition of human nature His own, we must answer . . . that we do not know."[95] His main complaint, which he reiterates in a number of works, is that in the Formula the two natures of Christ are united miraculously, not morally: "The person was the resultant of the two natures rather than the agent of their union."[96]

> The Roman or the Chalcedonian type of doctrine begins with the Incarnation, beyond experience but believed on authority, and then it descends on the Atonement; instead of beginning with the Atonement, in a moral departure, and going on from that experience to the Incarnation, since God only could atone. But between this and the evangelical position there is sought a *via media* which claims to be both evangelical and catholic. . . . [It is] taken by those who are engrossed with the Person of Christ as the Son of God in Whom we mystically live, but who do not give a first and crucial place to the New Creation in the Cross as the source of our life and the sum and crown and key of all the Person was. Christ is our food rather than our new Creation.[97]

Consistently with this he writes, "The doctrine of the Incarnation did not create the Church; it grew up (very quickly) in the Church out of the doctrine of the cross which did create it—in so far as that can be said of any doctrine, and not rather of the act and power which the doctrine tries to state."[98] All of this notwithstanding, "for thought, for theological science, Incarnation is the logical *prius*. It is at the rational base of Atonement, of Redemption, which was God's offering up of Himself in Christ. But that is to say it was God's Act in Christ more than his presence. The metaphysic is one of ethic, not of being; it is of will rather than thought."[99]

95. Forsyth, *The Person and Place of Jesus Christ*, 320.
96. Ibid., 223.
97. Forsyth, *The Church and the Sacraments*, 197. Cf. Forsyth, *God the Holy Father*, 39–40; Forsyth, *The Preaching of Jesus and the Gospel of Christ*, 120–21.
98. Forsyth, *The Cruciality of the Cross*, 50 n.
99. Forsyth, *The Justification of God*, 90.

It must be granted that Forsyth does recognize the negative service performed by the Chalcedonian Formula in blocking off untoward exits into heresies; and we might also note that the Chalcedonian authors were, happily, on Forsyth's side in declining, in the absence of knowledge, to speculate upon the question of the "mechanics" of the union of the two natures in Christ. For all his qualms about the Formula, it must be said that Forsyth's own positive affirmations are not altogether unproblematic, and it may even be suggested that in places his antithetical style trips him up. Thus, for example, he suggests that the God-man union in Christ may be thought of as "the mutual involution of two personal movements raised to the whole scale of the human soul and the divine."[100] If we can grasp this we may also be prepared to agree that "Our Redeemer must save us by his difference from us," but when he immediately adds, "He saves us because he is God and not man"[101] it is difficult not to think that he is led by antithesis towards docetism. Our perplexity at this point need not prevent our agreement with Forsyth's declaration that "a Christ that differs from the rest of men only in saintly degree and not in redeeming kind is not the Christ of the New Testament nor of a Gospel Church."[102] We may further agree on the following points: in Christ "we have the whole of God, but not everything about God, the whole heart of God but not the whole range of God"[103] (an echo of Fairbairn here); that in humbling himself (*kenosis*) the pre-existent Christ realized himself (*plerosis*); and that "The mighty thing in Christ is his grace and not His constitution."[104]

We may permit Forsyth to sum up his understanding of the person of Christ thus:

> What we have in Christ . . . is more than the co-existence of two natures, or even their interpenetration. We have within this single increate person the mutual involution of the two personal acts or movements supreme in spiritual being, the one distinctive of man, the other distinctive of God; the one actively productive from the side of Eternal God, the other actively receptive

---

100. Forsyth, *The Person and Place of Jesus Christ*, 333. Cf. 307.
101. Ibid., 342.
102. Forsyth, *The Church, the Gospel and Society*, 99.
103. Forsyth, *The Person and Place of Jesus Christ*, 257.
104. Ibid., 10. For further discussion of matters touched upon here see Sell, *Testimony and Tradition*, chs. 7 and 8.

from the side of growing man . . . The two supreme movements of spiritual being, redemption and religion, are revealed as being so personal that they can take harmonious, complete, and final effect within one person, increate but corporeal.[105]

At the time of the Leicester Conference of 1877 Forsyth was inclined towards the liberal theological wing, and in that gathering his great friend, J. Baldwin Brown (1820–1884)[106] took a prominent part on the liberal side. In the mid-eighteen-nineties, however, Forsyth was, in his own words, "turned from a Christian to a believer, from a lover of love to an object of grace."[107] From that time onwards Forsyth directed his fire against two principle classes of theological liberals. First, there were those who held that Christian thought must be expressed under the rubric of the prevailing philosophy—at the time, post-Hegelian immanentism. In Forsyth's opinion, this intellectualist approach yields either a mystical or an aesthetic mysticism. Supremely in his sights in this connection is R. J. Campbell (1867–1956),[108] minister of London's prominent (Congregational) City Temple, whose book, *The New Theology* (1907), provoked responses in books, pamphlets, and articles. Campbell declares that his starting-point is "a re-emphasis of the Christian belief in the Divine immanence in the universe and mankind."[109] By "the Divine," or God, Campbell means "the one reality I cannot get away from, for, whatever else it may be, it is myself."[110] Through this door we reach a decidedly reductionist Christology. No other person could display divine love as Christ did; the Christhood of every person is a reality; and "What we succeed in doing some of the time Jesus did all the time; when all men are able to do it all the time the Atonement will have

---

105. Forsyth, *The Person and Place of Jesus Christ*, 343–44.

106. For whom, see ODNB.

107. Forsyth, *Positive Preaching and the Modern Mind*, 193. See R. M. Brown, "The 'Conversion' of P. T. Forsyth," 236–44.

108. For whom, see ODNB. He was educated at University College Nottingham and Christ Church College, Oxford.

109. Campbell, *The New Theology*, 4. Forsyth and the High Church Anglican, Charles Gore (1853–1932) were at one on *this* matter. See Gore's *The Old Religion and the New Theology*, 43–44. "Were there no alternative," Forsyth wryly remarked, "Bishop Gore's gospel would make one put up, for the time at least, with his view of the ministry." See *The Principle of Authority*, (1915), 224. For Peter Hinchliff on Campbell, see *God and History*, ch. 9. See also Sell, *Theology in Turmoil*, 35–36.

110. Ibid., 18.

The Proliferation of Nonconformist Christology 1891–1950

become complete, and love Divine shall be all in all."[111] Not surprisingly, many felt that this approach seriously neglected, if it did not altogether repudiate, the *historic* incarnation (and it is only fair to note that having originated in the Church of England Campbell returned there, recanted his earlier views, and became a Canon of Chichester).

But, secondly, Forsyth is not enamoured of the reductionist approach of those historical critics of the Bible who, by elevating their "scientific" method, seem to be dispensing with as much of the text—the virgin birth, miracles, and the like—as they can. Forsyth has no problem with reducing the burden of belief laid upon Christians: "the old orthodoxy laid on men's believing power more than it could carry."[112] What concerns him is that "too many are occupied in throwing over precious cargo; they are lightening the ship even of its fuel."[113] Having thus cleared the decks, liberals of this kind are left with an exemplary Christ, and to Forsyth such a Christ is grossly inadequate: "For positive theology Christ is the object of faith; for liberal He is but its first and greatest subject . . . It is really an infinite difference. For only one side can be true."[114] Again, "with the person of Jesus comes a new religion, of which he is the object, and not simply the subject as its saint or sage."[115]

Despite the best efforts of Forsyth and others, W. B. Selbie was nevertheless able to write, on the occasion of the centenary of the Congregational Union of England and Wales in 1931, that in Congregationalism:

> There have always been those who have taken a strongly humanitarian view of the Person of Jesus Christ, while others again have insisted on all the implications of the historic creeds. While the majority of Congregationalists have succeeded in steering a middle course between these two extremes, they have never put forward any orthodox statement of Christology as essential to Church membership.[116] . . . At the same time it must be admitted

---

111. Ibid., 174.
112. Forsyth, *Positive Preaching and the Modern Mind*, 84.
113. Forsyth, *The Principle of Authority*, 261.
114. Forsyth, *Positive Preaching and the Modern Mind*, 143.
115. Forsyth, *The Person and Place of Jesus Christ*, 114. See further, Sell, *Theology in Turmoil*, chs. 5, 6.

116. Quite so, and this as the expression of longstanding reluctance on the part of Dissenters to subscribe to the words of men, and to allow that the Spirit may have more light to shed on the Word (see the following note). However, it has been customary for those being received at church members to profess their faith in Jesus Christ as Lord and Saviour.

that both the life and witness of the Congregational churches have at times been impaired by the prevalence of what is known as a reduced Christology.... Their churches have become democratic clubs, and the great Head of the Church a leader and example rather than a living presence and the Lord of all good life. They have failed to realize that their very *raison d'être* as churches is bound up with the loftiest possible conception of their Church's Lord.[117]

Alfred Ernest Garvie (1861–1945)[118] was educated at Edinburgh and Glasgow Universities, and at Mansfield College, Oxford, under A. M. Fairbairn. Following Congregational pastorates at Macduff and Montrose, in 1903 he became first Professor at Hackney and New Colleges, London, and then Principal of New College (united with Hackney College in 1924), where he remained until retirement in 1933. He was a prolific author who encompassed biblical studies, systematic theology, practical theology, and ethics, and his contribution as a pioneer modern ecumenist was significant. In Christology he was both down-to-earth and, in the then fashionable manner, psychologically speculative.

Garvie observes that in the past discussions of the person of Christ have set out from the divinity, and have failed to take due account of the humanity, of Jesus: "The manhood has not been conceived in accordance with the historical evidence, but to secure consistency with an abstract idea of God which had no relevance to the facts."[119] He does not deny that there was a descent from Godhead to manhood, but this is not a fact known, but an inference drawn from facts that are known. He welcomes the modern emphasis upon the humanity of Jesus, interest in which can now be pursued without risking the charge of Unitarianism—

---

117. W. B. Selbie, "Congregationalism and the Great Christian Doctrines," 135–36. One excruciating example will suffice: T. Rhondda Williams (1860–1945) who trained at Carmarthen Presbyterian College and became known as "the silver-tongued Welshman," declared that "there is still more light and truth to break forth *through the souls of men.*" See his book, *The Working Faith of a Liberal Theologian*, xiii (my italics). One can imagine the seventeenth-century John Robinson turning in his grave at thus being turned onto his head; for in his farewell sermon to the Pilgrims of 1620 he was "very confident that the Lord hath more truth and light yet to break forth out of his holy Word." From the account of the sermon by Edward Winslow in *Hypocrisie Unmasked*, 1646.

118. For whom, see DHT, ODNB, SI, WTW.

119. Garvie, *The Christian Doctrine of the Godhead*, 32.

albeit in some "reactionary theological circles" there are those who continue to speak not only of Christ's divinity, but of his deity, "intending thereby to ascribe to Christ, even in His earthly life, the possession and exercise of divine attributes inconceivable in combination with a real humanity."[120] In his view the true divinity is manifested in the real humanity, "But to assert the real humanity is not to affirm that Jesus was an ordinary man, and that we cannot believe of Him what we cannot believe of men generally, or that we must deny as facts whatever in the Gospels goes beyond what might be said of an ordinary man. We must allow the fact to modify our conception of real humanity,"[121] and we must give due place to Jesus's moral experience, and to the development of his human consciousness.[122] In the former connection we must give full weight to the temptations of Jesus, while understanding that, while not impeccable, he was sinless. Indeed, "To surrender His sinlessness is to surrender entirely the only possible object of a faith, reverence, and devotion such as the Christian Church has believed itself justified in offering to Him."[123] In the latter connection, it is not appropriate to speak of the pre-existence of Jesus, because "it represents an eternal relation as priority in the temporal process."[124] We need not suppose that Jesus's human consciousness was in continuity with the Logos; indeed, "In a developing human consciousness such a continuity is inconceivable."[125] In the case of Jesus himself, "the intuition of His eternal relation to God (pre-existence) came to Him as He was exposed to the derision of His foes."[126]

Garvie gives careful attention to the terms of the Chalcedonian Formula, the most important of which, in his view, is *homoousion*. He explains that the term *ousia* is ambiguous:

> It may mean either an *entity*, the subject of attributes, or a class, species, or genus. . . . Athanasius did not mean that Christ was an individual divine being, belonging to the same class of divine beings as the Father. That would have been polytheism, and he

120. Ibid.
121. Ibid.
122. See, for example, Garvie, *Studies in the Inner Life of Jesus*, 85–86.
123. Garvie, *The Christian Doctrine of the Godhead*, 50.
124. Ibid., 56.
125. Ibid.
126. Ibid., 195. Cf. 56.

> was combating polytheism in resisting Arianism. Neither did he mean that Christ and God the Father were one individual subject, for that would have been a relapse into the modalism which had been condemned as a heresy... He meant neither separation from nor identity with the Father; but a relation of difference in unity.... Accordingly, neither of the meanings of the word *ousia* is carried over unchanged in his use of the word *homoousion*. The rival word, *homoiousion*, would serve no better, as it would not affirm even that Christ belonged to the divine class.[127]

The problem is that "Without intention the Creed of Chalcedon takes advantage of the ambiguity of the term in using it for Christ's relation to man as well as to God. Here it cannot mean identity of subject, it can mean only inclusion in one class ... Christ is not one with as He is with the Father, but like us as belonging to the same species."[128]

A similar ambiguity arises *vis à vis* the term "generation" as used in the Athanasian Creed. In attempting

> to preserve a parallelism between the relation to the Father and to man, the same term is used in two senses. Generation out of the substance of the Father expresses, in the intention of the creed, distinction, but not separation: generation out of the substance of the mother involves separation. The language itself does not guard the unity of the Father and the Son. Again, the term generation, even when qualified by eternal, does suggest separation of one individual from another. The term *substance* ... when applied to the mother, means something more distinctly physical than its proper meaning as applied to God can bear.[129]

The upshot is that

> we are asked, nay, even required, by the Athanasian Creed, on pain of damnation if we don't, to confess three persons in one substance in the Godhead, and two substances (modified usually to natures) in one person in Christ. If we use the word person in the same sense as regards the Godhead as we do as regards Christ, we deny the divine unity and fall into tritheism. If we use the word substance in the same sense as regards Christ as we do as regards the Godhead, we deny the unity of His person, and fall into dualism. The creeds maintain an unstable equilibrium

---

127. Ibid., 130–31.
128. Ibid., 131.
129. Ibid., 131–32.

between the differences and the unity alike in the Godhead and in Christ.[130]

In Garvie's opinion the Chalcedonian Formula clearly intended to give due weight to both the divinity and the humanity of Christ in one person (albeit without explaining how this could be), but "the tendency of piety was to let the humanity be absorbed in the divinity, so that in the thought of Leontius of Byzantium and John of Damascus we find that the human nature is deified whilst the divine remains unchanged. The history of the doctrine at large suggests to Garvie that

> If we start from the difference of the natures we can never reach the unity of their relation. If we start from the unity of their relation and then ask how the natures are to be conceived, if the unity of relation is to be intelligible, we may hope for a solution to the problem. We do not then begin with God as infinite and eternal, but with God as present and active in the world of time and space.... As we rise from facts to faith, our thought must pass from the immanent to the transcendent.[131]

Garvie does not hesitate to award marks to the divines of yesteryear (and as he does so we note his custom of drawing morals for the churches of his day):

> Athanasius was right when he insisted on the *homoousion* to assert the unity of Christ with God, the Cappadocian fathers were wrong when they allowed the term to be used with a tendency to tritheism. Much of the popular religious speech to-day, even in the pulpit, is tritheistic. There is a divine class to which Father, Son, and Holy Spirit belong, not a divine personal unity existing and manifested as Father, Son, and Holy Spirit.... What we have to do is to show how we can apprehend Christ as God, and the Holy Spirit as God, indicating the reasons for which the Church hitherto has often failed in this apprehension.[132]

The greatest failure of the Chalcedonian Formula and of the creeds was to deem it a "monstrous doctrine" that "the divine nature of the only begotten is passible," for it was then impossible to think intelligently of the incarnation:

---

130. Ibid., 135–36.
131. Ibid., 186.
132. Ibid., 468.

> It is Christ's own consciousness of God as Father which we must fully accept if we are to understand the reality of His Sonship, His unity with God. . . . If God be conceived as love, the Incarnation ceases to be a mystery, as piety has often felt it to be, or a puzzle, as theology has sometimes done its worst to make it; it becomes a necessity. Love must give itself and find itself in the giving. It is God who gives Himself and finds Himself in Christ, not an inferior deity, or a being partly divine; and the humanity, so far from being a limitation is the very condition of God's most fully giving and finding Himself.[133]

While trenchant in his criticism of earlier kenotic theories which drove a wedge between the metaphysical and moral attributes, Garvie nevertheless maintains that love's self-limitation, or *kenosis*, at the incarnation is also love's *plerosis*, "to use a couple of terms that it would be well to give a permanent place in our theological vocabulary."[134]

Robert Sleightholme Franks (1871-1964)[135] was yet another of Fairbairn's Mansfield students. Following a tutorship at Mansfield College, a pastorate at Prenton Road, Birkenhead, and a tutorship at Woodbrooke, Birmingham, the Quaker study centre, he served as Principal of Western College, Bristol, from 1910 to 1939.[136] Franks ranged widely over the history of Christian thought, not excluding medieval philosophy, and while his major books concern the work of Christ and the Trinity, his position on the person of Christ is by no means without interest. Franks emerges as an apostle of "the principle of free critical investigation",[137] and as an opponent both of fundamentalist ways of understanding the authority of the Bible, and of appeals to the supreme

---

133. Ibid., 469.

134. Ibid., 470. He does not at this point acknowledge a debt to his senior colleague, Forsyth. In Garvie's judgment, Forsyth's "absorption in the Cross made him insensitive and unresponsive to the truth and grace which [the ministry of Jesus] disclosed. He depreciated any attempt to understand the inner life of Jesus, especially His relation as Son to God as Father." See "Placarding the Cross: The Theology of P. T. Forsyth," 352. See also his review of Forsyth's Christology in *The Christian Certainty amid the Modern Perplexity*, 460–74. Garvie himself, more influenced by questions regarding personality that were being aired in increasingly fashionable psychological circles, sought to redress the balance in his *Studies in the Inner Life of Jesus*. For more of his Christological reflections see *The Christian Faith*, 129–51.

135. For whom, see DHT, ODNB, SI, WTW; Sell, *Hinterland Theology*, ch. 10 and *passim*.

136. See further, Sell, *Hinterland Theology*, ch. 10 and *passim*.

137. Franks, "The Person of Christ in the Light of Modern Scholarship," 27.

The Proliferation of Nonconformist Christology 1891–1950

authority of the Church in doctrinal matters. He finds that in the ancient creeds Christ's human nature is impersonal, because "the personality of the Incarnate Word is that of the Eternal Word who became incarnate."[138] Today, however, we distinguish between the Jesus of history and the Christ of faith,[139] and "the Christology of the creeds . . . is not consistent with what we know of the Jesus of History."[140] Matters come to a head in connection with the humanity of Christ. In Franks's view the credal idea that the Logos assumed an impersonal human nature leads logically to the conclusion espoused by fundamentalists that Jesus was omniscient and omnipotent—a position that comes to grief on the fact that Jesus's expectation of the imminent coming of the Kingdom was not fulfilled. To turn from ancient credal formulations is not, however, to deny the divinity of Christ, who is "Divine in the peculiar *quality* and *content* of His humanity, which distinguished it from the humanity of the rest of us sinful men."[141] If we wish to give due place to the Jesus of history and the Christ of faith we should return to the Church's most original confession, namely, that Jesus is the Messiah,

> the earthly representative of God and God's plenipotentiary in His Kingdom. The meaning of the Messiahship is developed in the two great complementary titles, *Son of God* and *Son of Man*. The first name ascribes to Jesus a unique and perfect filial consciousness. The second describes Him and the Ideal Man, Who is the Divinely appointed head of Humanity. . . . Jesus does not hide God from us, or come between us and God. We see God in Him. We know God as our Father, because His Fatherhood is reflected in the Sonship of Jesus, the Christ. . . . Jesus is Divine because we find God uniquely in Him.[142]

---

138. Ibid., 28.

139. This matter was assiduously pursued by many, notably by the lay Baptist classical scholar, T. R. Glover (1869–1943), in his book, *The Jesus of History*. To pursue the theme in detail would take us too far into New Testament scholarship and away from more strictly doctrinal questions concerning the person of Christ. I have lost count as to whether New Testament scholars are currently in their third of fourth quest of the historical Jesus.

140. Franks, "The Person of Christ in the Light of Modern Scholarship," 33.

141. Ibid., 34.

142. Ibid., 36, 37, 38.

As I have elsewhere cautioned, "Clearly, we are intended to understand the concluding sentence as referring to the ground of our testimony, not to the cause of Christ's divinity."[143]

On a further matter Franks causes puzzlement. He thinks that we can bring Origen's valuable ideas "into correspondence with that fundamental Christian experience which we are making the starting-point of our theology. Let us say that we depend upon God the Father Himself for our very being and all that may sustain and develop it. We depend upon God revealed in Jesus Christ for our ideal of personal character, and we depend upon the Holy Spirit for the power to realize that ideal."[144] On this I have remarked that "It is the Christological sentence here which seems to represent a significant attenuation: we depend upon Christ for far more than is here specified. . . . Except that, at least on occasion, Franks does not like the word, we might almost call it a "paradox" that one who builds so strongly upon the experiential should at times have had such a thin way of specifying that experience."[145]

David Miall Edwards (1873–1941)[146] was educated at Bala-Bangor Theological College, whence he proceeded to Mansfield College—one of a number of Welsh Nonconformists of the period to do so—where he, like Garvie, Franks, and others, sat under the tutelage of Fairbairn. After Congregational pastorates at Blaenau Ffestiniog and Plough Church, Brecon, Edwards became Professor of Christian Doctrine and Philosophy of Religion at the Congregational Memorial College, Brecon, where he served from 1910 to 1934. To a degree of which Forsyth would by no means have approved, his theological liberalism was governed by the principle of the divine immanence as propounded by those theologians who were influenced by post-Hegelian idealism.[147] As Densil Morgan has explained, for Edwards, "Christianity begins with salvation interpreted as the believer's experience of the divine; it advances through Christology interpreted as Jesus of Nazareth's sense of sonship in relation to the Father; and concludes with a doctrine of God as the ground

---

143. Sell, *Hinterland Theology*, 461.

144. Franks, "The Fullness of God, Father, Son and Holy Spirit," 554.

145. Sell, *Hinterland Theology*, 495.

146. For whom, see DTCBP, DWBO, SI, WTW.

147. For a brief account of Edwards's philosophical position, see Sell, *The Philosophy of Religion 1875–1980*, 30–31, 96–97.

of all existence."[148] "It is apparent", wrote Edwards, "that we are working on the assumption that experience is the key to doctrine."[149] How, then, does he understand Christ's person? Simply as revealing "the sanctity of human life in all its interests and relations, the sacredness of that human nature which was found competent to be the abode of God."[150] Language of this kind suggests that unlike his Fairbairn-educated contemporary, Garvie, Edwards was less technical in Christological matters, and more akin to the visionary side of their Principal. Jesus, he claims, thus far epitomizes religious experience at its peak, though he does not rule out the possibility that Jesus's high degree of religious experience may be exceeded in the future; and he certainly thinks that the humanity of Jesus exemplifies that to which all persons may aspire. At the same time, Edwards is rooted in the Jesus of history and, unlike Fairbairn whose thought stopped short of him, Edwards reveals his affinity with the thought of Ritschl. This emerges in his concise paper on "The Doctrine of the Person of Christ."

Edwards regards his paper as "tentative and experimental," and he is well aware that any reconstruction of the doctrine of the person of Christ requires "a reconstruction of the historical facts of our Lord's life and teaching in the light of modern scholarship."[151] This, he thinks, is essential if the doctrine is to be made intelligible to serious-minded contemporaries. In a manner characteristic of his time he concedes that we are nowadays less certain of our metaphysic than were our forebears in the faith, but we are much better equipped from the point of view of psychology: "if we cannot speak so confidently of the 'substance' or 'essence' of things as the Church Fathers could, such terms as 'experience', 'consciousness', 'personality', 'will', mean much more to us than they did to them."[152] We can thus no longer rest content with a "two natures" doctrine "because it presents to us a Person of whose consciousness no in-

148. D. Densil Morgan, "A Chapter in the History of Welsh Theology," in Sell, ed., *The Bible in Church, Academy and Culture*, 242.

149. Ibid., 242, where D. D. Morgan quotes Edwards's *Bannaur' Ffydd* [*Pinnacles of Faith*], xiii.

150. D. M. Edwards, "The Christian Philosophy of Life in its Relation to the Social Problem," in Gwilym Davies, ed., *Social Problems in Wales*, 46–47. The social problem was an abiding preoccupation of Edwards. See Pope, *Seeking God's Kingdom*, 38–55 and *passim*. In the present paragraph I am much indebted to Pope's exposition.

151. Edwards, "The Doctrine of the Person of Christ," 454.

152. Ibid., 455.

telligible psychological account it possible."[153] Whereas the early divines set out from the conviction that Jesus was God and then considered how he could also be man, our method must be more empirical and inductive. He agrees that Christ's humanity is representative and universal, but his individuality is not thereby submerged.

The human, historical Jesus "*has in a unique sense 'the religious value of God' for Christian experience.*"[154] Edwards is well aware the he here echoes Ritschl, but he does not wish to be taken as affirming that God is unknown except in Jesus, or that the construction of a metaphysic of ultimate reality is an impossibility. He regards Ritschl's view of Christian value judgments "as a kind of 'interim report' in theology, in the interval in which we are trying to get rid of the encumbrances of an obsolete metaphysic and have not yet found another to take its place."[155] Indeed, he grants that Ritschl's distinction between facts and values ultimately fails, "For to the extent that our value-judgments can stand the test of a thoroughgoing intellectual criticism, they are also existential judgments."[156] Furthermore, "the Ritschlian theory of values needs to be purged of its associations with agnostic empiricism and with the suspicion of subjectivity that attaches to it."[157]

The preliminaries over, Edwards proceeds to discuss the relation of Jesus Christ to God. Here he adverts to Christ's personal experience—in particular, to his consciousness of God. *Pace* the Virgin Birth, Christ's sonship is not a physical matter, nor yet a metaphysical one; it is primarily ethical and religious; and "When we assert that Christ is absolutely one with the Father in Will, we have reached a point beyond which no advance is possible, for Will (if we accept the theistic hypothesis) is the ultimate reality of things."[158] Edwards does not think that the doctrine of Christ's pre-existence is essential, for his consciousness is revealed to us only in the historical Jesus. However, "What *is* absolutely essential is that the values embodied in Christ be regarded as pre-existent in God

---

153. Ibid., 456.
154. Ibid., 458. His italics.
155. Ibid., 460.
156. Ibid., 461.
157. Ibid.
158. Ibid., 463.

and therefore as revealing the real and eternal nature of God, and not as first coming to be in the historical Jesus."[159]

Some reflections upon the relation of the divine to the human elements in the person of Jesus bring the paper to its conclusion. "His Person," declares Edwards, "leaves on us the impression of a perfectly organised spiritual unity in which there are no discordant or disparate elements."[160] The framers of the Chalcedonian Formula rightly insisted upon the unity of the one person, but they "also made it impossible for us to apprehend that unity intelligently"[161] because they thought of two disparate natures that could be united only by irrational omnipotence or a miracle. Edwards prefers the monothelite formula of one divine-human energy. In other words, whereas the classical dogma sets out from two disparate natures, he begins from *"the spiritual affinity between God and man."*[162]

Edwards is at pains to distinguish his theory from that of the kenotic theologians, and from pantheistic Christologies. The former accept the two nature doctrine that he rejects; the latter make Christ a phase or mode of God, whereas Edwards "conceives of His will as a distinct function not merged in the will of God though in the most perfect harmony with it."[163] He admits that his Christology is anthropocentric rather than theocentric, albeit "with the important qualification that the *anthropos* is not the antithesis of *theos*, but is in Christ the abode of God."[164] He thinks it quite irrelevant that some may see the view of Paul of Samosata in his position, or wonder whether he is heretical or orthodox: "The only question that matters is whether [a Christological theory] does justice to the fundamental facts concerning the Jesus of history and of Christian experience, and whether it commends itself to our reason as not inconsistent with the findings of modern science, psychology, ethics, and philosophy."[165] The difficulty in specifying the "fundamental facts," and the fact that the psychological approach is not always so favourable to religion as Edwards supposed, cannot undermine the feeling that

---

159. Ibid., 465.
160. Ibid.
161. Ibid.
162. Ibid., 466. His italics.
163. Ibid., 467.
164. Ibid.
165. Ibid.

here we have early twentieth-century theological liberalism at its most elegant, if also near its terminus.

Robert Pope compares the position of Edwards on the Trinity with that of his slightly older contemporary, Thomas Rees (1869–1926),[166] the Fairbairn student whom Edwards succeeded at Brecon when Rees became Principal at Bala-Bangor College. He writes: "Thomas Rees appeared to adopt the Modalist position of successive revelation while Miall Edwards tended to mirror Paul of Samosata's heresy that Christ grew progressively in divinity."[167] Pope underlines the point with a quotation from Edwards concerning Rees: "I used to chaff him with being a Sabellian and he would retort by calling me a Samosatene or even an Arian! I think we were orthodox in spirit and intention, though somewhat heterodox in form. But we knew that theological labels solve no problems, and that technical orthodoxy is a matter of little importance in comparison with the experience of God in Christ which the orthodoxies and even the heresies endeavoured with varying degrees of success or failure to safeguard."[168]

Lest it be thought that Mansfield College alone produced scholars of Christological competence, I turn to two who sat under P. T. Forsyth at Hackney College, and also benefited from Garvie's teaching at New College. The senior by one year is Sydney Cave (1883–1953).[169] Cave saw

---

166. For whom, see DWB, SI, WTW. He was educated at the Presbyterian College Carmarthen and at Mansfield College Oxford.

167. Pope, *Seeking God's Kingdom*, 94.

168. Ibid., 95, quoting D. M. Edwards, "Dr. Thomas Rees of Bangor," 184. Not surprisingly, Edwards's position failed to commend itself to his Congregational colleague, J. E. Daniel (1902–62), of Bala-Bangor College, whose Barthian sympathies and sharply analytical mind found a prominent target in Edwards. See D. D. Morgan, "A chapter in the history of Welsh theology," 242–44. Daniel gained first class degrees in Greats and Theology at Jesus College, Oxford. In the online *Dictionary of Welsh Biography Online* article on Edwards, H. D. Lewis says, more generously, of *Pinnacles of Faith*, that in it Edwards "strove, with much success, to provide a comprehensive interpretation of the main Christian doctrines in terms of modern life and culture." It would seem that John Morgan Jones (1873–1946), who was educated at the Memorial College, Brecon, and at Mansfield College under Fairbairn, was even more doctrinally reductionist than Rees and Edwards. Of him Robert Pope writes that "he was completely unconcerned with doctrinal niceties. Instead, he based his faith on Jesus of Nazareth as an ethical teacher and his ability to inspire both personal and social regeneration." See *Wales and the Social Gospel*, 70. Following a pastorate at Tabernacle, Aberdare, Jones became Professor of Church History at Bala-Bangor College in 1913, and Principal there from 1926–46. See DWBO, SI.

169. For whom, see DHT, ODNB, SI, WTW.

service in India under the auspices of the London Missionary Society from 1908 to 1918, was President of Cheshunt College, Cambridge, from 1920 to 1933, and in the latter year joined the staff of New College, London. He was Principal there in succession to Garvie from 1936 until his death in 1953. Cave was among those who pioneered the study of world religions, in which field he published a number of works. Among his other publications are textbooks on various Christian doctrines, which give evidence of deep learning worn lightly, and are characterized by considered judgments crisply expressed. Among these works are *The Doctrine of the Person of Christ* (1925) and a more comprehensive study, *The Doctrines of the Christian Faith* (1931).

As he works out his Christology, Cave, like Edwards, has at the back of his mind the fact that

> [m]uch of our difficulty is due to the lack of a recognised philosophy, congruent with Christian values, and so able to supply Christian theology with its necessary categories. And this difficulty is increased by the retention in theology of categories [such as "substance"] which have lost their meaning, and which belong to a philosophy pagan, and not Christian, in origin. If Christianity be, as we believe, a religion, not of "deification," but of personal communion, then only a philosophy which sees in personality the highest category can be adequate for its expression.[170]

Cave's review of the scriptural evidence leads him to conclude that the paradox of New Testament Christianity is that "It centres in One who lived on earth a truly human life and who yet so belonged to the life of God that faith in Him was faith in God."[171] In his view, "The modern attempts to depict Jesus as man alone, though the noblest of men, have not failed because of any lack of learning or insight on the part of their authors. They have failed, because His life cannot be thus explained."[172] Jesus is truly God and truly man, but to accept this is not to accept the two-nature doctrine. It came subsequently to be seen that the Chalcedonian Formula entailed that Jesus had two wills, and this both contradicts all that we know of human personality and there is no suggestion in the New Testament that Jesus willed now as God, now as

---

170. Cave, *The Doctrine of the Person of Christ*, 240.
171. Cave, *The Doctrines of the Christian Faith*, 207.
172. Ibid., 208.

man.[173] From Schleiermacher's criticism of traditional formulae we can learn the necessity of making our doctrines of Christ's person and of the Godhead cohere:

> [T]he Western orthodoxy of the so-called "Athanasian" Creed, in its doctrine of the Trinity, so emphasizes the unity of the Godhead, that the three "persons" denote little more than eternal aspects of the Godhead. Yet in its doctrine of Christ's person, the dominant view has seen in Him the Son of God incarnate. But how can an eternal "aspect" of the Godhead become incarnate? We have to make our choice. If we emphasize the "oneness" of the Godhead, then we must seek for an interpretation of Christ's person which is congruous with this emphasis; or if we hold a conception of Christ's person which involves the triality, the "three-ness", of the Godhead, then that triality must be candidly acknowledged. We must not profess a unitary view of the Godhead and at the same time give an interpretation of Christ's person impossible on that unitary view."[174]

In this we hear an echo of Garvie's teaching. Cave proceeds to say that while we may learn from Calvinism that there is a great gulf between the holy and the profane, we may nevertheless, against Calvinism, hold that "the finite is capable of receiving the infinite, or rather, for such spatial metaphors are here out of place, that in a life lived in human conditions God can be made manifest to men. And however unpopular Ritschlianism may at present be, we may learn from it to begin with the known and not the unknown, with the actual revelation of God in the historic Christ as received by the corporate experience of the Church, and not with *a priori* ideas of the nature of God's eternal and triune life."[175] But two major interpretations of this experience have been offered. According to the first Christ is the supremely God-filled man;[176] according to the latter he is the Son of God incarnate. Of the two, and despite the fact that it is not as easy to grasp, Cave affirms the latter view,

---

173. Cf. Cave, *The Doctrine of the Person of Christ*, 120.

174. Cave, *The Doctrines of the Christian Faith*, 209–10. Cf. Cave, *The Doctrine of the Person of Christ*, 233–34.

175. Cave, *The Doctrines of the Christian Faith*, 210.

176. On the view that Jesus is "only the greatest of all teachers" Cave comments, "we are not thus bound to give Him that surrender which is another name for Christian faith. His revelation of God might be imperfect, and, as we could not be sure just where that imperfection lay, we could excuse ourselves for our partial acceptance of His ethical and spiritual ideals." Cave, *The Doctrine of the Person of Christ*, 246.

The Proliferation of Nonconformist Christology 1891–1950

provided that the real humanity of Christ be not obscured. Thomasius expounded the theory of *kenosis* by way of expressing this humanity, but we must begin with what has been revealed, and not, as he did, with the divine attributes of the Trinity. It is in the incarnate Christ that we see that "in the limits of a human life the Divine has been revealed."[177] Moreover, Jesus "did not come to tell men that God was triune, but to reveal the greater wonder of God's holy love"[178]—the supreme emphasis of Cave's other teacher, Forsyth. A complete explanation of the mystery of Christ's person will for ever elude us, "and yet in His person we have the answer to our deepest need. Differences of interpretation are thus of subordinate importance. . . . [Christ] becomes to us less a problem to be explored than a Gospel to be known and preached."[179]

Cave is utterly persuaded that

> it is in the life and death of Jesus that we have the perfect revelation of the character of God. . . . If by faith in God, we mean faith in a God of holy love, then belief in the divinity of Christ is not a burdensome addition to this faith, but its one adequate support. We can be sure of God the Father only when we find in Christ the Son. . . . If, instead of speaking as if Christ were the unknown quantity which had to be resolved in terms of God and man, we begin with the historic Christ, and find in His life the revelation of the holy love of God, then the doctrine of His divinity becomes the concern of every believing man. . . . It is not just one of many Christian doctrines. It is the foundation of them all, and every Christian doctrine is an explication of its truth.[180]

The second of Forsyth's students to whom I wish to refer is Harry Francis Lovell Cocks (1894–1983),[181] who, after pastorates at Winchester, Hove, and Headingly Hill, Leeds, became Professor at Yorkshire United Independent College, Bradford (1932–1948), and then Principal of Western College, Bristol, from 1948 to 1962. Like the majority of Nonconformist theologians, Lovell Cocks has more to say concerning Christ's work than his person; he is firmly in the line of those who main-

---

177. Ibid., 214. Cf. *The Doctrine of the Person of Christ*, 234–39.
178. Cave, *The Doctrines of the Christian Faith*, 215.
179. Ibid., 216.
180. Cave, *The Doctrine of the Person of Christ*, 243, 244, 245.
181. For whom, see ODNB, SI, WTW; Sell, *Commemorations*, ch. 13.

tain that "What Christ is can only appear in what He has done for us."[182] Nevertheless, in a series of lectures on Christology he tackles Lessing's celebrated claim that "accidental truths of history can never become the proof of necessary truths of reason."[183] Far from agreeing that historical truths are accidental, Lovell Cocks holds that history "is the very sphere in which the reality of things is made manifest," and that "history can be declared accidental or contingent only under the presupposition that God is not to be found there"[184]—which would be to beg the question. From Garvie he learned his criticisms of the Chalcedonian Formula, and from Forsyth he received the caution that we must not allow impersonal categories such as being and substance to obscure the religious and ethical datum of the communion of Jesus with God.[185]

On his own account Lovell Cocks declares, "I believe it belongs to the essence of the Incarnation that the Son of God can become man only by becoming a man—the particular man Jesus of Nazareth, who lived at a particular time and in a particular place. Jesus is unique with the uniqueness of John Smith as well as with that uniqueness he shares with no other."[186] If we were to look at Jesus, as it were, from the outside as one of us, we might think of him as a religious genius or prophet. This, however, will not suffice, for there is more to Jesus than the sonship that belongs to every person as God's creature. Jesus is more than our example, there is an un-likeness to us which is signified by the term "only begotten". That is to say, "Though Christ is our brother, his sonship and ours are not of the same order. His is an absolute, ours a mediated sonship. He is for God only, we for God in him."[187] Again, "Jesus is human nature at its best, and human nature at its best is the most perfect

---

182. Cocks, untitled paper on Christology, 6. The Lovell Cocks papers (LCP) to which I refer are at Dr. Williams's Library, London.

183. Lessing, "On the Proof of the Spirit and of Power," in *Lessing's Theological Writings*, 53. See further, Sell, *Confessing and Commending the Faith*, 194–97.

184. Cocks, "Is Our Problem Historical?" LCP, 1.

185. Cocks, "P. T. Forsyth's *The Person and Place of Jesus Christ*," 194.

186. Cocks, "Reinterpretation of the fact of Christ," LCP, 2. Lovell Cocks delivered this paper at the Thirteenth Congregational Conference held in Oxford in July 1939. The theme was "The Person of Christ." According to the reporters, H. I. Frith and John Marsh, "Outstanding in the Conference, by general consent, was the finely evangelical paper by Principal Lovell Cocks." See Frith and Marsh, "The Person of Christ," 496. The compliment is the more impressive since, among other lectures, that of C. H. Dodd is described as "brilliant."

187. Cocks, "Reinterpretation of the fact of Christ," 5.

The Proliferation of Nonconformist Christology 1891–1950

revelation of God our minds can receive."[188] If we wish to know what being made in God's image, and being a child of God, means, this is where we must look. But we may not stop there for Jesus also reveals what human beings are not, namely, free from sin. He can do this because he himself is sinless, *the Man*. Thus, "it will not do to say that a sinless Jesus could not have been truly man, since all men have sinned. For on any showing sin, although part of the average man, is no part of the normal or typical man. It is definitely an intrusion in our humanity, a pathological element."[189]

What we have in Christ are parallel revelations of God and man. Not, indeed, that Lovell Cocks wishes to reinstate the two-nature doctrine of Christ's person:

> On the contrary, I suggest that the parallel revelations are one and the same act of divine grace. The man Jesus is the Son of God incarnate—the Son of God or Logos revealed within the forms and limitations of our finite, temporal experience. That is to say, Jesus Christ is not a man indwelt by the Spirit of God or human nature assumed by the Logos. He is the Son *as man*. This conception may be as full of heresies as a sponge of holes, but it does seem to give full value to the formula that the Word became flesh. . . . The difference between him and us is twofold. In the first place he is the uncreated image of God—the "express image" of the Father's person, the Alter Ego of the Father, the eternal Son. But he is this under the forms and limitations of our temporal life, i.e. as *the Man*. But in the second place he is the mediator of our sonship. He is not only the revelation of God's gracious purpose to call us into loving communion with Himself, but the earnest of its fulfilment. He is the only-begotten Son; we are sons by creation, i.e. by the adoption of grace. His sonship is an unbroken communion; our sonship is a distorted relation until he restores it. . . . His work of reconciliation not only re-establishes our filial relation to God but also our fraternal relations with one another.[190]

It is interesting to set alongside the Christologies of Franks, Cave and Lovell Cocks, that of Nathaniel Micklem (1888–1976), who was educated at New and Mansfield Colleges, Oxford, and at Marburg, and was Principal at Mansfield from 1932 to 1953. Micklem is convinced that we

---

188. Ibid.
189. Cocks, "The Manhood of Jesus," LCP, 1.
190. Cocks, "Reinterpretation of the Fact of Christ," 10–11.

cannot deny that Jesus was very God and very man without at the same time denying the Christian revelation. But if we affirm the revelation, what meaning can we give to it? It has been denied that Jesus was God, and that he was man. Jesus has been called divine because his character is God-*like*, while on the other hand it has been claimed that whereas all human beings have the capacity for the divine, Jesus, as the perfect man, has it to perfection. The latter view Micklem finds to be popular at the present time, and it is highly problematic. It

> misses the heart of the matter because it fails to give expression to the divine initiative and Condescension. . . . [T]his doctrine, that Jesus Christ as perfect man is thereby "divine", bears no relation to the dynamic and cataclysmic teaching of the Gospels concerning the advent of the supernatural Kingdom, of the Son of Man, and of the New Covenant "in His blood". Or, again, this view gives no place to the Christian conviction that we are not redeemed by man, even by the perfect man, but by the "mighty act" of God.[191]

Micklem thus rules out all adoptionist views, for Jesus was not a deified man; he considers that while kenotic theories do not deny the incarnation, they do not illuminate it; and he concedes that the Ritschlian idea that Christ has for us the value of God may be spiritually helpful, but it is not intellectually clear, for if it "does not mean that Christ is God, but rather that He is somehow different, it is precisely this difference that Christology must define."[192] Micklem is thus left with the two-nature doctrine. He then confesses to a radical change of mind. He used to reject the Christological affirmations of the Chalcedonian Formula because in the light of modern psychology he could not readily conceive of a human being as having two minds and two wills; and he also thought, with Herrmann, that the two-nature doctrine contradicted the Nicene faith that "we meet with God in the man Jesus Christ."[193] He has now come to the conclusion, however, that "Christ was truly man, but not that He was *a* man [the converse of Lovell Cocks's and others' conviction]; there was no man, Jesus of Nazareth, to whom was added divinity [with which Lovell Cocks and others agree]. Christ, we say, assumes human nature but not a human personality [which Lovell Cocks

---

191. Micklem, *What is the Faith?*, 152.
192. Ibid., 168.
193. Ibid., 155.

and others deny]."[194] Micklem's reasoning is that the Son of God did not assume fallen nature and become a sinner like ourselves, for otherwise he would have needed redemption, which he did not. Micklem reiterates his point that "He took our flesh, but not a human personality."[195] In the case of Jesus, "the hypostasis of human nature was not a fallen personality, but the eternal Word of God."[196] This, Micklem insists, safeguards the fact that in Christ we meet God; his is determinedly a Christology "from above."

What, then of the classical teaching that Christ had a divine and a human will? Micklem solves this problem to his own satisfaction by seeking to show that "will" here does not bear its normal meaning. He argues that in every living thing there is an urge to attain its end, "Therefore the Incarnate Word being made man shared in the human will. There must be conceived to be in God that which is analogous to the human will, but in His case it must be the will, not to become what He is not yet, but to be what He is. The Two Wills doctrine, therefore, follows naturally from the idea of Incarnation."[197] At the same time, "In our modern sense of the word "will," as indicating the expression of the whole personality, [Christ] had one will."[198] Micklem immediately adds that here we are confronted by "unfathomable mystery" and, no doubt, few would be inclined to disagree. For his part, he cannot at the present time see any satisfactory alternative to the two-natures doctrine, though he grants that this does not confirm the doctrine. He further admits that "the Christian 'story' can be told without any reference to 'two wills' or 'two minds' or 'two energies,' but it cannot be told without the assertion (in some form of words or other) that God 'was made man'—that is, that He assumed our nature without loss of His own."[199]

The sequence of broadly orthodox Christologies considered thus far in this chapter should not blind us to the fact that alternative views were also to hand. In 1933 the Congregational minister Thomas Wigley (1891–1961)[200] an alumnus of Cheshunt College, Cambridge,

194. Ibid.
195. Ibid., 160.
196. Ibid., 163.
197. Ibid., 165.
198. Ibid.
199. Ibid., 169.
200. For whom, see SI, WTW.

and minister at Blackheath from 1927 to 1961, founded the Union of Modern Freechurchmen. A number of Congregational and other ministers joined the Union. Their objective was a reasonable faith abreast of modern scholarship and alive to the issues of the day. Notwithstanding that Barth had already spoken, they were firmly in the tradition of the older liberal theology. On 9 February 1933 a letter, signed by Wigley and five others, appeared in *The Christian World* under the heading "A restatement of Christian thought." Nathaniel Micklem found neither the Trinity nor redemption in the letter, and took up his pen. His reply appeared in the same paper on March 9. Micklem was one of the so-called "Genevan" Congregationalists who were persuaded of the inadequacy of theological liberalism, and who sought a return to Congregationalism's Reformed roots, and a revival of the fullness of its worship. As I elsewhere put it, "Albert Peel, the non-'Genevan,' afterwards observed, in a statement skilfully blending puzzlement, humour and point-scoring, that 'most Congregationalists are not disposed to wander with the wizards on the Blackheath, nor do they propose to fall down and worship the dogmatic image which Nathaniel the Principal set up.'"[201]

Micklem himself pulled no punches when speaking on his own account:

> However we put it, we believe in Christ not merely as a Man amongst men, the best, the wises, the kindest of mankind, not merely as one who by His perfection shows us what God is like, but rather as one who, being Man, is also God Himself, so that the coming of Christ is the coming of God, that what He did for the redemption of mankind upon the Cross is what God alone can do, and that He is to us what God alone can be.
>
> This is the common Confession of the whole Church universal; this is the Word of God or Gospel which is the beginning and the end of the Reformers' faith; it is the fundamental *Credo* to which we bear witness, when we ask this question alone of those who would "join the Church"—"Do you believe in our Lord Jesus Christ?" Congregationalism, based upon faith in God made known to us in Jesus Christ our Saviour, and venturing

---

201. Sell, *Nonconformist Theology*, 99, quoting Albert Peel, *Inevitable Congregationalism*, 113. Peel (1887–1949), was educated at Leeds University and Yorkshire United Independent College, and did research at Oxford. He was, among other things, a considerable historian of early Dissent, the historian of the Congregational Union of England and Wales, founder and editor of *The Congregational Quarterly*. See ODNB, SI, WTW.

The Proliferation of Nonconformist Christology 1891–1950 165

its whole polity upon trust in the Holy Spirit present within the Church, might perhaps claim that more than any other polity it is an expression of the Trinitarian faith. Our boasted liberty is a freedom to express the Gospel, not to question it.[202]

Here is the "Genevan"-*cum*-classical accent; here also is the implication of Christology for polity; here, finally, is the dissuasive against the Modern Freechurchmen—a dissuasive more than hinted at on the next page, where Micklem writes, "We [Congregationalists] are not Rationalists nor Unitarians nor unbelievers, but, little as some of us are aware of it, Rationalism, Unitarianism and unbelief have eaten into our denomination."[203]

Elsewhere, some were decided Unitarians, and they continued to reflect on Jesus during the twentieth century, and this in a variety of ways. Fred Kenworthy (1909–1974),[204] Principal of his *alma* mater, Manchester Unitarian College from 1955 until his death had a high view of the life and teaching and death of Jesus: "The claim of Christianity to be a historical religion, and to have its foundation in the life, teaching and death of one who was supremely what he taught, is soundly based. . . . [T]he life, teaching and death of Jesus Christ remain for us an imperishable standard against which we in the West must always judge and measure our attainments."[205] Bruce Findlow (1922–1974),[206] an alumnus of Harris-Manchester College, of which he was Principal from 1975 to 1985, declared that Jesus "will always be important because he shows that possibility of living in the presence of God fulfilled in his life, and a way of living which promises the same fulfilment to us."[207] To the Welsh Unitarian, D. Jacob Davies (d. 1974, aged 57), "Jesus is a sure Leader and his teaching and example a firm handrail to the acceptable life."[208] From an undated and unpaginated pamphlet issued by the Unitarian Information Department entitled, *Unitarian Views of Jesus* we learn the following:

202. Micklem, *Congregationalism To-day*, 28–29.

203. Ibid., 29.

204. For whom, see UGAYB, 1975; Leonard Smith, ed., *Unitarian to the Core*, ch. 6. He also studied at Strasbourg University.

205. Kenworthy, "Jesus and the Gospel," 125–26.

206. For whom, see UGAYB, 1994–95.

207. Quoted by D. E. Davies, *They Thought for Themselves*, 27.

208. Ibid., 180, quoted from Davies's "Outline of a Declaration of Faith," 1961.

Jesus was the last of the great Hebrew/Jewish prophets.... The encouragement and inspiration provided by Jesus lies not only in his proclamation of what was deepest and truest in Judaism but in the embodiment of that faith in his own life and death. (Peter Godfrey)

[A]ll that is best in the faith of Israel is summed up in the life and teaching of that astonishing first century rabbi, Jesus of Nazareth, one of the greatest religious geniuses of all time, and the very embodiment of the Liberal Christian brand of Unitarianism to which I have always given my allegiance.... I find increasingly [Jesus] can become, in a symbolic or mythological sense, a true image of the divine—a window through which we can catch some authentic glimpse of that Reality which he was not afraid to think of in terms of a daring metaphor built out of the tender experience of human parenthood. (Arthur Long)[209]

Jesus to me means following his teaching as an example to live by, something to strive for. (Betty Smith)

While Jesus was, like all people, a unique individual, he was not other than human.... Jesus was, and is, the focus of a dynamic community dedicated to the remaking of humankind. (Cliff Reed)

I count [Jesus] amongst the greatest of the children of God: a beautiful poetic genius who lived out the wisdom he taught. ... The Way to Salvation, wholeness of person, is revealed in the paradigm of the life and teachings of Jesus. Its flower is the experience of union or nirvana, where we shed the delusions of time and separateness. (David Doel)

[D]espite the defects of his heritage, his example and his teachings, as presented through scripture and the Churches, have helped countless people to live better lives. Of course he is important to me—whoever he was. (Philip Silk).

Perhaps most striking of all is a paper by Tony Cross, sometime Principal of Harris-Manchester College, Oxford, entitled "Towards a Unitarian Christology." He writes,

---

209. Arthur Long served as Tutor at Principal of Manchester Unitarian College from 1959–74, and was Principal there from 1974 to 1988. See his four-part article, "The Human and the Divine."

> Having for centuries laboured to warn our fellow Christians against the distortions of "orthodox" Christology, Unitarians would indeed themselves be castaways if they abandoned the historical Jesus and floated upwards into cloudy existentialist regions with the mythical Christ. Only an historically rooted, psychologically plausible Jesus is adequate grounding for a Unitarian Christology.... As we Unitarians drift seemingly helplessly into the metaphysical vacuities of "Religious Humanism", perhaps we could pause for a while to consider whether Jesus Christ is really irrelevant. Certainly he speaks to my condition and I make no bones about it.[210]

It would seem that Jesus had quite a lot to say to Mr. Cross, for a note appended to his paper reads as follows: "Although I still hold many of the opinions advanced in this chapter... I am no longer a Unitarian—I am a member of the Roman Catholic Church."[211] What becomes clear from these Unitarian affirmations is that there is no strong desire to repudiate Jesus altogether, a concern stronger among some than others to heed the biblical record of his life and work, and an inclination on the part of some to place other religious leaders on a par with him. Over all the flavour is of Christological humanitarianism, with Jesus as the great example of, and for, living in the presence of the divine. To a Micklem this would have been a reductionist—indeed, an emaciated, Christology.

It is a bracing, not to say a jolting, experience to move from these Unitarian opinions to a defence of full-blooded Chalcedonianism. Aubrey Russell Vine (1900–1973),[212] who had studied under Garvie at New College, London, and then served pastorates at Greenwich and Reading, was Professor of Church History and New Testament at Yorkshire United Independent College (1951–1957), before becoming General Secretary of the Free Church Federal Council. He had already published a work on *The Nestorian Churches* (1937) when his London D.D. thesis was published in 1948 under the comprehensive and self-explanatory title, *An Approach to Christology: An Interpretation and Development of some Elements in the Metaphysic and Christology of Nestorius as a Way of Approach to an Orthodox Christology compatible with Modern Thought*. This is as intricate a Christology as any published by a Nonconformist in any century, an impression underscored by the

---

210. D. G. Wigmore-Beddowes, ed., *Concerning Jesus*, 82, 84.
211. Ibid., 85.
212. For whom, see URCYB 19743/4, SI.

fact that—as if classical technical terms were not enough—Vine does not hesitate to coin neologisms in order to explicate, or at least label, his complex ideas. Nicely combining accuracy with gentle humour, Lovell Cocks, a predecessor of Vine's at Yorkshire College, opened his review of Vine's book in characteristic style, thus:

> Father Tyrrell used to say that theological books were either gaseous, liquid, or solid. In the last category he included the works of his friend Von Hügel, as capable of being read only by archangels in retreat. If by this time the archangels have digested Von Hügel, this book of Dr. Vine's may be added to their list of required reading.... Here is metaphysical theology in the grand manner. Here is Christology *more geometrico*. For Dr. Vine is the tidiest of thinkers. In a closely wrought texture of argument he distinguishes and defines and refines until his readers expect that he will shortly formulate the doctrine of the Incarnation in a series of equations. For what he gives us is indeed the higher mathematics of theology.[213]

At issue is the hypostatic union of Godhood and manhood in Jesus. Cyril of Alexandria defended this union, but Nestorius could think only in terms of a union of *ousias*; but such a union would yield a new *ousia* such that the humanity and divinity of Christ would be obliterated. Hence Nestorius' conclusion that Jesus's union with the Word was voluntary, not metaphysical, and conditioned both by God's will and Jesus's obedience *qua* prophet. In the view of his Alexandrian opponents Nestorius had scuppered the incarnation by concluding to the juxtaposition of the human and the divine in Jesus, thereby denying their genuine union. Vine's thesis is that "Nestorius had stumbled upon a mode of approach to the Christological problem which had greater possibilities than could be realised by his methods; . . . more can be gained by delving into his thought processes than we shall ever gain by regarding him as no more than a mere foil to Cyril."[214]

To follow the details of Vine's argument is here impossible. His conclusions, however, are clearly and concisely stated, and I shall summarize them. He finds that Nestorius' metaphysic is capable of rectification in such a way as to support the terms of the Chalcedonian Formula. Thus, concerning "*Son*":

---

213. Cocks, review of A. R. Vine, *An Approach to Christology*, 24.
214. Vine, *An Approach to Christology*, 32.

The Proliferation of Nonconformist Christology 1891–1950 169

God the Word . . . was "Son" before the Incarnation in the sense both of mode of existence within the Godhead and of mode of harmony within the Godhead. God the Word possesses "sonship" after the Incarnation in the additional sense that He had allowed Himself to undergo a process of integration in utero Virginis as nearly as possible the kind that is undergone by ordinary human beings. . . . He also thus became "Son" of God in the sense of self-restricting emergence into this continuum from the totality of Godhead, as though He were being derived from that totality by emission or egression, though . . . there was no emission or egression in a separative sense—God the Word as Jesus Christ was still in the unbroken continuity and unity of the Godhead, was truly God and truly and indiscriminably of Godhead.[215]

"*Begotten of the Father.*" "Sonship and Fatherhood are both eternal and continuous within the Godhead, The Son is indeed begotten of the Father. But there never was when He was not, and there never is when He is not being begotten."[216]

"*Perfect in Godhead, truly God, consubstantial with the Father as to the Godhead.*" "Jesus Christ was perfect in Godhead, truly God, because He was God the Word and no other, and at any moment God the Word could have released Himself from all implication with humanity, could have escaped from the integration into which He had entered." [Theoretically, perhaps, but surely not if the divine salvific purpose were to be achieved. Here is a point at which the person of Christ is best understood through his work].

"*Perfect in manhood, truly man, consubstantial with us as to the manhood.*" "Jesus Christ was perfect in manhood because He had revealed, for the only time in the history of the world, what perfect manhood should be."[217]

"*Of a reasonable soul.*" Vine understands by this "the intermeshing of centrum vitae and spirit . . . [which] seems to be the only way of accounting for the difference between animal and human mental life and the only way of providing for at once the interrelation and distinction of space-temporal and exoschematizable qualities."[218] If Jesus did not have a "reasonable soul" we should land in a version of Apollinarianism.

215. Ibid., 403.
216. Ibid., 404.
217. Ibid., 405.
218. Ibid.

Positively, "Jesus Christ possessed a truly human spirit, God the Word particularizing Himself voluntarily thereto. . . . The true humanity of Jesus Christ arose from the ideally perfect human endohypostasis within God the Word."[219]

"*Body.*" "We do not doubt in any way the complete similarity of Jesus Christ's body to an ordinary human body."[220] ["Similarity"? Would it not have been safer to say that the physical body of Jesus was human in all respects?]

"*In (of) two natures.*" "Jesus Christ was by origin of two natures, the divine and the human, and He was during the period of the biotic integration in two natures, the divine and the human. As of the Godhead, God the Word was certainly in the divine nature, and nothing but His own will retained Him in the humanity of Jesus Christ. He could at any moment have disintermeshed Himself. There was no abrogation of His divine nature, no "kenosis" (in the modern understanding of that word); there was indeed anapausis of certain divine attributes, but they would have been instantly reactive at His will. As Jesus Christ, God the Word . . . was truly in human nature. God the Word was truly in the divine nature and truly in human nature: in both, not in a nature fused from both. Monophysitism is definitely excluded."[221]

"*Unconfusedly.*" "[T]he two natures were . . . not fused into one new or composite nature."[222]

"*Immutably.*" "The divine nature remained essentially unaffected by its linkage with human nature, and the human nature became by the linkage simply that which was its highest destiny to become, that which alone could make it perfect human nature."[223]

"*Indivisibly, inseparably.*" The union of the two natures in Jesus Christ "was a real union and not a mere juxtaposition."[224] [However, on p. 385 Vine declares that "omniawareness was actual in {Jesus Christ} in that He was Godhead, but was ignored. He actually knew everything, but He restricted Himself to the use of such knowledge as came to Him through the particularized focus." Robert Franks plunged in the knife at

219. Ibid., 406, 407.
220. Ibid., 407.
221. Ibid.
222. Ibid., 408.
223. Ibid.
224. Ibid., 409.

this point: "It seems to me that Dr. Vine's theory results in a far worse schism than anything he fears: he is constrained not merely to speak of accommodation, but actually also to recognize a double knowledge, Divine and human, in Jesus . . . What can this imply, but a schism of His personality with a vengeance?"[225] I find that on more than one occasion Vine takes the "high priori" line that might have been tempered by closer reference to the New Testament witness.[226]]

"*One prosôpon.*" "Jesus Christ was certainly one person . . . in the objective sense . . . for [he] was none other than God the Word, and during the duration of Jesus Christ God the Word manifested Himself in this continuum in no other way than as Jesus Christ."[227]

"*One hypostasis.*" "Jesus Christ was certainly one person . . . in the sense of discrete individuality, one personality in our sense of the term."[228]

In the light of the foregoing analysis Vine finds that he can accept the Chalcedonian Formula. Thus, despite the fiery darts of theological liberalism, the period of greatest Christological activity in modern Nonconformity ends on a classical, albeit at times a faintly discordant, note.[229]

225. Franks, Review of *An Approach to Christology*, 173.

226. To put it otherwise, it sometimes seems to me that Vine knows more about things divine than I think are knowable. An analogy might be with those present-day expounders of the Trinity who seem to project upon the Trinity those characteristics of the divine community that they deem appropriate, and then proceed to draw inferences therefrom regarding the right workings of the empirical Church.

227. A. R. Vine, *An Approach to Christology*, 410.

228. Ibid.

229. Readers may note that it is some time since I referred to a Methodist theologian. The facts are (1) In 1903 the Methodist George Jackson (1864–1945) was able to say that "Theology as yet has not come into its own among us." See *The Old Methodism and the New*, 56. (2) That during the twentieth century English and Welsh Methodists have not produced a substantial systematic work on the person of Christ as such. They have published more on the atonement, and Vincent Taylor's biblical studies of Christ's person and work are valuable. (3) That in William Strawson's comprehensive study of "Methodist Theology 1850–1950" there is not a section labelled "Christology." (4) Strawson himself acknowledges that "with one or two notable exceptions, Methodist theology is mainly of interest within the family of Methodism. Methodism has not in fact produced many outstanding scholars, and has depended upon other Churches for leadership in theological matters." See his chapter in Rupert Davies, A. Raymond George and Gordon Rupp, *A History of the Methodist Church in Great* Britain, III, 230. It would seem that the several theological disciplines flourish now here, now there. For example, the Methodists produced some fine New Testament scholars during the middle decades of the twentieth century: C. K. Barrett, W. F. Flemington, W. F. Howard,

C. L. Mitton and V. Taylor among them. In the same period the Baptists well nigh cornered the market in Nonconformist Old Testament experts: among them G. Henton Davies, A. R. Johnson, H. Wheeler Robinson, T. H. Robinson and H. H. Rowley. All of this granted, I nevertheless feel somewhat embarrassed to find that the bulk of those who wrote on the person of Christ during what I regard as the vintage period of modern Nonconformist activity in that field (1891–1950) belonged to my own Congregational/ United Reformed tradition. It is difficult to avoid the conclusion that this is at least in part owing to the presence in Congregational Colleges of expatriate Scots, who in their divinity schools breathed stronger systematic/dogmatic air than their English-educated contemporaries; and to the influence of their students. Thus, Fairbairn came to Airedale College in 1877 and proceeded to Mansfield College in 1886, where D. Miall Edwards, Robert Franks, A. E. Garvie, and Thomas Rees were among his students. Robert Mackintosh came to Lancashire Independent College in 1894, where E. J. Price and George Phillips (my teacher of the History of Doctrine) were among his students. P. T. Forsyth came to Hackney College in 1901, where he taught S. Cave and H. F. Lovell Cocks. A. E. Garvie taught at Hackney and New Colleges from 1903, and had Cave, Lovell Cocks and Aubrey Vine in his classes.

8

The Decline of Nonconformist Christological Endeavour 1950–2000

WHILE IT IS SOMETIMES possible to infer the Christological positions of Nonconformist scholars of the period 1950 to 2000 from the relatively few book-length studies they have produced of such authors as Barth, Tillich, Bonhoeffer, Moltmann, and others, as well as from some works on the Trinity and the atonement, the period is not noted for substantial systematic Nonconformist treatments specifically of the person of Christ. Certainly, as compared with the quantity of offerings from 1890 to 1950 one experiences a decided tailing off of Christological endeavour. This is, of course, explained in part by the numerical decline of mainline Nonconformity—a decline that has been marked since the end of World War II, one aspect of which is that there is no longer the critical mass of mainline Nonconformist systematicians that there was from 1890 to 1950. A corresponding decline has occurred in the number of denominational theological colleges, and hence in church-provided academic posts (though some of the newly-established universities have presented new opportunities of theological academic employment, some of them seized by Nonconformists). There are also indications that the attention of some systematicians has, to some extent, been diverted from the person of Christ to certain aspects of ecclesiology that have received fresh impetus owing to the challenges and concerns of the modern ecumenical movement, and the proliferation of local, national and international dialogues between members of the several Christian world communions.[1] Others have sought to respond to the need to provide theological foundations to Christian socio-ethical

---

1. See Sell, *Nonconformist Theology*, ch. 3.

discussion. The period is not, however, altogether devoid of concern with the person of Christ, and what follows is a miscellany of items of interest in chronological order.

Huw Parri Owen (1925–1995),[2] the Welsh Presbyterian who taught at Aberyswyth, Bangor, and King's College London, emerges as a staunch defender of the Chalcedonian Formula. He values the Formula because it maintains the full deity and humanity of Christ, and affirms the distinctness, inseparability and unity of the two natures in Christ. He understands "person" in an ontological, not a psychological sense; and he accuses those who complain that the Formula leaves the two natures juxtaposed rather than united of unfairly employing the *argumentum ex silentio*. He invokes Cyril of Alexandria in support of his claim that "The Chalcedonian Fathers were not required to pronounce on the relation between the two natures. However, if they had been asked they would certainly have said that the natures were interrelated in the closest possible ways, and in particular that Christ's human nature was continuously activated by his divine nature."[3] When considering the charge that the Formula endorses a Christology from above, rather than from below, Owen invokes the distinction between the order of being and the order of knowing:

> Within the order of being the Incarnation is by its very nature "from above"; . . . Within the order of knowing belief in the Incarnation both must be and can be "from below." It must be so in so far as we know Christ's deity only through his humanity. It can be so in so far as it is possible for someone to begin by believing in Jesus as merely a man and then to apprehend him as also divine. Yet even in the order of knowing a "Christology from above" finally takes precedence in so far as we can finally understand Jesus and his humanly perfect response to God only in terms of God's prior act in becoming man for our sake.

While Owen has no objection to attempted reformulations of Christological doctrine, "we must not expect that we can move outside the limits set by the Chalcedonian formula and the reflections of the Cappadocians."[4]

---

2. For whom, see Sell, *Convinced, Concise and Christian. The Thought of Huw Parri Owen*.

3. Owen, *Christian Theism*, 42. He was educated at Jesus College, Oxford.

4. Owen, *The Christian Knowledge of God*, 44; cf. ibid., 309.

In the middle decades of the twentieth century we find some corporate doctrinal reflection on the part of some Nonconformist denominations. The General Assembly of Unitarian and Free Christian Churches was constituted in 1928. In due course it appointed a commission, the product of which was a report entitled, *A Free Religious Faith* (1945). The commission, chaired by Raymond V. Holt (1885–1957)[5] of the Unitarian College, Manchester, comprised thirteen ministers. The report contained both agreed sections and some minority reports, none of them signed—an inducement to speculation in Unitarian circles of the day.

Three denominations gave thought to their statements of faith. In 1957 the Presbyterian Church of Wales published "A Short Confession of our Faith" which includes one sentence specifically on the person of Christ, thus: "We believe in Jesus Christ, [God's] Only Begotten Son, our Lord and Saviour."[6] In 1966 the National Assembly of Strict Baptist Pastors and Deacons published, *We Believe: Strict Baptist Affirmation of Faith 1966*. The two paragraphs of interest to us (which are in accord with, though not as detailed as, the comparable clauses in the Particular Baptist *Second London Confession* of 1677) are as follows:

> United in the one essence of God there are three Persons, the Father, the Son and the Holy Spirit. These are separate Persons since the Father is not the Son and not the Holy Spirit, and the Son is not the Holy Spirit. Each of these Persons possesses the entire divine essence undivided, and therefore the perfections which belong to God belong to each of the three Persons. . . .
> The nature of God's Covenant of Grace necessitates the office of a Mediator to bring about the reconciliation of sinful man with a holy God. This need God, in His wisdom and grace, has met in the Person of Jesus Christ, who, truly God, became also truly man, being born of the virgin Mary by the agency of the Holy Spirit whereby the two natures, Divine and human, are mystically joined in one glorious Person, called in the Scriptures the Mediator of the new covenant.[7]

The most substantial confessional product of the middle decades of the twentieth century was the *Declaration of Faith* (1967) of the

---

5. For whom, see UGAYB, 1956; L. Smith, ed., *Unitarian to the Core*, ch. 6.
6. Anon., *The Presbyterian Church of Wales Book of Order*, 118.
7. Anon., *We Believe*, 5, 11.

Congregational Church in England and Wales. This was truly a corporate undertaking in that draft documents were circulated to every local church, comments were received from churches, individuals and groups—and were heeded, and the result was to a high degree owned by the Church at large.[8] The main paragraph respecting the person of Christ is as follows:

> We believe in God the Son. We see Jesus first as a man who knows the will of God and does it with freedom and love exceeding what is expected in a servant and found only in a son. His role in the world is unique: the Spirit-anointed Servant-Lord depicted in the Old and New Testaments as Messiah or Christ. Manhood was uniquely perfected in the response of Jesus to God the Father. In him there is a sonship without defect or strain. This sonship, we believe, has a foundation in God other than the sonship by creation and adoption to which the rest of mankind may aspire. We affirm that it was the eternal Son of God who came to the world in Jesus of Nazareth. His words come home to us as the words of God himself. His deeds come home to us as the deeds of God himself. His redeeming compassion comes home to us as the redeeming compassion of God himself. All three, taken to their climax in the dying and resurrection of Jesus, convince us that we have found God not only through Jesus but in him. Exalted now to the majesty of divine power and love, he is our living Lord and Saviour Jesus Christ. We acknowledge him, so exalted, to be at all times God the Son eternally united with the Father in the one life of God.[9]

As might be expected in a declaration of faith, the affirmations are made (albeit without the employment of classical technical language), but such questions as how Christ can be both God and man are not addressed. The quoted paragraph is not, however, the only locus of references to Christ's person. Thus, for example, as to the divinity of Christ we learn that "God identifies himself with the human race, in the person of Jesus Christ." History has, "as its central event the life of God made man in Jesus of Nazareth." The humanity of Christ is no less emphasized. Jesus's "life was a perfect expression of human love to God and to his fellow-men. We believe that it was also a deed of grace done by God, yet

---

8. See further, Sell, *Nonconformist Theology in the Twentieth Century*, 84–89; Sell, *Dissenting Thought*, 54–56.

9. Anon., *A Declaration of Faith*, 20.

done in manhood common with our own." "In Jesus Christ we affirm the presence and action of God as well as the effort and achievement of a man [not of Micklem's 'man']. In transparent goodness Jesus achieved the full stature of manhood . . . ['achieved' is problematic: might it not have been safer to say that he exemplified it?]" "In our flesh [if this means 'sinful flesh' we have a further contrast with Micklem's view] and in our world Jesus gave to God the obedience man should be giving. Alone among men [Jesus] was guiltless of surrendering to temptation or of promoting evil." Jesus "kept his own manhood clear of sin"—thereby revealing true humanity.[10]

An occasion of corporate reflection on Christology was thrust upon the Baptist Union when in 1971 Michael Taylor (1936-), the Principal of Manchester Baptist College from 1969 to 1985, addressed the Union Assembly on the subject, "The Incarnate Presence: How much of a Man was Jesus Christ?" It was not his intention to repudiate the Nicene Creed, or to distress the faithful, but he said, "I think I must stop short of saying categorically, Jesus is God. . . . I do say with the New Testament that God was in Christ or that I encounter God in Jesus";[11] and he elucidated his Christology, according to which the difference between Jesus and ourselves was one of degree, not of kind. This caused considerable discussion in Baptist circles; the governors of Manchester College stood by their Principal, notwithstanding that a few churches withdrew support from the College and the number of student applications declined; but members of the Baptist Revival Fellowship were far from content, and some—Stephen Holmes speculates "perhaps several dozen"[12]—churches and ministers seceded from the Union. These were among the twentieth century's very few secessions sparked by Christological disagreement.

After the Baptist Christological bang came the constructive Christological whimper. As far as I have been able to discover the only book[13]

---

10. The quoted clauses in this paragraph are on the following pages of the *Declaration*: 12, 13, 16–17, 11, 14 (2). See further Tomes, ed., *Christian Confidence*.

11. Quoted by Shepherd, *The Making of a Northern Baptist College*, 232. See further, ibid., 228–34; and Randall, *The English Baptists of the Twentieth Century*, 366–82.

12. Holmes in Cross and Wood, eds, *Exploring Baptist Origins*, 125. In Shropshire, for example, the churches at Grosvenor Park/Upton, Chester, Bradley Road, Wrexham, left the Baptist Union. See Collis, *An Account of the Baptist Churches of Shropshire*, 36, 54, 112.

13. I do not feel it appropriate to discuss my own book of 2000, *Christ Our Saviour*, because, although considerable research lies behind it, it is different in character from the works here introduced. It is the second volume of a trilogy entitled, *Doctrine and*

by a Nonconformist on the person of Christ published between 1970 and 2000 is *Yesterday and Today: A Study of Continuities in Christology* (1983) by Colin Gunton (1941–2003).[14] A Congregationalist educated at Hertford and Mansfield Colleges, Oxford, who continued into the United Reformed Church, and spent his entire academic career at King's College, London, Gunton finds Christologies "from below" no less inadequate that Christologies "from above." Indeed he queries the way in which Christological stalls have thus been set out, thereby risking the removal of Jesus either from eternity or from history. He defends orthodox Christology, not by denying the varieties of Christological expression in the New Testament, but by arguing that underlying all is the witness to Jesus as human and divine. From the same source flows the degree of Christological continuity that Gunton discerns throughout the Christian ages. Furthermore, in the incarnation he finds both the basis of reconciliation (because who the Saviour is determines what he can savingly do) and the value of human life. "That the Word became flesh," he argues, "speaks volumes for the value to God, and therefore the eternal value and importance, of human life in its temporality. It forbids the mistreatment of any member of the human family to escape from human relationships in the various ways that have been, and are always being, invented by our fertility in evil."[15] In the wake of the intellectual, personal and ecclesial skirmishes that discussions of the person of Christ have fomented, or to which they have contributed, or for which they have been the pretext, or for which they have been blamed, during the Nonconformist centuries, it is pleasant to close on a refreshingly humane note.

Devotion—an attempt on my part to inject content into devotions and to enliven doctrine with warmth.

14. For whom, see ODNBO, SI, URCYB 2004, WTW.
15. Gunton, *Yesterday and Today*, 63.

9

Epilogue

IN THIS STUDY OF English and Welsh Nonconformist reflection upon the person of Christ, it has proved possible to discern orthodox views on the subject throughout the period from 1600 to 2000. The prominent themes discussed were the eternal generation of the Son; the relation of the Son to the Father; the humanity and divinity of Christ; kenotic theories; and modern reappraisals of the Chalcedonian Formula. It has also been shown that variations upon these themes have been many, and that some of them had ecclesial repercussions that helped to shape the map of English and Welsh Nonconformity as we have come to know it. It has become clear that ecclesial changes could occur in a variety of ways. In some cases the progression of a local church from orthodoxy to heterodoxy occurred without disruption. Sometimes the departure (voluntary or "encouraged"[1]) of the minister sufficed to forestall the continuation of doctrinal strife. In many cases, however, secessions occurred as either the orthodox or the heterodox departed, with a view to establishing causes to their own doctrinal liking. On occasion secessions were prompted by doctrinal considerations alone; in other cases the motives of the seceders were mixed.

We have also seen that the advent of modern biblical criticism, the influence of modern historical method, the turn to experience and the psychological interest prompted a number of authors to offer fresh appraisals of the person of Christ; and that for a variety of reasons publications by Nonconformists on Christ's person significantly declined in number between 1950 and 2000. Happily, a revival of interest in the

---

1. We shall never know how frequently in Dissenting history the will of the saints, if not necessarily of that of the Holy Spirit, prevailed because the saints kept their money at home.

person of Christ—and, indeed, in other doctrines—in Nonconformist circles cannot be ruled out. We recall that D. W. Simon's lament of 1891 over the doctrinal void that he perceived was followed almost at once by a considerable upsurge in doctrinal activity, to which, in the event, he himself contributed. In this connection it is encouraging to note the arrival on the scene since 2000, the terminus date of this study, of a number of younger Nonconformist systematic theologians, not all of them drawn from the ranks of the ministry. It is not impossible that some of these may offer fresh insights into the person of Christ. At the same time, and at the risk of sounding faithless, one cannot help wondering what it would take to galvanize some of our present-day Nonconformist ministers, ordinands, and church members with doctrinal enthusiasm.[2] That I am not the first to have reflected thus is confirmed by some remarks of Caleb Scott (1831–1919),[3] Professor at Lancashire Independent College from 1865, and President there from 1869 to 1902:

> I cannot understand how any man can occupy the position of a Congregational minister devoid of a conviction, which is becoming ever stronger, of the reality of the incarnation, the life, the death, the resurrection, of the Word who was with God, who was God, the eternal Son of the Great Father. If we are in doubt about any of these great truths, what is the message of good news we have to deliver to our fellow-men? What is the "glorious Gospel of the blessed God" which we have to preach to a world groaning under a load of sin and sorrow?[4]

What, indeed? I have always believed that the faithful preaching of the gospel of God's grace in Christ, rooted in clear, solid (but not stodgy), non-patronizing biblical exposition, is the right place to begin.[5]

---

2. In the late nineteenth and early twentieth centuries "Doctrine divides, service unites," and "Not doctrine, but life" were among the liberal slogans of the day. More than once of late I have been advised that "spirituality [construed a-doctrinally] is the new ecumenism." It sounds as jolly as, I fear, it is empty. P. T. Forsyth put the point more formally but not less bluntly: "A spirituality without positive, and even dogmatic, content is not Christianity." *The Person and Place of Jesus Christ*, 4. For "Some Reformed reflections on spirituality," see my *Enlightenment, Ecumenism, Evangel*, ch. 8.

3. For whom, see SI; *The Congregational Year Book*, 1920, 112–13. He was educated at Airedale College during the principalship of his father, Walter (1779–1858), for whom see SI.

4. Waddington quotes from a paper by Scott on "Christian Individualism," *Congregational History 1850 to 1880*, 407.

5. After I had attempted this three weeks ago in my capacity of visiting preacher,

Moreover, such proclamation should flow from deep gratitude for that very grace, and should not be undertaken as a ploy on the instrumentalist ground that perhaps the gospel is the only thing left than may reverse a disturbing statistical trend in church membership. I suspect that such a misbegotten policy would not be likely to succeed, nor would it deserve to do so.

It seems entirely likely that, while Christians and non-Christians alike may properly discuss what has been written about the person of Christ through the centuries, theologians who have, by the Spirit through the Word, become acquainted with the significance of Christ's saving work will be most likely to have fresh insights into his person, and least likely to perpetuate that doctrinal aridity from which Christological reflection has not always been immune.[6] This is because (to reiterate a running theme of the book) while temporally and logically the incarnation precedes the Cross, the question, "Who is Jesus Christ?" is most clamantly raised as the significance of his supremely salvific *act* at the Cross is brought home to individual experience by God the Holy Spirit. It seems to me that a competent view of Christ's person will be inspired by, and will take due account of, the realisation that God alone can save and Jesus Christ is Saviour; and that Proper Man alone can make the "full, perfect and sufficient" oblation to his Father on behalf of sinners.

As I muse upon the quantity and variety of writings on the person of Christ that I have here reviewed, one methodological consideration in particular occurs to me as I ponder the shape that Christology might take in the years to come. I find it interesting that during what I called the hey-day of modern reflection upon Christ's person A. E. Garvie was found carefully analysing the Chalcedonian Formula with a view to separating the Christological wheat from the metaphysical chaff, while at the same time Miall Edwards was regretting that there was not a prevailing modern metaphysic in terms of which Christological reflection might be expounded. It is a huge subject, and one that has preoccupied me for many years. To hazard a bald summary statement: on the one hand, metaphysics cannot be extruded from theological affirmations; on the other hand, while in the interests of communication it is well that

---

a faithful, longstanding, church member ruefully confided to me that "Nowadays we hardly ever hear a sermon that mentions God."

6. See further Sell, *Enlightenment, Ecumenism, Evangel*, ch. 13, entitled, "May we still glory in the Cross?"

theologians engage with prevailing thoughts forms, they should always remember that if the gospel is not to be attenuated, their role in relation to the language of prevailing "isms," is that of terminological anabaptist ("*logos*" qualified by "made flesh" is not synonymous with "*logos*"; the absolute of philosophical idealism is not synonymous with "the God and Father of our Lord Jesus Christ"); and that among their requisite skills is that of distinguishing between positive and negative analogies.[7]

This study of the ways in which Nonconformists have treated the person of Christ, and of ecclesial consequences that their thinking has sometimes had, has, as I cautioned at the outset, been abstractive in character; for Christology permeates all Christian doctrines and is itself illuminated by them. In conclusion I would remark that as well as implications for other doctrines, convictions concerning the person of Christ have ethical implications also. Sydney Cave was not wide of the mark when, alluding in part to the words of Jesus himself, he declared,

> It is useless to call Him Lord, Lord, unless we seek to do the things which He commanded; useless to proclaim Him very God and very man, unless we are trying to think after Him His thought of God and man, to trust the God whom we have seen in Him, and show, in deed as well as word, that we are judging of life, so far as we are able, by the values He reveals.[8]

---

[7] See further Sell, *Defending and Declaring the Faith*, ch. 4; Sell, *Philosophical Idealism and Christian Belief*; and, in relation to the quest of a viable starting-point for Christian apologetics, *Confessing and Commending the Faith*.

[8] Cave, *The Doctrine of the Person of Christ*, 247.

Bibliography

Abel, George. *A History of the Presbyterian Congregational United Reformed Church in Salisbury 1662-1978*. Typescript, 1978.
Adeney, Walter F. *A Century's Progress in Religious Life and Thought*. London: Clarke, 1901.
———. *The Christian Conception of God*. London: Law, 1909.
———. *The Greek and Eastern Churches*. Edinburgh: T. & T. Clark, 1908.
———. *The New Testament Doctrine of Christ*. London: Jack, 1909.
———. *The Theology of the New Testament*. London: Hodder and Stoughton, 1894. 2nd ed. 1895.
———. "The Trinity." In *Studies in Christian Evidences. Series I*. London: Kelly, n.d.
Anon. *A Declaration of Faith*. London: Congregational Church in England and Wales, 1967.
———. *A Fac-Simile Copy of the Original Covenant of the Protestant Dissenters Worshipping at Angel Street Congregational Church, Worcester*. Worcester, UK: Published by the church, 1888.
———. *An Authentick Account of Several Things Done and Agreed Upon by the Dissenting Ministers Lately Assembled at Salters-Hall*. London: Clark, 1719.
———. *An Evangelical Free Church Catechism for Use in Home and School*. In *Protestant Nonconformist Texts III: The Nineteenth Century*, edited by David Bebbington, et al, 52-58. Aldershot, UK: Ashgate, 2006.
———. "Baptist Churches in the Weald," *The Baptist Quarterly* 2 (1924-25) 374-84.
———. *The Castle Gate [Nottingham] Church Book*. Dr. Williams's Library, London. MS.201.33.8.
———. *Confession of Faith of the Calvinistic Methodists, or the Presbyterians of Wales*. 1823. E.T. Caernarfon, UK: The Bookroom, for the General Assembly. 1827.
———. "The Covenant and Confession of Faith of the Church of Christ Meeting in Blanket-Row, Kingston-upon-Hull, 1770." *Congregational Historical Society Transactions* 9 (1924-26) 249.
———. *A Free Religious Faith*. London: Unitarian and Free Christian General Assembly, 1945.
———. *Independency Accused by Nine Several Arguments: Written by a Godly and Learned Minister, to a Member of Mr. John Goodwin's Congregation, and Acquitted by Severall Replyes to the Said Arguments by a Member of the Same Church*. London: Overton, 1645.
———. Obituary of James Wells. *The Baptist Handbook* (1873) 209.
———. Obituary of John Gadsby. *The Earthen Vessel and Gospel Herald* 49 (1893) 341.
———. Obituary of Thomas Row. *The Gospel Herald* 37 = N.S. 5 (1868) 39.
———. Obituaries of William Palmer. *The Earthen Vessel* 29 (1873) 165-70; *The Gospel Herald* 4 (1873) 155-59.

———. *Observations on the Rev. James Manning's Sketch of the Life and Writings of the Rev. Micaijah Towgood*. London: Johnson, 1792.

———. *The Presbyterian Church of Wales Book of Order*. Caernarvon, UK: C. M. Book Agency, 1958.

———. *Reasonable Religion: A Series of Twelve Tracts for the Times*. London: British and Foreign Unitarian Association, 1893.

———. *A Short and Compendius Confession of Faith held by the Church of Christ Meeting at Aulcester in the County of Warwick who are Baptized by Immersion upon a Personal Profession of Faith*. 1711.

———. "A Sussex Lay Preacher Seeing Camp Meetings in America. John Burgess 1785–1819." *The Baptist Quarterly* 4 (1928–29) 317–26.

———. *We Believe: Strict Baptist Affirmation of Faith 1966*. Hadleigh, UK: Frost, 1966.

———. *The Westminster Confession*, 1647, numerous editions.

Argent, Alan. "Henry Allon at Union Chapel, Islington." In *The Congregational History Circle Magazine* 1.3 (1993) 12–31.

Atkinson, James. *Jesus Christ the Son, Essentially the Same with God the Father*. 1722.

———. *The Father, the Word (or Son), and the Holy Ghost, the One True God; Together with the Necessity of Believing it. Prov'd and Apply'd in Two Sermons, on I John v. 7, with a Dedication Plainly Showing the Unreasonableness, Impiety, and Dreadful Effects of Denying Christ to be the Most High God*. 1726.

Ball, John. *Some Remarks on a New Way of Preaching Propos'd in an Ordination Sermon Preach'd at Taunton*. London: Buckland, 1736.

Bassett, T. M. *The Welsh Baptists*. Swansea, UK: Ilston House, 1977.

Beard, Charles. "Jesus Christ." In *Reasonable Religion: A Series of Twelve Tracts for the Times*. London: British and Foreign Unitarian Association, 1893.

Belsham, Thomas. *A Calm Enquiry into the Scripture Doctrine Concerning the Person of Christ; Including a Brief Review of the Controversy between Dr. Horsley and Dr. Priestley, and a Summary of Various Opinions Entertained by Christians on this Subject*. London: Johnson, 1811.

———. *Letters upon Arianism, and Other Topics in Metaphysics and Theology, in Reply to the Lectures of the Rev. Benjamin Carpenter*. London: Johnson, 1808.

Bennett, T. *Laws against Nonconformity That Have Stood upon the Statute Book of England*. Grimsby: Roberts & Jackson, 1913.

Benson, George. *The Reasonableness of the Christian Religion as Delivered in the Scriptures*. 2 vols. London: Waugh, 1759.

Benson, Joseph [work begun by J. W. Fletcher]. *A Rational Vindication of the Catholic Faith: Being the First Part of a Vindication of Christ's Divinity; Inscribed to the Rev. Dr. Priestley*. London, 1790.

———. *Socinianism Unscriptural: Or the Prophets and Apostles Vindicated from the Charge of Holding the Doctrine of Christ's Mere Humanity: Being the Second Part of a Vindication of his Divinity; Inscribed to the Rev. Dr. Priestley*. London, 1790.

Bettenson, Henry, ed. *Documents of the Christian Church*. 2nd ed. London: Oxford University Press, 1963.

Biddle, John. *A Confession of Faith Touching the Holy Trinity, According to the Scripture*. London, 1648.

———. *XII Arguments Drawn out of Scripture: Wherein the Commonly-Received Opinion Touching the Deity of the Holy Spirit is Clearly and Fully Refuted*. London, 1647.

———. *A Twofold Catechism: The One Simply Called A Scripture Catechism; The Other, A Brief Scripture Catechism for Children*. London, 1654.

Bibliography

Bland, S. K. "Samuel Collins of Grundisburgh." *The Gospel Herald* 49 (1881) 257–60, 321–25, 353–56.

Blyth, Samuel, *The Good Soldier of Jesus Christ Characterized. In a Sermon Preached at Birmingham, March 31, and at Coseley, April 7. Occasioned by the Sudden and Much-Lamented Death of the Reverend Mr. S. Bourn, Who Died March 22, 1754, in the 66th Year of his Age.* London: Bourn, 1754.

Bolam, C. G. et al. *The English Presbyterians.* London: Allen & Unwin, 1968.

Bourn, Samuel the Younger. *An Address to Protestant Dissenters: or an Inquiry into the Ground of Their Attachment to the Assemblies Catechism; Whether they Act upon Bigotry or Reason.* London: Roberts, 1736.

———. *A Dialogue between a Baptist and a Churchman.* London: Roberts, 1739.

Bourn, Samuel, III. *Discourses on Various Subjects of Natural Religion and the Christian Revelation.* London: Griffiths, 1760.

Briggs, John H. Y. *The English Baptists of the Nineteenth Century.* Didcot, UK: The Baptist Historical Society, 1994.

Brine, John. *A Vindication of Some Truths of Natural and Revealed Religion: In Answer to the False Reasoning of Mr. James Foster.* London: Ward, 1746.

Brown, Raymond. *The English Baptists of the Eighteenth Century.* London: The Baptist Historical Society, 1986.

Brown, Stuart, ed. *Dictionary of Twentieth-Century British Philosophers.* London: Continuum, 2005.

Budden, H. D. *The Story of Marsh Street Congregational Church, Walthamstow.* Margate, UK: Bobby, 1923.

Burgess, W. H. *The Story of Dean Row Chapel, Wilmslow, Cheshire.* Hull, UK: Elsom, 1924.

Burnaby, John, *The Belief of Christendom: A Commentary on the Nicene Creed*, London: SPCK, 1959.

Bury, Arthur. *The Naked Gospel. Discovering I. What was the Gospel which Our Lord and His Apostles Preached. II. What Additions and Alterations Latter Ages Have Made In It. III. What Advantages and Damages have Thereupon Ensued. Part 1. Of Faith. By a True Son of the Church of England*, 1690.

Calamy, Edmund. *An Historical Account of My Own Life.* 2 vols. London: Colburn and Bentley, 1829.

Calvin, John, *Institutes of the Christian Religion.* 2 vols. Translated by Ford Lewis Battles, edited by J. T. McNeil. Philadelphia: Westminster, 1961.

Campbell, R. J. *The New Theology.* London: Chapman and Hall, 1907.

Caston, M. *Independency in Bristol.* London: Ward, 1860.

Cave, Sydney. *The Doctrine of the Person of Christ.* 1925. Reprint. London: Duckworth, 1952.

———. *The Doctrines of the Christian Faith.* 1931. Reprint. London: Independent, 1952.

Chambers, Ralph F. *The Strict Baptist Chapels of England IV: The Industrial Midlands.* London: Fauconberg, 1963.

Chandler, Samuel. *A Letter to the Rev. Mr. John Guyse.* London: Gray, 1730.

———. *The Motives and Obligations to Love and Good Works, Represented in a Sermon Preached at the Ordination of Mr Edward Harwood, of Bristol, and the Reverend Benjamin Davis of Marlborough . . . by the Rev. Mr. Thomas Amory. To Which is Annexed the Rev. Mr. Harwood's Confession of Faith, and a Charge Delivered by Samuel Chandler, D.D.* Bristol: Farley, 1765.

———. *A Second Letter to the Rev. Mr. John Guyse*. London: Gray, 1730.
Clarke, Adam. *The Holy Bible Containing the Old and New Testament . . . with a Commentary and Critical Notes*. 6 vols. 1810–24. Reprint. London: Ward, Lock, n.d.
Clarke, Samuel. *The Scripture Doctrine of the Trinity*. London: Knapton, 1712.
Cocks, H. F. Lovell. "Christology." Unpublished paper in the Lovell Cocks papers at Dr. Williams's Library, London.
———. "Is Our Problem historical?" Unpublished paper in the Lovell Cocks papers at Dr. Williams's Library, London.
———. "The Manhood of Jesus." Unpublished paper in the Lovell Cocks papers at Dr. Williams's Library, London.
———. "P. T. Forsyth's *The Person and Place of Jesus Christ*." *The Expository Times* 44 (1953) 195–98.
———. "Reinterpretation of the Fact of Christ." Unpublished paper in the Lovell Cocks papers at Dr. Williams's Library, London.
———. Review of A. R. Vine, *An Approach to Christology*. *The Presbyter* 7 (1949) 24–27.
Coleman, Thomas. *Memorials of the Independent Churches in Northamptonshire*. London: Snow, 1853.
Colligan, J. H. *The Arian Movement in England*. Manchester: Manchester University Press, 1913.
Collis, Michael J. *An Account of the Baptist Churches in Shropshire and the Surrounding Areas*. Newtown, UK: Shropshire Group of Baptist Churches, Heart of England Baptist Association, 2008.
Cross, Anthony R., and Nicholas J. Wood, eds. *Exploring Baptist Origins*. Oxford: Regent's Park College, 2010.
Cross, Tony. "Towards a Unitarian Christology." In *Concerning Jesus*, edited by D. G. Wigmore-Beddowes, London: Lindsey, 1975.
Dale, R. W. *Christian Doctrine: A Series of Discourses*. 1894. Reprint. London: Hodder and Stoughton, 1903.
———. *Essays and Addresses*. London: Hodder and Stoughton, 1899.
———. *Fellowship with Christ and Other Addresses delivered on Special Occasions*. London: Hodder and Stoughton, 1900.
———. *The Old Evangelicalism and the New*. London: Hodder and Stoughton, 1889.
Davies, D. Elwyn, *"They Thought for Themselves": A Brief Look at the Story of Unitarianism and the Liberal Tradition in Wales and beyond its Borders*. Llandysul, UK: Gomer, 1982.
Davies, Gwilym, ed. *Social Problems in Wales*. London: SCM, 1913.
Davies, J. M. "The Present-Day Theology of Wales." In *Wales: To-day and Tomorrow*, edited by T. Stephens. Cardiff: Western Mail, 1907.
Davies, Rupert, et al., eds. *A History of the Methodist Church in Great Britain. III.* Peterborough, UK: Epworth, 1983.
Denney, James. *Studies in Theology*. London: Hodder and Stoughton, 1894.
Densham, W., and J. Ogle, *The Story of the Congregational Churches of Dorset*. Bridport, UK: Mate, 1899.
Deweese, Charles W. *Baptist Church Covenants*. Nashville, TN: Broadman, 1990.
Ditchfield, Grayson M. "Anti-Trinitarianism and Toleration in Late Eighteenth-Century British Politics: The Unitarian Petition of 1792." *The Journal of Ecclesiastical History* 2 (1991) 39–67.

Dodson, Joseph. *Moderation and Charity, Recommended in a Sermon Preach'd at Keswick, to the Associated Protestant Dissenting Ministers of Cumberland and Westmorland.* London: Matthews, 1720.
Drummond, James. *Via, Veritas, Vita: Lectures on Christianity in its Most Simple and Intelligible Form.* London: Williams and Norgate, 1894.
———. *Some Thoughts on Christology.* London: Green, 1902.
Dyer, George. *Memoirs of the Life and Writings of Robert Robinson.* London, 1796.
Dykes, J. Oswald. "The Person of Our Lord." *The Expository Times* 17 (1905–6) 7–10, 55–59, 103–7, 151–56.
Edwards, D. Miall. *Bannaur 'Ffydd [Pinnacles of Faith].* Wrexham, UK: Hughes, 1929.
———. "The Christian Philosophy of Life in its Relation to Social Problems." In *Social Problems in Wales*, edited by Gwilym Davies. London: SCM, 1913.
———. "The Doctrine of the Person of Christ." *The Hibbert Journal* 23 (1924–25) 454–67.
———. "Dr. Thomas Rees of Bangor." *Welsh Outlook* (1926) 184.
Edwards, Lewis. *The Doctrine of the Atonement.* London: Hodder and Stoughton, 1886.
Edwards, Maldwyn. "Adam Clarke the Man." *The London Quarterly and Holborn Review* (1964) 146–53.
Edwards, Thomas. *Gangraena.* London, 1646.
Edwards, Thomas Charles. *The God-Man.* London: Hodder and Stoughton, 1895.
Elliot, Ernest. *A History of Congregationalism in Shropshire.* Oswestry, UK: Woodhall, Minshall, 1898.
Emlyn, Thomas, *An Humble Enquiry into the Scripture Account of Jesus Christ: Or a Short Argument concerning His Deity and Glory, according to the Gospel.* London, 1702.
———. *A True Narrative of the Proceedings of the Dissenting Ministers of Dublin against Mr. Thomas Emlyn*, 1691.
———. *The Works of Mr. Thomas Emlyn.* 4th ed. London: Noon, 1846.
Evans, Caleb. *Christ Crucified; Or the Scripture Doctrine of the Atonement.* Bristol: Pine, 1789.
Evans, David. *The Proper Deity of our Lord Jesus Christ [Duwdod Priodol ein Harglwydd Iesu Grist]*, 1840.
Evans, G. E. *Midland Churches: A History of the Congregations on the Roll of the Midland Christian Union.* Dudley: Herald, 1899.
Fairbairn, A. M. *The Place of Christ in Modern Theology.* London: Hodder and Stoughton, 1893.
———. *Studies in the Life of Christ.* 11th ed. London: Hodder and Stoughton, 1899.
Forsyth, P. T. *The Church and the Sacraments.* 1917. London: Independent, 1953.
———. *The Church, the Gospel and Society.* London: Independent, 1962.
———. *The Cruciality of the Cross.* 1909. Reprint. London: Independent, 1948.
———. *God the Holy Father.* London: Independent, 1957.
———. *The Justification of God: Lectures for War-Time on a Christian Theodicy.* 1916. Reprint. London: Independent, 1953.
———. *The Person and Place of Jesus Christ.* 1909. Reprint. London: Independent, 1961.
———. *Positive Preaching and the Modern Mind.* 1907. Reprint. London: Independent, 1964.
———. *The Preaching of Jesus and the Gospel of Christ.* (Articles reprinted from *The Expositor*, 1915). Blackwood, South Australia: New Creation, 1987.
———. *The Principle of Authority.* 1915. Reprint. London: Independent, 1952.

Frankland, Richard. *Reflections on a Letter Writ by a Nameless Author to the Reverend Clergy of both Universities, and on his Bold Reflections on the Trinity*. London: Churchill, 1697.

Franks, Robert S. "The Fullness of God, Father, Son and Holy Spirit." *The Congregational Quarterly* 7 (1929) 549–56.

———. "The Person of Christ in the Light of Modern Scholarship." *The Congregational Quarterly* 10 (1932) 27–38.

———. "The Theology of Andrew Martin Fairbairn." *Transactions of the Congregational History Society* 13 (1939) 140–50.

———. Review of A. R. Vine, *An Approach to Christology*. *The Congregational Quarterly* 27 (1949) 172–74.

Frith, H. I., and John Marsh. "The Person of Christ." *The Congregational Quarterly* 4 (1939) 494–97.

Fuller, Andrew. *The Calvinistic and Socinian Systems Examined and Compared, as to their Moral Tendency*. Market Harborough, UK: Harrod, 1793.

———. Letter to William Carey of 2 May 1796. MSS.BMS Vol. 1, Angus Library, Regent's Park College, Oxford.

———. *Socinianism Indefensible on the Ground of its Moral Tendency*. London, 1797.

———. *The Works of Andrew Fuller*. 1841. Reprint with an introduction by Michael A. G. Haykin. Edinburgh: Banner of Truth, 2007.

G., W. B. Obituary of Matthew Anstis in *The Monthly Repository*, XVIII, December 1823, 731.

Garvie, A. E. *The Christian Certainty amid the Modern Perplexity*. London: Hodder and Stoughton, 1910.

———. *The Christian Doctrine of the Godhead*. London: Hodder and Stoughton. 1925.

———. *The Christian Faith*. London: Duckworth, 1936.

———. "Placarding the Cross: The Theology of P. T. Forsyth." *The Congregational Quarterly* 21 (1943) 343–52.

———. *Studies in the Inner Life of Jesus*. London: Hodder and Stoughton, 1907.

Gibson, Hugh. *A Brief History of Tockholes Congregational Chapel 1662–1962*. Privately printed, 1962.

Gill, John. *An Answer to the Birmingham Dialogue-Writer*. London, 1739.

———. *A Complete Body of Doctrinal and Practical Divinity: or A System of Evangelical Truths Deduced from the Sacred Scriptures*. 2 vols. 1767. Reprint. Grand Rapids: Baker, 1978.

Glover, T. R. *The Jesus of History*. London: SCM, 1917.

Gordon, Alexander. *Addresses Biographical and Historical*. London: Lindsey, 1922.

———. *Historical Account of Dob Lane Chapel, Failsworth*. Manchester: Rawson, 1904.

Gore, Charles. *The Old Religion and the New Theology*. London: Murray, 1907.

Gosden, J. H. *Memoir and Letters of James Kidwell Popham*. London: Farncombe, 1928.

Granger, James. *A Biographical History of England from Egbert the Great to the Revolution*. London: Nicholson, 1804.

Gray, Marshall N. G. *Presbyterianism in Kendal: A Historical Sketch*. Kendal, UK, 1908.

Green, Samuel G. "Deity and Humanity of Christ." In *The Ancient Faith in Modern Light: A Series of Essays*. Edinburgh: T. & T. Clark, 1897.

Grieve, A. J. "The Nineteenth Century." In *Congregationalism through the Centuries*. London: Independent, 1937.

Grove, Henry. *The Works of the Reverend and Learned Mr. Henry Grove, of Taunton Containing All the Sermons, Discourses, and Tracts Published in His Life-Time*. 6 vols. Reprint. Bristol: Thoemmes, 2000.

Gunton, Colin E. *Yesterday and Today: A Study of Continuities in Christology*. London: Darton, Longman and Todd, 1983.

Guyse, John. *Christ the Son of God the Great Subject of a Gospel Ministry*. 2nd ed. London, 1730.

Halley, Robert. *Lancashire: Its Puritanism and Nonconformity*. 2 vols. Manchester: Tubbs and Brook, 1869.

Hamilton, Barry W. "The 'Eternal Sonship' Controversy in Early British Methodism." *Wesleyan Theological Journal* 40 (2005) 220–38.

Harris, Joseph. *Bwyall Crist yng Nghoed Anghrist [Christ's Axe in Satan's Trees]*. Swansea, UK: Voss, 1804.

Hart, Trevor A., ed. *The Dictionary of Historical Theology*. Carlisle, UK: Paternoster, 2000.

Harwood, Edward. *A Sermon Occasioned by the Death of the Rev. John Taylor, D.D., Late of Norwich, Professor of Divinity and Morality in the Academy at Warrington, Lancashire: with Some Account of his Character and Writings*. London, 1761.

Hayden, Roger. *Continuity and Change: Evangelical Calvinism among Eighteenth-Century Baptist Ministers Trained at Bristol Academy, 1690–1791*. Milton under Wychwood, UK: Lynn (for the Baptist Historical Society), 2006.

Haykin, Michael A. G., ed. *"At the Pure Fountain of Thy Word": Andrew Fuller as an Apologist*. Carlisle, UK: Paternoster, 2004.

Henderson, A. R. *History of Castle Gate Congregational Church, Nottingham, 1655–1905*. London: James Clarke, 1905.

Henry, Matthew. *The Life of the Rev. Philip Henry, A.M.* 1698. Corrected and enlarged by J. B. Williams. Edinburgh: Banner of Truth, 1974.

Herford, R. Travers. *Memorials of Stand Chapel*. Prestwich, UK: Allen, 1893.

Herford, R. Travers, and E. D. Priestley Evans, eds. *Historical Sketch of the North and East Lancashire Unitarian Mission and its Affiliated Churches 1859–1909*. Bury, UK: Fletcher and Speight, 1909.

Hetherington, H. J. W. *The Life and Letters of Sir Henry Jones*. London: Hodder and Stoughton, 1924.

Hinchliff, Peter. *God and History: Aspects of British Theology 1875–1914*. Oxford: Clarendon, 1992.

Holmes, Stephen R. "The Dangers of Just Reading the Bible: Orthodoxy and Christology." In *Exploring Baptist Origins*, edited by A. R. Cross and N. J. Wood, 123–37. Oxford: Regent's Park College, 2010.

Hopkins, Mark. *Nonconformity's Romantic Generation: Evangelical and Liberal Theologies in Victorian England*. Milton Keynes, UK: Paternoster, 2004.

Horsey, John. *Lectures to Young Persons on the Intellectual and Moral Powers of Man; the Existence, Character and Government of God; and the Evidences of Christianity*. London: Leigh, 1828.

Hunsworth, George. *Baxter's Nonconformist Descendants; or Memorials of the Old Meeting Congregational Church Kidderminster*. Kidderminster, UK: Parry, 1874.

Inglis, John. *Reminiscences of the United Presbyterian Church of Kendal for One Hundred Years*. Kendal, UK, 1865.

Jackson, George. *The Old Methodism and the New*. London: Hodder and Stoughton, 1903.

James, T. S. *The History of the Litigation and Legislation respecting Presbyterian Chapels and Charities in England and Ireland between 1816 and 1849*. London: Adams, 1867.

Jones, J. Puleston. "Principal Thomas Charles Edwards, M.A., D.D." In *Welsh Religious Leaders in the Victorian Era*, edited by J. Vyrnwy Morgan. London: Nisbet, 1905.

Jones, R. Tudur. *Congregationalism in Wales*. Edited by Robert Pope. Cardiff: University of Wales Press, 2004.

Jordan, E. K. H. *Free Church Unity: History of the Free Church Council Movement 1896–1941*, London: Lutterworth, 1956.

Kensett, Emily. *History of the Free Christian Church Horsham from 1721 to 1921*. Horsham, UK: Free Christian Church Public Library, 1921.

Kentish, John. *The Moral Tendency of Genuine Christian Doctrine*. 2nd ed. London: Johnson, 1798.

Kenworthy, Fred. "Jesus and the Gospel." In *Essays in Unitarian Theology*, edited by Kenneth Twinn, London: Lindsey, 1959.

Knowles, John. *An Answer to Mr. Ferguson's Book, Intituled Justification Onely upon a Satisfaction*. Printed for J.J., 1668.

Knox, R. Buick. *Voices from the Past. History of the English Conference of the Presbyterian Church of Wales 1889–1938*. Llandyssul, UK: Gomer, 1969.

Lessing, G. E. *Lessing's Theological Writings*. Translated by Henry Chadwick. Palo Alto, CA: Stanford University Press, 1957.

Lewis, Donald M, ed. *Dictionary of Evangelical Biography*. Oxford: Blackwell, 1995.

Lindsey, Theophilus. *An Examination of Mr. Robinson of Cambridge's Plea for the Divinity of Christ*. London: Johnson, 1785.

Livingstone, E. A., ed. *The Oxford Dictionary of the Christian Church*. 3rd ed. Oxford: Oxford University Press, 1997.

Lloyd, John Edward, and R. T. Jenkins, eds. *The Dictionary of Welsh Biography*. London: Honourable Society of Cymmrodorion, 1959.

Locke, Don. *A Fantasy of Reason: The Life and Thought of William Godwin*. London: Routledge & Kegan Paul, 1980.

Locke, John. *An Essay concerning Human Understanding*. Edited by Peter H. Nidditch. Oxford: Clarendon, 1975.

Long, Arthur. "The Human and the Divine." Series of four articles in *Unitarian Christian Herald* 26–29 (1977–78).

Lumpkin, William L. *Baptist Confessions of Faith*. Rev. ed. Valley Forge, PA: Judson, 1969.

Mackintosh, Robert. *Historic Theories of Atonement*. London: Hodder and Stoughton, 1920.

———. "The Genius of Congregationalism." In *Essays Congregational and Catholic*, edited by A. Peel, 103–25. London: Congregational Union of England and Wales, 1931.

McLachlan, H. *The Methodist Unitarian Movement*. Manchester: Manchester University Press, 1919.

———. *The Unitarian Movement in the Religious Life of England*. London: Allen & Unwin, 1934.

McLachlan, H. John. *Socinianism in Seventeenth-Century England*. Oxford: Oxford University Press, 1951.

Mander, W. J., and Alan P. F. Sell, eds, *Dictionary of Nineteenth-Century British Philosophers*. Bristol: Thoemmes, 2002.
Manning, James. *A Sketch of the Life and Writings of the Rev. Micaijah Towgood*. Exeter: Grigg, 1792; abbreviated in *The Protestant Dissenter's Magazine*, (October 1794) 385–93, (November 1794) 425–32.
Mansfield, Reginald. *Charlesworth Independent Chapel: Triple Jubilee Commemoration 1798-1948*. Privately printed, 1948.
Marriott, Ernest S. *A History of Gower Street Chapel, London, 1820-1917-1920*. London: Farncombe, 1921.
Martineau, James. *Endeavours after the Christian Life*. 10th ed. London: Longmans, Green, 1900.
———. *Essays, Reviews and Addresses*. 4 vols. London: Longmans, Green, 1890–91.
Matthew, Colin, and Brian Harrison (and continuing online, Lawrence Goldman) eds. *The Oxford Dictionary of National Biography*. Oxford: Oxford University Press, 2004.
Matthews, A. G., *The Congregational Churches of Staffordshire: With Some Account of the Puritans, Presbyterians, Baptists and Quakers in the County during the Seventeenth Century*. London: Congregational Union of England and Wales, 1924.
———, ed. *The Savoy Declaration of Faith and Order 1658*. London: Independent, 1959.
Miall, J. G. *Congregationalism in Yorkshire*. London: Snow, 1868.
Micklem, Nathaniel. *Congregationalism To-day*. London: Hodder and Stoughton, 1937.
———. *Ultimate Questions*. London: Geoffrey Bles, 1955.
———. *What is the Faith?* London: Hodder and Stoughton, 1936.
Morgan, D. Densil. "A Chapter in the History of Welsh Theology." In *The Bible in Church, Academy and Culture: Essays in Honour of John Tudno Williams*, edited by Alan P. F. Sell. Eugene, OR: Wipf & Stock, 2011.
Morgan, Vyrnwy. *The Life and Sayings of the late Kilsby Jones, Congregational Minister, Llandrindod*. London: Stock, 1896.
Morgan, William. *Memoirs of the Life of the Rev. Richard Price, D.D., F.R.S.* London. 1815.
Muirhead, J. H. *Reflections of a Journeyman in Philosophy on the Movements of Thought and Practice in his Time*. London: Allen & Unwin, 1942.
Murch, Jerom. *A History of the Presbyterian and General Baptist Churches of the West of England*. London: Hunter, 1835.
"Naphtali". "Pre-Existarian Errors." *The Earthen Vessel* 13 (1857) 268–70.
———. "Reply to Mr. Row of Little Gransden." *The Earthen Vessel* 11 (1855) 207–10.
Nettles, Tom J. "Christinaity Pure and Simple: Andrew Fuller's Contest with Socinianism." In *"At the Pure Fountain of Thy Word": Andrew Fuller as an Apologist*, edited by Michael A. G. Haykin, 139–73. Carlisle, UK: Paternoster, 2004.
Nicholson, Francis, and Ernest Axon. *The Older Nonconformity in Kendal*. Kendal, UK: Wilson, 1915.
Nightingale, Benjamin. *Lancashire Nonconformity*. 6 vols. in 3, Manchester: Heywood, 1890–93.
Nuttall, Geoffrey F., ed. *Calendar of the Correspondence of Philip Doddridge, D.D (1702-1751)*. London: HMSO, 1979.
Nye, Stephen. *A Brief History of the Unitarians, Called Also Socinians: In Four Letters Written to a Friend*. London, 1687.

Oliver, Robert. *History of the English Calvinistic Baptists 1771–1892*. Edinburgh: Banner of Truth, 2006.
Orton, Job. *Letters to Dissenting Ministers, and to Students for the Ministry, . . . To Which are Prefixed Memoirs of His Life. By S. Palmer*. 2 vols. London: Hurst, Rees and Orme, 1806.
Ottley, R. L. *The Doctrine of the Incarnation*. 2 vols. London: Methuen, 1896.
Owen, H. P. *The Christian Knowledge of God*. London: Athlone, 1969.
———. *Christian Theism*. Edinburgh: T. & T. Clark, 1984.
Owen, John. *The Works of John Owen*. Edited by W. H. Goold. 16 vols. 1850–53. Reprint. London: Banner of Truth, 1968.
Packer, Brian A. *The Unitarian Heritage in Kent*. London: London District and South Eastern Provincial Assembly of the Unitarian and Free Christian Churches, 1991.
Patchett, Benjamin. *A Short Inquiry into the Proper Qualification of Gospel Ministers: with Some Directions How We, Who Are Hearers, May Know Whether the Doctrines our Ministers Deliver from the Pulpit Are According to God's Mind and Will, or Not*. 1759.
Paul, S. F. *Historical Sketch of the Gospel Standard Baptists*. Harpenden, UK: Gospel Standard Baptist Trust, 1945.
Payne, George. *Lectures on Christian Theology*. Edited by Evan Davies. 2 vols. London: Snow, 1850.
Peach, W. Bernard, ed. *The Correspondence of Richard Price. III*. Durham, NC: Duke University Press, 1994.
Peel, Albert, ed. *Essays Congregational and Catholic*. London: Congregational Union of England and Wales, 1931.
———. *These Hundred Years: A History of the Congregational Union of England and Wales*. London: Congregational Union of England and Wales, 1931.
Peirce, James. *The Evil and Cure of Divisions*. Exeter: Brice, 1719.
———. *Plain Christianity Defended*. London: Noon, 1719.
Perry, J. C. "Unitarianism an Affirmative Faith." In *Reasonable Religion: A Series of Twelve Tracts for the Times*, no editor. London: British and Foreign Unitarian Association, 1893.
Philpot, J. C. "The Eternal Sonship of Christ." *The Gospel Standard* 10 (1844) 36–39.
———. *The True, Proper, and Eternal Sonship of the Lord Jesus Christ, the Only Begotten Son of God*. 1861. Reprint. Harpenden, UK: Gospel Standard Trust, 1926.
Pope, Robert. *Seeking God's Kingdom: The Nonconformist Social Gospel in Wales 1906–1939*. Cardiff: University of Wales Press, 1999.
Pope, W. B. *A Higher Catechism of Theology*. London: Woolmer, 1883.
———. *The Person of Christ: Dogmatic, Scriptural, Historical: The Fernley Lecture for 1871*. 2nd ed. London: Wesleyan Conference Office, 1875.
Popham, J. C. "An Opening Word." *The Gospel Standard* (1926) 5–19.
Powicke, F. J. "An Apology for the Nonconformist Arians of the Eighteenth Century." *Transactions of the Unitarian Historical Society* 1 (1817) 101–28.
———. *A History of the Cheshire County Union of Congregational Churches*. Manchester: Griffiths, 1907.
Price, Richard. *Sermons on the Christian Doctrine as Received by the Different Denominations*. Dublin: Exshaw, 1787.
Priestley, Joseph. *A Discourse on the Occasion of the Death of Dr. Price; Delivered at Hackney, on Sunday, May 1, 1791*. London: Johnson, 1791.

———. *The History of the Corruptions of Christianity*. 1782. Volume 5 of *The Theological and Miscellaneous Works of Joseph Priestley, LL.D., F.R.S.*, Edited by J. T. Rutt. Reprint. Bristol: Thoemmes, 1999..
———. *The Theological and Miscellaneous Works of Joseph Priestley, LL.D., F.R.S.* Edited by J. T. Rutt. 1817–32. Reprint. Bristol: Thoemmes, 1999.
Pyle, Andrew, ed. *Dictionary of Seventeenth-Century British Philosophers*. Bristol: Thoemmes, 2000.
Ramsbottom, B. A. *The History of the Gospel Standard Magazine 1835–1985*. Carshalton, UK: Gospel Standard Societies, 1985.
Randall, Ian M. *The English Baptists of the Twentieth Century*. Didcot, UK: The Baptist Historical Society, 2005.
Redford, George. *Declaration of the Faith, Church Order, and Discipline of the Congregational, or Independent Dissenters*. In *Protestant Nonconformist Texts III*, edited by David Bebbington, et al, 39–44. Aldershot, UK: Ashgate, 2006.
Rees, Thomas. *The Racovian Catechism, with Notes and Illustrations*. London: Longman, 1818.
Ridgley, Thomas. *A Body of Divinity*. 2 vols. 1731. New York: Carter, 1855.
———. *The Unreasonableness of the Charge of Imposition Exhibited against Several Dissenting Ministers In and About London*. London, 1719.
Rivers, Isabel, and David L. Wykes, eds. *Joseph Priestley: Scientist, Philosopher and Theologian*. Oxford: Oxford University Press, 2008.
Roberts, Brynley F., ed. *The Dictionary of Welsh Biography Online*. http://wbo.llgc.org.uk/en/index.html.
Roberts, H. P. "Nonconformist Academies in Wales (1662–1862)." *Transactions of the Honourable Society of Cymmrodorion* (1930) 1–98.
Robinson, Robert. *A Plea for the Divinity of Our Lord Jesus Christ: In a Pastoral Letter Addressed to a Congregation of Protestant Dissenters, at Cambridge*. Cambridge: Fletcher and Hodson, 1776.
———. *Miscellaneous Works, with a Memoir of His Life and Writings by B.F.* B. Flower]. 4 vols. Harlow, UK: Flower, 1807.
Robson, Douglas W. *Origins and History of Elder Yard Chapel, Chesterfield*. Chesterfield, UK, 1924.
Row, Thomas. "Remarks on a Second and Third Sermon by Mr. Philpot." *The Gospel Herald* 20 (1852) 9–11.
———. "The Soul and Sympathy of Christ." *The Earthen Vessel* 13 (1857) 268–70.
———. "True Freedom by the Son of God." *The Earthen Vessel* 11 (1855) 152–54.
Ruston, Alan. "English Approaches to Socinianism." In *Faustus Socinus and his Heritage*, edited by Lech Szczucki, 423–33. Kraków: Polska Akademia Umiejętnóski, 2005.
Selbie, W. B. *Congregationalism*. London: Methuen, 1927.
———. "Congregationalism and the Great Christian Doctrines." In *Essays Congregational and Catholic*, edited by A. Peel, London: Congregational Union of England and Wales, 1931.
Sell, Alan P. F. *Alfred Dye, Minister of the Gospel*. London: Fauconberg, 1974.
———. *Aspects of Christian Integrity*. 1990. Reprint. Eugene, OR: Wipf & Stock, 1998.
———. "Caleb Ashworth of Daventry: His Academy, Church and Students." Forthcoming.
———. *Christ Our Saviour*. Shippensburg, PA: Ragged Edge, 2000.

———. *Church Planting: A Study of Westmorland Nonconformity*. 1986. Reprint. Eugene, OR: Wipf & Stock, 1998.

———. *Commemorations: Studies in Christian Thought and History*. 1993. Reprint. Eugene, OR: Wipf & Stock.

———. *Confessing and Commending the Faith. Historic Witness and Apologetic Method*. 2002. Reprint. Eugene, OR: Wipf & Stock, 2008.

———. *Convinced, Concise and Christian: The Thought of Huw Parri Owen*. Eugene, OR: Pickwick, 2012.

———. *Defending and Declaring the Faith: Some Scottish Examples 1860–1920*. Exeter, UK: Paternoster, 1987.

———. *Dissenting Thought and the Life of the Churches: Studies in an English Tradition*. Lewiston, NY: Edwin Mellen, 1990.

———. *Enlightenment, Ecumenism, Evangel: Theological Themes and Thinkers 1550–2000*. Milton Keynes, UK: Paternoster, 2005.

———. *The Great Debate: Calvinism, Arminianism and Salvation*. 1983. Reprint. Eugene, OR: Wipf & Stock, 1998.

———. *Hinterland Theology: A Stimulus to Theological Construction*. Milton Keynes, UK: Paternoster, 2008.

———. *John Locke and the Eighteenth-Century Divines*. 1977. Reprint. Eugene, OR: Wipf & Stock, 2006.

———. *Nonconformist Theology in the Twentieth Century*. Milton Keynes, UK: Paternoster, 2006.

———. *Philosophical Idealism and Christian Belief*. 1995. Reprint. Eugene, OR: Wipf & Stock, 2006.

———. *Philosophy, Dissent and Nonconformity 1689–1920*. 2004. Reprint. Eugene, OR: Wipf & Stock, 2009.

———. *The Philosophy of Religion 1875–1980*. 1988. Reprint. Bristol: Thoemmes, 1996.

———. *Saints: Visible, Orderly and Catholic: The Congregational Idea of the Church*. Allison Park, PA: Pickwick, 1986.

———. *Testimony and Tradition: Studies in Reformed and Dissenting Thought*. Aldershot, UK: Ashgate, 2005.

———. *Theology in Turmoil: The Roots, Course and Significance of the Conservative-Liberal Debate in Modern Theology*. 1986. Reprint. Eugene, OR: Wipf & Stock, 1998.

———, ed. *The Bible in Church, Academy and Culture: Essays in Honour of John Tudno Williams*. Eugene, OR: Wipf & Stock, 2011.

Sellers, Ian. "The Old General Baptists, 1811–1915." *The Baptist Quarterly* 24 (1971) 30–41.

Sharman, Edward. *A Caution against Trinitarianism: Or, an Inquiry Whether Those Who Now Follow the Example of the Ancient Fathers, by Invoking God's Servant the Messiah as Supreme Deity, are the Only True Worshippers of the One Almighty God Revealed in the Bible, or Do Not Deserve the Name of Idolaters: In Five Letters Addressed to the Reverend Mr. David, of Wigston, Leicestershire, Containing Some Remarks upon His Late Publication, Stiled, a Caution against Socinianism. By a Northamptonshire Farmer*. Market Harborough, UK: Harrod, 1799.

———. *A Letter on the Doctrine of the Trinity, Addressed to the Baptist Society at Guilsborough, Northamptonshire*. London: Johnson, 1795.

———. *A Second Caution against Trinitarianism; or, An Inquiry Whether that System Has Not Some Tendency to Lead People unto Deism and Atheism, in a Letter Addressed to The Rev. Mr. Fuller, Kettering*. Market Harborough, UK: Harrod, 1800.

———. *A Second Letter on the Doctrine of the Trinity*. Market Harborough, UK: Harrod, 1796.

Shepherd, Peter. *The Making of a Northern Baptist College*. Manchester: Manchester Baptist College, 2004.

Sherlock, William. *A Vindication of the Doctrine of the Holy and Ever Blessed Trinity*. 2nd ed. London: Rogers, 1691.

Sibree, John, and M. Caston. *Independency in Warwickshire*. Coventry, UK: King, 1885.

Simon, D. W. "The Present Direction of Theological Thought in the Congregational Churches of Great Britain." In *The International Congregational Council, London, 1891. Authorised Record of Proceedings*. London: Clarke, 1891.

———. *Reconciliation by Incarnation: The Reconciliation of God and Man by the Incarnation of the Divine Word*. Edinburgh: T. & T. Clark, 1898.

R. Slate, *A Brief History of the Rise and Progress of the Lancashire Congregational Union; and of the Blackburn Independent Academy*. London: Hamilton, Adams, 1840.

Sloss, James. *A Vindication of the Answer to the Sixth Question in the Assembly's Shorter Catechism*. London: Woodfall, 1738.

Smith, John Pye. *The Scripture Testimony to the Messiah*. 3 vols. 2nd ed. London: Holdsworth, 1829.

Smith, Leonard, ed. *Unitarian to the Core: Unitarian College Manchester 1854–2004*. Manchester: Unitarian College, 2004.

Spears, R. *The Unitarian Handbook of Scriptural Illustrations & Expositions*. Newcastle-on-Tyne, UK: Lambert, 1861.

Spurgeon, C. H. *An All-Round Ministry*. 1900. Reprint. London: Banner of Truth, 1960.

Stennett, Joseph. *The Christian Strife for the Faith of the Gospel. A Sermon Preach'd at the Revd Mr. Hill's Meeting-Place, in Thames-Street, the 9th of February, 1738*. London: Ward, 1738.

Stevens, John. "The Man Christ Jesus is Personally God." *The Gospel Herald* 5 (1837) 158–59.

———. *A Scriptural Display of the Triune God and the Early Existence of Jesus's Human Soul*. London, 1813.

———. *Verses on the Sonship of Christ and the Pre-Existence of His Human Soul*. London, 1812.

Strawson, William. "Methodist theology 1850–1950." In *A History of the Methodist Church in Great Britain. III*, edited by R. Davies, et al. Peterborough, UK: Epworth, 1983.

Streiff, Patrick. *Reluctant Saint? A Theological Biography of Fletcher of Madeley*. Translated by G. W. S. Knowles. London: Epworth, 2001.

Strong, James. *The Suddenness of Christ's Coming Consider'd and Improv'd*. London, 1738.

Summers, W. H. *History of the Congregational Churches in the Berks, South Oxon and South Bucks Association*. London: Memorial Hall, 1905.

Tarrant, W. G. *The Story and Significance of the Unitarian Movement*. London: Green, 1910.

Taylor, Abraham. *The Scripture Doctrine of the Trinity Vindicated in Opposition to Mr. Watts's Scheme of One Divine Person and Two Divine Powers*. London: Roberts, 1726.

———. *The True Scripture-Doctrine of the Holy and Ever-Blessed Trinity, Stated and Defended, in Opposition to the Arian Scheme*. 2 vols, London: Roberts, 1727.

Taylor, John. *The Lord's Supper Explained upon Scripture Principles*. London: Waugh, 1756.

———. *A Narrative of Mr. Joseph Rawson's Case: or, an Account of Several Occurrences Relating to His Being Excluded from Communion with the Congregational Church in Nottingham. With a Prefatory Discourse in Defence of the Common rights of Christians*. 2nd ed. London: Fenner, 1742.

———. *A Scheme of Scripture Divinity*. London, 1762.

———. *The Scripture Account of Prayer*. London, 1761.

———. *The Scripture Doctrine of Original Sin*. London, 1740.

Taylor, John, and Clyde Binfield, eds. *Who They Were in the Reformed Churches of England and Wales, 1901–2000*. Donington, UK: Tyas, 2007.

Taylor, William. *Calling the Generations: A History of the Independent Protestant Dissenters of Billericay (1672–1972)*. Privately printed, 1972.

Thomas, D. O. *The Honest Mind. The Thought and Work of Richard Price*. Oxford: Clarendon, 1977.

Thomas, Joshua. *A History of the Baptist Association of Wales from the Year 1650, to the Year 1790*. London, 1795.

Timpson, Thomas. *Church History of Kent*. London: Ward, 1859.

Tomes, Roger F., ed. *Christian Confidence: Essays on A Declaration of Faith of the Congregational Church in England and Wales*. London: SPCK, 1970.

Tomkins, M. *The Case of Mr. Martin Tomkins, Being an Account of the Proceedings of the Dissenting Congregation At Stroke Newington, Upon Occasion of a Sermon Preach'd by him July 13, 1718*. London: Clark, 1719.

Toplady, A. M. *The Complete Works of Augustus M. Toplady, B.A. Late Vicar of Broad Hembury, Devon*. London: Cornish, 1869.

———. *Historic Proof of the Doctrinal Calvinism of the Church of England*. 2 vols. London, 1774.

Torbet, Robert G. *A History of the Baptists*. Valley Forge, PA: Judson, 1950.

Toulmin, Joshua. *Memoirs of the Rev. S. Bourn*. Birmingham, 1808.

———. *The Practical Efficacy of the Unitarian Doctrine Considered, in a Series of Letters to the Rev. Andrew Fuller*. 1796. Reprint. London: Johnson, 1801.

Turner, J. Horsfall. *Nonconformity in Idle*. Bradford: J. Brear, Saltaire: A. Holroyd, Brighouse: J. S. Jowett, 1896.

Turner, W. *The Warrington Academy*. Warrington, UK: Library and Museum Committee, 1957.

Twinn, Kenneth, ed. *Essays in Unitarian Theology*. London: Lindsey, 1959.

Tyerman, Luke. *The Life and Times of the Rev. John Wesley*. London: Hodder and Stoughton, 1872.

Urwick, William, ed. *Historical Sketches of Nonconformity in the County Palatine of Chester*. London: Kent, 1864.

———. *Nonconformity in Herts*. London: Hazel, Watson and Viney, 1884.

Various. *The Ancient Faith in Modern Light: A Series of Essays*. Edinburgh: T. & T. Clark, 1897.

———. *Congregationalism Through the Centuries*. London: Independent, 1937.

———. Notices following the Death of Charles W. Banks. *The Earthen Vessel* 42 (1886) 113–49; *The Earthen Vessel* 43 (1887) 183.

———. Notices following the Death of John Gadsby. *The Gospel Standard* (1893) 507–27.

———. *Reasonable Religion: A Series of Twelve Tracts for the Times.* London: British and Foreign Unitarian Association, 1893.

———. *Unitarian Views of Jesus.* London: Information Department, Unitarian Headquarters, n.d.

Vickers, John A., ed. *A Dictionary of Methodism in Britain and Ireland.* Peterborough, UK: Epworth, 2000.

Vidler, William. *God's Love to His Creatures Asserted and Vindicated.* London: Teulon, 1799.

———, ed. *The Universalist's Miscellany; or, Philanthropist's Museum. Intended Chiefly as an Antidote against the Antichristian Doctrine of Endless Misery.* 5 vols. London, 1797–1801.

Vine, Aubrey R. *An Approach to Christology: An Interpretation and Development of Some Elements in the Metaphysic and Christology of Nestorius as a Way of Approach to an Orthodox Christology Compatible with Modern Thought.* London: Independent, 1948.

———. *The Nestorian Churches.* London: Independent, 1937.

Waddington, John. *Congregational History, 1700–1800.* London: Longmans, Green, 1876.

———. *Congregational History, 1850 to 1880.* London: Longmans, Green, 1878.

Ward, Mrs. Humphry. *Unitarians and the Future.* London: Green, 1894.

Watson, Richard. *Remarks on the Eternal Sonship of Christ and Use of Reason in Matters of Revelation: In a Letter to a Friend.* London: Cordeaux, 1818.

———. *The Works of Richard Watson.* 12 vols. London: Mason, 1834–37.

Watson, Thomas. *A Body of Divinity.* 1692. Reprint. London: Banner of Truth, 1965.

Watts, Isaac, *The Ruin and Recovery of Mankind: Or, an Attempt to Vindicate the Scripture Account of These Great Events upon the Plain Principles of Reason.* London: Hett and Brackstone, 1740.

Wesley, John. *The Character of a Methodist.* 7th ed. Bristol: Farley, 1751.

———. *The Doctrine of Original Sin according to Scripture, Reason and Experience.* Bristol, 1757.

———. *The Letters of the Rev. John Wesley.* Edited by John Telford. 8 vols. London, 1931.

Whale, John S. *Christian Doctrine.* 1941. Reprint. London: Collins Fontana, 1957.

Whiston, William. *Memoirs of the Life and Writings of Mr. William Whiston.* London, 1749.

Whitehead, Thomas. *History of the Dales Congregational Churches.* Keighley: Feather, 1930.

Whitley, W. T. *The Baptists of London.* London: Kingsgate, 1928.

———. ed. *Minutes of the General Assembly of the General Baptist Churches in England.* London: Baptist Historical Society, 1909.

Wigmore-Beddowes, D. G., ed. *Concerning Jesus: A Symposium.* London: Lindsey, 1975.

Wiles, Maurice F. *Archetypal Heresy: Arianism through the Centuries.* Oxford: Clarendon, 1996.

Williams, G. Bernard. *Albany United Reformed Church Haverfordwest. 350th Anniversary 1638–1988.* Haverfordwest, UK: Published by the church, 1988.

Williams, J. B. *Memoir of the Life and Character of the Rev. Matthew Henry.* 1828. Reprint. Edinburgh: Banner of Truth, 1974.

Williams, T. Rhondda. *The Working Faith of a Liberal Theologian.* London: Williams and Norgate, 1914.

Willis, Alfred. *A History of Bridge Street Congregational Church, Walsall*. Walsall, UK, 1893.

Wilson, Walter. *The History and Antiquities of Dissenting Churches and Meeting-Houses in London, Westminster and Southwark*. 4 vols. London: Button, 1808–12.

Winslow, Edward. *Hypocrisie Unmasked*, 1646.

Wood, Arthur Skevington. *Revelation and Reason: Wesleyan Responses to Eighteenth-Century Rationalism*. Oakham, UK: The Wesley Fellowship, 1992.

Woodger, Phyllis L., and Jessie E. Hunter, *The High Chapel: The Story of Ravenstonedale Congregational Church*. Kendal: Wilson, 1962.

Wykes, David L. "Joseph Priestley, Minister and Teacher." In *Joseph Priestley: Scientist, Philosopher and Theologian*, edited by I. Rivers and D. L. Wykes, Oxford: Oxford University Press, 2008.

Yolton, John, et al., eds, *Dictionary of Eighteenth-Century British Philosophers*. Bristol: Thoemmes, 1999.

Index of Persons

Abel, George, 70
Adams, William, 52
Adeney, W. F., 138–41
Allen, John, 107–8
Allen, Richard, 19
Allon, Henry, 99–100
Allt, William, 94
Amory, Thomas, 69, 71
Anselm, 132
Anstis, Matthew, 46
Apollinarius, 5
Argent, Alan, 99
Arius, 5, 11, 14, 27, 35, 111
Ashworth, Caleb, 23, 25, 46, 49, 50,
    52, 53, 64–65, 70, 74, 75, 77,
    80, 81, 91, 96
Astley, Thomas, 74
Athanasius, 5, 134, 147
Atkinson, James, 38–39
Aubrey, Richard, 77–78, 92
Augustine, 34
Avery, Benjamin, 37
Axon, Ernest, 21, 39, 46, 67

Badland, Thomas, 19, 20
Ball, John, 37
Banks, Charles Walter, 109
Barnes, Thomas, 88, 92
Baron, Peter, 24
Barrett, C. K., 171
Barrett, John, 80
Barth, Karl, 164, 173
Bassett, T. M., 83, 87, 88
Bates, Samuel, 66
Bates, William, 21
Baxter, Richard, 14

Bealey, Joseph, 91–92
Beard, Charles, 115, 116
Beard, John Relly, 96
Bebbington, David, 98, 101
Beddome, John, 35
Belsham, Thomas, 49–50, 51,
    52–53, 56, 77, 92, 93, 94, 112
Benion, J., 73
Bennett, T., 21
Benson, George, 32
Benson, Joseph, 54
Bettenson, Henry, 5
Biddle, John, 13–14
Bland, S. K., 109
Blyth, Samuel, 38
Bolam, C. G., 11
Bonhoeffer, D., 173
Booth, Abraham, 49
Bourn, Samuel (1689–1754), 27–28,
    38, 42–43, 67, 80, 85
Bourn, Samuel (1714–1796), 45–46
Bradburn, Samuel, 102
Bridge, William, 9
Briggs, J. H. Y., 95, 101
Brine, John, 22, 44, 62, 105
Brown, Mr., 19
Brown, J. Baldwin, 144
Brown, John, 94
Brown, Raymond, 38, 64
Brown, R. M., 144
Bruce, A. B., 135
Buckley, William, 80–81
Budden, H. D., 76
Bull, George, 39–40
Bunting, Jabez, 102
Burder, Samuel, 79

199

Burgess, W. H., 76
Burnaby, John, 5
Burnet, John, 73
Burnett, George, 65
Burroughes, Jeremiah, 9
Bury, Arthur, 36
Bushnell, Horace, 141
Butler, Mr., 66

Caffyn, Matthew, 16–18, 19
Caird, John, 134
Calamy, Edmund, 37
Calvin, John, 63, 78, 126
Campbell, R. J., 144–45
Cardale, Paul, 46, 62
Carey, William, 59, 60
Carpenter, Benjamin, 49–50
Carpenter, Joseph Estlin, 113
Caston, M., 69, 71, 79
Cave, Sydney, 156–59, 161, 172, 182
Cerinthus, 14
Chadwick, George, 75
Chalmers, Thomas, 90
Chambers, Ralph F., 109
Chandler, Samuel, 29, 32, 40, 41, 71
Channing, William Ellery, 113
Chauncy, 20
Chidlaw, John, 73
Chorlton, John, 65
Clark, Samuel, of St. Albans, 29
Clark, Samuel, 50
Clarke, Adam, 102–6, 107, 110, 117
Clarke, Samuel, 36, 38, 40, 49
Cocks, H. F. Lovell, 2, 159–61, 162, 168, 172
Coke, Thomas, 102
Coleman, Thomas, 93
Coleridge, S. T., 70
Colligan, J. H., 11
Collins, Samuel, 108, 109
Collins, Thomas, 67–68
Collis, Michael J., 19, 73
Conder, John, 50
Cooke, Joseph, 104
Cornish, William, 69

Cox, John Hayter, 79
Crabb, Habakkuk, 80
Cromwell, Oliver, 14
Cross, Anthony, R., 17, 177
Crosley, David, 56
Cross, Tony, 166–67
Cyril of Alexandria, 168, 174

Dale, R. W., 12, 123–27
Daniel, J. E., 156
Darby, Abraham, 76
Darracott, Ridson, 69
David, Rees, 83
Davies, David Charles, 136
Davies, D. Elwyn, 84, 86, 87, 165
Davies, D. Jacob, 165
Davies, Gwilym, 153
Davies, G. Henton, 172
Davies, J. M., 136
Davies, James, 85
Davies, Owen, 88
Davies, Rupert, 171
Davis, David, 84
Dawson, Joseph, 74
Dean, Arthur, 78
Dean, Peter, 90–91
Delacourt, Mary B., 94
Denney, James, 123
Densham, W., 68, 72, 75, 77, 94
Deweese, Charles W., 56
Dewhirst, Edward, 75
Ditchfield, Grayson M., 47, 53
Dix, Kenneth, 62, 98, 101, 107, 109
Dixon, Thomas, 32
Dobson, Joseph, 94
Dodd, C. H., 160
Doddridge, Philip, 27, 29, 50, 53, 62, 69, 70, 76, 77, 79, 92, 96
Dodson, Joseph, 31, 38
Doel, David, 166
Doolittle, Samuel, 65
Doolittle, Thomas, 65
Dorner, I. A., 134, 140
Drummond, James, 113, 128–29
Dyer, George, 49

Index of Persons

Dykes, J. Oswald, 101, 129–34, 136

Edwards, Mr., 25
Edwards, D. Miall, 152–56, 157, 172, 181
Edwards, Lewis, 116, 134, 135, 136
Edwards, Maldwyn, 102
Edwards, Thomas, 12, 13, 26
Edwards, Thomas Charles, 116, 134–36
Elliot, Ernest, 70, 81
Emlyn, Thomas, 33–35
Enfield, William, 75, 92
Enty, John, 24
Erbury, William, 13
Evans, Caleb, 55
Evans, David, 112
Evans, E. D. Priestley, 94
Evans, Edward, 85
Evans, G. E., 23
Evans, Hugh, 44
Evans, James, 75
Evans, Thomas (1764–1833), 87
Evans, Thomas, 26

Fairbairn, A. M., 119, 129, 132, 136–38, 143, 146, 150, 152, 156, 172
Fawcett, Benjamin, 27, 80
Fawcett, Joseph, 76
Findlow, Bruce, 165
Firmin, Giles, 46
Firmin, Thomas, 20
Fleming, Caleb, 43
Flemington, W. F., 17
Fletcher, John William, 54–55
Fordyce, James, 78
Forsyth, P. T., 2, 3, 129, 141–45, 150, 152, 159, 172, 180
Foskett, Bernard, 35, 44
Foster, James, 43–44
Fownes, Joseph, 81
Frankland, Richard, 21, 65

Franks, R. S., 137, 150–52, 161, 170, 172
Frith, H. I., 160
Fry, John, 13
Fry, Richard, 79–80
Fuller, Andrew, 22, 23, 56–60, 88
Fuller, Andrew Gunton, 23

Gadsby, John, 108
Gadsby, William, x
Gale, John, 35–36, 43
Gardner, John, 73
Garvie, A. E., 146–50, 152, 153, 157, 158, 167, 172, 181
Gaskell, William, 96, 128
Gentleman, Robert, 81
George, A. Raymond, 171
Gess, W. F., 135
Gibson, Hugh, 70
Gill, George, 75
Gill, John, 22, 23, 41–43, 44, 105, 107
Gill, John (1730–1809), 79
Glover, T. R., 151
Godfrey, Peter, 166
Godwin, John, 76
Godwin, William, 76
Goodwin, John, 13, 26
Goodwin, Thomas, 9, 31
Gordon, Alexander, 78, 88
Gore, Charles, 144
Goring, Jeremy, 11
Gosden, J. H., 111
Granger, James, 26
Gray, Marshall N. G., 46
Green, Samuel G., 121–23, 125
Gregory of Nyssa, 123
Grieve, Alexander James, 100
Griffiths, Roger, 69, 84
Gronow, David, 26
Grove, Henry, 11, 30, 37, 67, 68, 69, 71
Grundy, 88
Gunton, Colin E., 178

Index of Persons

Guyse, John, 29, 40–41

Halley, Robert, 28, 47
Hamilton, Barry W., 105
Hanson, John (?), 6
Hardman, Samuel, 64
Harries, Solomon, 84
Harris, James Reed, 74–75
Harris, Joseph, 86, 87
Harris, Thomas, 86
Harrop, Robert, 64, 70
Hart, Cheney, 81–82
Harwood, Edward, 71
Haughton, John, 70
Hayden, Roger, 35, 42, 44
Haykin, Michael A. G., 56
Hazlitt, William, 68, 70
Head, Geoffrey, 96
Henderson, A. R., 67
Henry, Matthew, 14, 35, 73
Henry, Philip, 14
Herford, R. Travers, 78, 94
Hetherington, H. J. W., 115
Hewley, Lady Sarah, 96
Heywood, Oliver, 21
Hill, Thomas Wright, 80
Hinchliff, P., 137, 144
Hirons, Jabez, 79
Hobson, Paul, 13
Hoffman, Melchior, 16–17
Holmes, Stephen R., 17, 177
Holt, Raymond V., 175
Hopkins, Mark, 101, 127
Hopkinson, John, 94
Horsey, John, 92–93
Howard, W. F., 171
Howen John, 34
Howell, William (1714–1776), 69, 92
Howell, William (1740–1822), 92
Hügel, F. von, 168
Hughes, Hugh Price, 101
Hughes, Obadiah, 67
Hunsworth, George, 80

Hunt, Jeremiah, 43
Hunter, Jessie E., 67
Hussey, Joseph, 22
Hyatt, Charles James, 93

Ifans, Dafydd, 174
Illingworth, J. R., 126
Ingham, John, 93
Inglis, John, 46
Irenaeus, 140

Jackson, George, 171
James, John, 112
James, John Angell, 77
James, T. S., 43
James, William, 117
Janes, Thomas, 71
Jekyl, Joseph, 37
Jenkins, David, 84
Jenkins, Jenkin, 86
Jenkins, John, 88
Jennings, David, 71, 73, 76
Jennings, John, 29
John of Damascus, 149
Johnson, A. R., 172
Jollie, Timothy, 29, 65
Jones, Daniel, 26
Jones, Henry, 115
Jones, James Rhys Kilsby, 117
Jones, Jenkin, 83
Jones, Jenkin, of Haverfordwest, 84–85
Jones, John Morgan, 156
Jones, John Morris, 115
Jones, John Puleston, 136
Jones, R. Tudur, 84
Jones, Samuel, 83, 84
Jones, Thomas, 88
Jordan, E. K. H., 101
Josselin, Ralph, 13
Jowett, Benjamin, 134

Keach, Benjamin, 19
Kell, Robert, 77, 94

Index of Persons

Kenrick, Timothy, 53, 112
Kensett, Emily, 19
Kentish, John, 57–58
Kenworthy, Fred, 165
Key, Mark, 19
Kippis, Andrew, 76
Kirkpatrick, John, 77
Knowles, John, 28
Knox, R. Buick, 117

Lake, John Neal, 76
Lambert, George, 73, 75
Langdon, Luke, 37
Lardner, Nathaniel, 37, 46, 50, 68
Latham, Ebenezer, 28, 62, 68, 70, 81
Leggatt, Richard, 75
Leontius of Byzantium, 149
Lessing, G. E., 160
Lewis, H. D., 156
Lewis, Jenkin, 40
Lindsey, Theophilus, 46, 47, 48, 51, 52, 56, 87
Lloyd, Charles, 84
Lloyd, David, 114
Lloyd, Evan, 87
Llwyd, Dafydd, 84
Lob, Susanna, 66
Lobb, Stephen, 21
Locke, Don, 76
Locke, John, 32, 105
Long, Arthur, 166
Lucas, S., 49
Lumpkin, William L., 8, 16, 17, 18, 64
Luther, Martin, 134

Mackintosh, Robert, 99, 172
McLachlan, Herbert, 32, 105, 113
McLachlan, H. John, 13, 14, 28
Manning, James, 25, 30, 47
Mansfield, Reginald, 70
Mardon, Benjamin, 95
Marriott, Ernest S., 111
Marsh, John, 156

Marsom, Mr., 49
Martensen, H. L., 135
Martineau, James, 32, 89, 113, 114–15, 128
Mather, Nathaniel, 21
Matthews, A. G., 7, 23, 30, 76, 77
Maurice, F. D., 124
Meanley, Richard, 68
Means, Joseph Calrow, 95
Mercer, Samuel, 70
Miall, J. G., 6, 25, 26, 61, 65, 74, 75
Micklem, Nathaniel, 4, 161–63, 164–65, 177
Mills, Benjamin, 68
Mitton, Leslie C., 172
Moltmann, J., 173
Monk, Thomas, 17
Moore, John (d. 1730), 24
Moore, John (d. 1760), 24
Morgan, D. Densil, 152, 153, 156
Morgan, Vyrnwy, 118
Morgan, William, 52
Morison, James, 119, 136
Muirhead, J. H., 113
Murch, Jerom, 23, 46, 53, 66, 72, 95
Murrell, George, 109

Nestorius, 5, 168
Nettles, Tom, 56
Newton, Habakkuk, 19
Newton, Richard, 19
Nicholson, Francis, 21, 39, 46, 67
Nightingale, Benjamin, 75, 77, 78, 81, 92
Nye, John, 20
Nye, Philip, 9, 20
Nye, Stephen, 20

Ogle, J., 68, 72, 75, 77, 94
Oliver, David, 87
Oliver, Robert, 107
Origen, 134
Orton, Job, 27, 62, 81
Ottley, R. L., 123

Owen, Huw Parri, 174
Owen, James, 69, 73
Owen, John, 9–10, 14–16

Packer, Brian A., 19, 62
Palmer, Samuel, 27
Palmer, William, 109
Parker, Joseph, 90
Parker, Theodore, 113
Parry, William, 93
Patchett Benjamin, 25
Pattison, Mark, 134
Paul of Samosata, 14, 156
Paul, S. F., 108, 109
Payne, George, 74, 106–7
Payne, William, 29
Peel, Albert, 90, 98, 101, 164
Peirce, James, 27, 36
Perrot, Thomas, 69, 85
Perry, J. C., 115
Phillipps, Samuel, 72
Phillips, Daniel, 28
Phillips, George, 172
Philpot, Joseph Charles, 109–11
Picton, James Allanson, 100
Pike, Joseph, 66
Pope, Robert, 84, 153, 156
Pope, William Burt, 117–19
Popham, James Kidwell, 111–12
Powicke, F. J., 28, 62, 68
Price, E. J., 172
Price, Rees, 73
Price, Richard, 30, 47, 49, 50, 51–52
Price, Samuel, 51
Priestley, Joseph, 23, 46, 47, 48–49,
    50–52, 54, 55, 56, 57, 68, 74,
    76, 79, 87, 89
Procter, Henry, 23
Pugh, Philip, 84

Ramsbottom, B. A., 108, 109
Randall, Ian M., 177
Rattray, James, 26
Rawson, Joseph, 67

Reader, Simon, 77
Reader, Thomas, 77
Rees, Abraham, 76, 77
Redford, George, 98
Reed, Cliff, 166
Rees, Josiah, 86
Rees, Owen, 86
Rees, Richard, 85
Rees, Thomas (1777–1864), 12, 80
Rees, Thomas (1869–1926), 156,
    172
Reynall, John, 23
Richard of St. Victor, 134
Richards, William, 87
Ridgley, Thomas, 41–42, 71, 104,
    107
Rigby, Richard, 65
Ritchie, James, 25, 66–67
Ritschl, Albrecht, 141, 153, 154
Rivers, Isabel, 50
Roberts, H. P., 86
Roberts, John, 88
Robins, Thomas, 53, 76, 91
Robinson, Revd Mr., 66
Robinson, H. Wheeler, 172
Robinson, John, 146
Robinson, Robert, 47–49, 56
Robson, Douglas W., 74
Rogers, Henry, 124
Rooker family, 73
Rooker, James, 74
Rooker, Samuel, 72
Rose, John de la, 65
Rotheram, Caleb, 68
Row, Thomas, 111
Rowley, H. H., 172
Rupp, E. Gordon, 171
Ruston, Alan, 33, 98, 101
Rutt, J. T., 49

Santeen, James, 66
Saville, David, 93
Schwenckfeld, Caspar, 17
Schleiermacher, F. D. E., 141, 158

Index of Persons

Scott, Caleb, 180
Scott, James, 70, 73–74, 95
Scott, Robert, 75, 76
Scott, Walter, 180
Seddon, John, 81
Selbie, W. B., 124, 137, 145
Selina, Countess of Huntingdon, 23, 75
Sell, Alan P. F., 2, 11, 18, 21–23, 26–27, 29, 30–32, 35, 37, 39, 40–41, 43–44, 46, 50, 56, 63–64, 67–69, 73–74, 91, 93, 96, 98–99, 101, 105, 107, 112, 114–15, 117, 119, 124, 126, 128–29, 137–39, 143–45, 150, 152, 159, 160, 164, 173–74, 176, 181–82
Sellers, Ian, 95
Sellon, Walter, 26
Sharman, Edward, 59
Shepherd, Peter, 177
Sherlock, William, 20, 33, 34
Sibree, John, 69, 79
Silk, Philip, 166
Simon, David Worthington, 100, 119–20, 127–28, 129, 180
Simpson, Sidrach, 9
Skepp, John, 22
Slate, Richard, 78, 96
Sloss, James, 43, 67, 69
Smith, Betty, 166
Smith, John Pye, 106
Smith, Leonard, 96, 165
Smyth, John, 8
Socinus, 11, 28, 35, 50
Sozzini, Fausto Paolo. *See* Socinus
Spears, R., 113
Spurgeon, C. H., 63, 101, 127
Stapp, Benjamin, 81–82
Stennett, Joseph, 44
Stennett, Samuel, 49
Stevens, John, 107
Strawson, William, 171
Streiff, Patrick, 55

Strong, James, 30
Summers, W. H., 65, 73, 77

Tarrant, W. G., x, 114
Tayler, John James, 113, 128
Taylor, Abraham, 39, 41
Taylor, Dan, 63, 95
Taylor, John, 31, 47, 54, 67, 71
Taylor, Michael, 177
Taylor, Vincent, 171, 172
Taylor, William, 80
Thames, Shad, 19
Thomas, Caleb, 33
Thomas, D. O., 47
Thomas, Joshua, 83, 86
Thomas, Micah, 88
Thomas, Samuel, 84, 86
Thomas, Thomas, 94
Thomas, William, 87
Thomasius, Gottfried, 132, 159
Tillich, Paul, 173
Timpson, Thomas, 40, 68
Toller, Thomas, 70
Tomes, Roger, 177
Tomkins, Martin, 36, 37
Toplady, A. M., 26
Torbet, Robert G., 19
Toulmin, Joshua, 46, 57–58
Towgood, Micaijah, 11, 25, 29, 30, 46–47, 53
Turner, J. Horsfall, 74
Turner, William, 47
Tyerman, Luke, 26
Tyrrell, George, 168

Urwick, William, 65, 66, 73, 79

Vidler, William, 59
Vine, Aubrey Russell, 167–71, 172
Vowell, Benjamin, 69
Vowell, Thomas, 69

Waddington, John, 82, 93, 97, 99, 100, 180

Wadsworth, John, 65
Warner, James, 67
Walrond, Henry, 24
Ward, Mrs. Humphry, 122
Waterland, Daniel, 38
Watkins, Joshua, 87
Watson, Richard, 102, 105–6, 117
Watson, Thomas, 9–10, 20, 21
Watts, Isaac, x, 3, 39, 51, 54, 68, 94, 107
Watts, Robert, 119, 137
Webb, Thomas, 12, 13
Wells, James, 109, 111
Wesley, Charles, x, 3
Wesley, John, 26, 46, 54, 102, 104
Wesley, Samuel, 54
Wesley, Susanna, 54
Westcott, B. F., 134
Whale, John S., 4
Whiston, William, 36
Whitaker, Thomas, 25
Whitaker, Thomas (d. 1778), 25
Whitaker, William, 25
Whitby, Daniel, 40
Whitefield, George, 46, 94
Whitehead, Benjamin, 69
Whitehead, James, 70
Whitehead, Thomas, 67
Whitley, W. T., 18, 62
Wiche, John, 68
Wicksteed, Philip Henry, 113
Wigley, Thomas, 163–4
Wigmore-Beddowes, D. G., 167
Wilde, Gervase, 69
Wiles, Maurice F., 11
Williams, Benjamin, 70
Williams, Daniel, 20. 11
Williams, Edward, 88
Williams, G. Bernard, 85
Williams, J. B., 35
Williams, Moses, 87
Williams, Nathaniel, 86
Williams, T. Rhondda, 146
Williams, William, x
Wilson, Job, 28, 29
Wilson, Walter, 43, 62, 63, 107
Witty, John, 68
Wood, Nicholas J., 17, 177
Woodger, Phyllis L., 67
Wordsworth, Elias, 65
Wright, John, 71
Wright, Thomas, 71
Wykes, David L., 50

Index of Places

Aberdare, 86, 87, 156
Aberystwyth, 97
Alcester, 35
Alston, 25
Atherstone, 81
Aylesbury, 16, 17

Bala, 97
Barnstaple, 24
Bath, 13
Beaconsfield, 76
Bedfordshire, 17
Billericay, 79
Birkenhead, 150
Birmingham, 42, 67, 69, 77, 79, 94, 96, 124, 150
Bishops Hull, 69
Blackheath, 164
Blaenau Ffestiniog, 152
Bolton, 92
Bradford, 74, 121, 159
Brecon, 152
Bridport, 67
Bristol, 13, 44, 62, 71, 88, 150, 159
Buckinghamshire, 16, 17, 18
Bury, 77

Caeronnen, 84
Capel-y-groes, 84
Cambridge, 47, 157
Cardiganshire, 83
Carlton, 6
Carmarthen, 87
Carmarthenshire, 87
Chalfont St. Giles, 73
Charlesworth, 65, 70

Charmouth, 75
Cheshire, 29, 64, 81
Chester, 73
Chesterfield, 74
Cilgwyn, 84
Ciliau Aeron, 84
Cirencester, 80
Cockey Moor, 92
Colyton, 46
Coseley, 67, 80
Cottingham, 75
Cranbrook, 19, 62, 92
Crug-y-maen, 84
Cumberland, 25
Cwm-y-glo, 85, 86

Daventry, 52, 53
Debenham, 76
Denbigh, 88
Deptford, 40
Derbyshire, 70
Devonshire, 24, 46
Ditchling, 85
Dorset, 37, 67, 77, 94
Dover, 62
Dukinfield, 81

East Anglia, 18
Edinburgh, 127
England, 1, 11–12, 20–21, 45, 47, ch. 4, 86, 88, 90–91, 95
Essex, 12, 79
Evesham, 62
Exeter, 27, 44, 53, 62

Failsworth, 92

Index of Places

Faringdon, 31

Gellionnen, 86
Germany, 129
Glamorganshire, 85, 86, 87
Gloucester, 13
Greenwich, 167
Grundisburgh, 109
Gwernllwyn Uchaf, 85

Hale, 65
Halifax, 6, 28
Hatherlow, 65
Haverfordwest, 84
Headcorn, 62, 95
Heckmondwike, 70, 95
Henley-in-Arden, 35
Hertford, 66
Hertfordshire, 17
Hinckley, 94
Hinton, 95
Holland, 7, 13
Honiton, 37
Hove, 159
Hull, 73, 74, 75

Idle, 74
Ilminster, 75

Kendal, 46
Kent, 16, 18, 19, 68
Kidderminster, 27, 80, 81

Lancashire, 47, 70, 75, 77, 88, 93, 96
Leeds, 25, 121, 159
Leek, 75
Leicester, 100
Little Gransden, 111
Llandyfân, 87
Llanfair PG., 115
Llangefelach, 87
Llwynrhydowen, 83, 84
London, 12, 36, 38, 47, 51, 66, 71,
    73, 95, 101, 107, 109, 128,
    138, 141

Long Sutton, 95

Macduff, 146
Maidstone, 68
Manchester, 88
Marlborough, 31
Marple Bridge, 64
Middlewich, 29
Milborne Port, 69
Mixenden, 25, 26, 66
Monmouthshire, 85
Montrose, 146
Moulton, 59

Nantwich, 68
Northampton, 92
Northamptonshire, 18, 34, 117
Northwich, 29
Norwich, 31, 47
Nottage, 87
Nottingham, 43, 67, 69, 70, 80, 94

Oldham, 65
Oxford, 13, 17, 128

Pant Teg, 87
Pantycreuddan, 83
Pant-y-defaid, 84
Penruddock, 31, 38
Plymouth, 24
Pontbrenaraeth, 87
Poole, 72

Rathmell, 65
Ravenstonedale, 25, 66
Rawtenstall, 93
Reading, 65, 167
Rochdale, 105
Rotherham, 61, 65
Ruthin, 88

Saffron Walden, 95
Salisbury, 70
St. Albans, 79
St. Neots, 109

Index of Places

Sheffield, 65
Sherborne, 69
Shrewsbury, 19, 70, 81
Shropshire, 70
Smarden, 19
Somerset, 69
Southwark, 22
Sowerby, 28
Stafford, 23
Staffordshire, 64, 72
Stainland, 6
Stainton, 38, 95
Stand, 77–78, 92
Stoke Newington, 36
Stone, 23
Stony Stratford, 55
Stretton-under-Fosse, 79
Suffolk, 12, 76
Sussex, 16, 18, 95
Swanland, 75
Swansea, 84, 92

Taunton, 77
Tiverton, 24
Tockholes, 70, 95
Trecynon, 86

Wakefield, 61
Wales, 1, 45, 64, ch. 5, 87, 88–92, 97, 135, 136
Walsall, 64, 67, 72, 90
Walthamstow, 76
Wareham, 77, 94
Warrington, 75, 81
Warminster, 66
Warwickshire, 79, 81
Wem, 70
West Country, 18, 36, 44
West Hatch, 69
West Midlands, 64
Wick, 87
Wiltshire, 66
Winchester, 159
Wirksworth, 14
Worcester, 19, 52, 53, 98

York, 61
Yorkshire, 25, 28, 61, 74, 75, 95, 96

Index of Academies, Colleges, and Universities

Aberdeen University, 2, 141
Abervagenny Academy, 69, 73, 84, 86, 88
Airedale Academy/College, 96, 172, 180
Attercliffe Academy, 29, 52, 65

Bala-Bangor Theological College, 152, 156
Bala Calvinistic Methodist College, 116, 134
Bedworth Academy, 77
Berlin University, 10, 116
Blackburn Academy, 96
Brasenose College Oxford, 9, 13, 124
Bridgewater Academy, 29
Bridport Academy, 74, 79
Bristol Baptist College, 6, 86, 88
Brynllywarch Academy, 83, 84

Cambridge University, 21, 34. *See also* individual colleges
Carmarthen Academy, 26, 28, 69, 80, 84–86, 92, 114
Cheshunt College, 157, 163
Christ Church College Oxford, 14, 26, 144
Christ's College Cambridge, 8, 21
Clerkenwell Academy, 50
Congregational Memorial College Brecon, 152, 156

Daventry Academy, 23, 25, 27, 46, 50, 52, 53, 58, 64, 70, 74–77, 80, 81, 91, 93, 96

Edinburgh University, 43, 73, 119, 129, 146
Emmanuel College Cambridge, 9, 10
Erlangen University, 129, 132
Exeter Academy, 25, 43, 53, 112

Findern Academy, 28, 31, 46, 62, 70, 81
Frankland's (peripatetic) Academy, 65

General Baptist Academy, 95
Glasgow University, 25, 26, 29, 32, 45, 67, 70, 74, 86, 98, 99, 106, 113, 114, 128, 146
Gloucester Academy, 29
Gosport Academy, 77
Göttingen University, 2, 141

Hackney Academy, 52, 58
Hackney College, 141, 146, 156
Halle University, 100
Harris-Manchester College Oxford, 165
Harvard University, 21
Heckmondwike Academy, 71, 75, 95
Heidelberg University, 100, 129
Hertford College Oxford, 178
Homerton College, 76, 79, 80, 93
Horton College, 121
Hoxton Academy (1701–1785), 30, 46, 58, 71, 77, 78, 92
Hoxton Academy (1778–1850), 98, 106

Index of Academies, Colleges, and Universities

Idle Academy, 96
Islington Academy, 65

Jena University, 99
Jesus College Oxford, 156, 174

Kendal Academy, 68
Kibworth Academy, 29, 53, 67
King's College London, 174, 178
King's Head Academy, ix, 50

Lancashire Independent College, 100, 128, 138, 180
Leeds University, 164
Leiden University, 27, 29, 36, 43, 46
Leipzig University, 100
Lincoln College Oxford, 116, 134
Llwynllwyd Academy, 30
London University, 121
Lyme Academy, 37

Magdalen Hall Oxford, 9
Manchester Academy (1699–1713), 27, 65
Manchester Academy (1786–1803) 88
Manchester Baptist College, 177
Manchester College York, 113 128
Manchester New College, 113, 128
Manchester Unitarian College, 165, 166, 175
Mansfield College Oxford, 4, 96, 100, 124, 136, 137, 146, 150, 152, 156, 172, 178
Marburg University, 4, 99
Mile End Academy, 49, 50
Moorfields Academy, 71

New College Edinburgh, 99
New College London, 2, 138, 146, 157, 167
New College Oxford, 4
Northampton Academy, ix, 27, 50, 69, 70, 76, 77, 79, 96
Northowram Academy, 29

Oswestry Academy, 73
Oxford University, 21. *See also* individual colleges

Pembroke College Cambridge, 65
Presbyterian College Carmarthen, 84, 156
Presbyterian Theological College London. *See* Westminster College Cambridge
Queens' College Cambridge, 13
Queen's College Oxford, 7, 9

Rotherham Academy, 96

Saffron Walden Academy, 29, 43
St. John's College Cambridge, 46
Scottish Congregational College, 127
Shrewsbury Academy, 29, 69, 73
Spring Hill College, 96, 124, 127
Stepney College, 121
Stourbridge Academy, 37
Strasbourg University, 165
Sulby Academy, 34

Taunton Academy, 11, 24, 30, 67, 69, 71
Tewkesbury Academy, 29
Tiverton Academy, 24
Trefeca College, 23, 75
Trinity College Cambridge, 21
Trinity College Dublin, 113

United Theological College Aberystwyth, 174
University College Aberystwyth, 100, 134
University College London, 90, 95, 113
University College Nottingham, 144
University College of North Wales Bangor, 174
Utrecht University, 27, 37, 46

Warrington Academy, ix, 74, 75, 81, 88, 92
Wellclose Square Academy, 73, 76
Wesleyan Theological Institute, 102, 117
Western Academy/College, 77, 150, 159
Westminster College Cambridge, 101, 130
Whitehaven Academy, 31, 32, 68
Woodbrooke College, 150
Worcester College Oxford, 109
Wymondley Academy, 70, 93, 94

Yorkshire United Independent College, 159, 164, 167, 168

Index of Subjects

adoptionism, 17, 22, 104, 107, 127, 162, 176
Arians/ism, 3, 11, 12, 17, 21, 23, 25–30, 32–33, 36–37, 39, 40–42, 44–47, 49–55, 62, 64–9, 71–77, 79–81, 83–88, 91–92, 94, 96–97, 103–7, 112, 130, 139, 148, 156
Arminianism, 3, 26, 84, 86, 105

Baptist/ists, ix, x, 1, 6, 7, 13, 22, 33, 35–36, 41–44, 47–49, 55–60, 63–64, 73, 79, 80, 88, 121, 125, 151, 172
    Earthen Vessel churches, 111, 112
    General, 8, 16–19, 25, 38, 43–44, 45, 62, 64, 68, 86–87, 95, 98
    Gospel Standard churches, 108–12
    Missionary Society, 127
    National Assembly of Strict Baptist Pastors and Deacons, 175
    New Connexion, 63, 64, 76, 95
    Particular, 8, 38, 59, 62, 83, 86, 87, 98, 107, 175
    Strict, 6, 107–12, 175
    Union, 95, 98, 101, 177

Calvinistic Methodists. *See* Presbyterian Church of Wales
Calvinism, 3, 6, 30, 38, 56, 59, 62, 82, 87, 88, 98, 158

Chalcedonian Formula, 3, 4, 5, 106, 122, 129, 142–43, 147–50, 155, 157, 160, 162, 168–71, 174, 179, 181
Christ, divinity of, 2–3, 5, 8, 20, 39, 40, 48, 51, 54–55, 78, 97, 102–3, 105–6, 108, 115–16, 121, 125, 130, 133, 138, 140–41, 146–47, 149, 151–52, 156, 159, 162, 168, 176, 179
    humanity of, 5, 46, 48, 53–54, 97, 105–6, 108, 115–17, 121–22, 125, 130, 132, 134–35, 137–38, 140–41, 146–47, 149–51, 153–54, 159, 168–70, 174, 176–77, 179
Church of England, 11, 12, 13, 20, 36, 47, 79, 89, 109, 126, 145
Confession of Faith of the Calvinistic Methodists, 97
Congregational/ism/ists, ix, x, 1, 2, 6–7, 9, 13, 20–21, 43, 61, 63, 65–67, 69–70, 72–73, 75–79, 82–87, 89–90, 92–93, 96–98, 100–101, 106, 117, 119–20, 124, 127, 136, 138, 144–46, 152, 160, 163–65, 172, 176, 192
    Church in England and Wales, 176
    Fund Board, 21, 86
    "Genevans," 164–65
    International Congregational Council, 119
    Union of England and Wales, 90, 98–100, 145, 164

Index of Subjects

Countess of Huntingdon's Connexion, 102
covenants
  Alcester, 35
  Blanket Row, Hull, 74
  Stand, 78
  Stony Stratford, 55
  Worcester, 19–20

Declaration of the Faith... Congregational, 98–99
denominations, 6

eternal generation/Sonship, 3, 5, 8, 10, 11, 15, 17, 22, 33, 39, 40–42, 90, 101–12, 118, 127, 134, 179

Free Church Federal Council, 167

Gospel Herald, 108, 111

Holy Spirit, 7–8, 12–15, 35, 42, 51, 74, 97–98, 101, 110, 128, 149, 152, 165, 175, 179, 181

kenosis, 3, 117, 119, 121, 123, 132–37, 140, 143, 150, 155, 159, 162, 170, 179

Leicester conference, 100, 101, 144
London Missionary Society, 157

Melchiorism, 17–18
Methodists/ism, ix, x, 1, 21, 26, 53, 81, 89, 102, 105, 171
  Methodist New Connexion, 102
  Wesleyans, 6, 104, 117
Methodist Unitarian Association, 105

National Council of Evangelical Free Churches, 101

pre-eistarianism, 22, 107, 108, 111

Presbyterians/ism, x, 1, 6, 9–10, 13–14, 20–23, 25–30, 32–33, 35–38, 40, 43, 46, 50, 61, 63, 65–70, 72–77, 79, 81–82, 84–86, 89–90, 92, 96, 101, 116–17, 119, 129, 137, 146, 174
  Church of Scotland, 90
  Free Church of Scotland, 90
  Presbyterian Church in England, 90
  Presbyterian Church of England, 1, 90
  Presbyterian Church of Wales, 89, 102, 117, 175
  United Free Church of Scotland, 90

Roman Catholics, 1
Racovian Catechism, 11–13, 15

Salters' Hall, 21, 24, 36–39, 41, 44, 65
Savoy Declaration, 7–9, 20, 88, 99
Second London Confession, 8–9, 163
Short Confession of Our Faith, 175
Scripture sufficiency, 11, 14, 28, 30–35, 37–38, 51, 53, 58, 113
Socinians/ism, 11–15, 17, 19–21, 23, 26, 28, 30, 33, 35, 39, 41–44, 46, 49, 50–52, 54–57, 62, 106, 112
Standard Confession, 16

Trinity, 3, 9–13, 15–18, 20–22, 27, 31, 33, 34, 36–37, 40, 42, 48–49, 51–53, 59, 67, 86, 95, 97, 101–3, 106–8, 111, 118, 126, 130, 134–35, 141, 150, 156, 158–59, 164, 171, 173
True Confession, 7–8
XX Articles, 8
Twofold Catechism, 14

Index of Subjects

two nature doctrine, 2, 131, 155, 157, 161, 162. *See also* Christ, humanity, divinity

Union of Modern Freechurchmen, 164

Unitarians/ism, x, 1, 3, 6, 11, 20, 23, 26, 32–34, 45–51, 53, 56–59, 61–64, 68, 70, 72, 74–80, 84–97, 99, 101, 104–6, 112–15, 117, 122, 127–29, 140–41, 146, 165, 166, 167

General Assembly of Unitarian and Free Christian Churches, 175

Home Missionary Board, 96

South Wales Unitarian Association, 86, 115

Westminster Assembly, 9, 20, 72

Westminster Confession, 8, 37, 43, 67, 122

Westminster Shorter Catechism, 10, 20

www.ingramcontent.com/pod-product-compliance
Lightning Source LLC
Chambersburg PA
CBHW052340230426
43664CB00041B/2500